American Beliefs

JOHN HARMON McELROY

American Beliefs

WHAT KEEPS A BIG COUNTRY
AND A DIVERSE PEOPLE
UNITED

Ivan R. Dee
CHICAGO   1999

Cone ornament, the *Sequoia sempervirens* (Coastal Redwood), by John Herrera McElroy.

Library of Congress Cataloging-in-Publication Data:
McElroy, John Harmon.
    American beliefs : what keeps a big country and a diverse people united / John Harmon McElroy.
        p.   cm.
    Includes bibliographical references and index.
    ISBN 1-56663-231-5 (alk. paper)
        1. National characteristics, American.   2. Values—United States.
3. Pluralism (Social sciences)—United States.   4. United States—
Social life and customs.   I. Title.
E169.1.M156 1999
306'.0973—dc21   98-45603

For

Celeste, Connor, Danielle,

Eric, Max, Natalie, Oni, Sara,

Theah, and Tiernan

"The American . . . acts upon new principles."

—Michel-Guillaume-Saint-Jean de Crèvecoeur,

farmer, 1782

"I'm not black or white. I'm an American."

—George Foreman, boxer, 1984

Contents

Preface   xi
1 What Do We Mean by "Culture"?   3
2 How American Culture Was Formed   10
3 Primary Beliefs of American Culture   37
4 Immigrant Beliefs   60
5 Frontier Beliefs   93
6 Religious and Moral Beliefs   108
7 Social Beliefs   148
8 Political Beliefs   165
9 Beliefs on Human Nature   206
10 American Culture Today, and Tomorrow   220
Appendix: List of American Cultural Beliefs   227
Notes   229
Bibliography   239
Acknowledgments   253
Index   255

Preface

THIS BOOK considers what makes America one nation and Americans one people. My audience is everyone who may be curious about what it means to be an American—something that I maintain has always been determined by beliefs rather than birthplace or skin color.

In identifying beliefs of the American people, I have looked for those large patterns of behavior from generation to generation that express continuing convictions, especially belief-behaviors that stand out in comparison to those of other peoples. Travel books by foreign visitors recording their observations of American life, and the letters of immigrants about their experiences in America to those they left behind in "the old country," have also provided primary sources of information. (Being outsiders, these travelers and immigrants were perhaps best able to notice the distinctiveness of American beliefs.) Additional sources of information have been found in assessments by historians of "the American mind," "American thought," "the American character," "American manners," "the American spirit," "American genius," and the characteristics and tendencies of American religion, economics, politics, and sociology. Writings by Americans active in public affairs, such as Benjamin Franklin, whose life (1706–1790) spanned the century in which American beliefs led to the American Revolution, have likewise been helpful. Another influence on my understanding of American beliefs has been my thirty-four years of teaching American literature.

And not least in making me aware of American beliefs have been my experiences in other cultures while teaching at four universities in Europe and South America and my travels in twelve countries of the Americas and thirteen countries in North Africa, Europe, and the Middle East.

The twentieth-century American expatriate James Baldwin articulated a simple truth when he wrote, "From the vantage point of Europe, an exile discovers his own country." The remark echoes Ralph Waldo Emerson's observation in the nineteenth century that Americans who go to Europe are "Americanized" (his word) and Thomas Jefferson's statement in the eighteenth century: "My God! how little do my country men know what precious blessings they are in possession of, and which no other people on earth enjoy. I confess I had no idea of it myself [until I came to Europe]."[1] It was during my own residence in Europe in 1968–1969 that I began to discover my Americanness. As a Fulbright Professor of American Studies that year at the University of Salamanca in Spain, I was asked to give a weekly lecture on *La historia cultural de los Estados Unidos* throughout the academic year, and in preparing those lectures I had to think seriously and systematically for the first time in my life about what we mean when we refer to culture, why different cultures have formed, and how the culture of the United States of America differs from other cultures in the Americas and Europe.

J. H. M.

January 1999

American Beliefs

CHAPTER ONE

What Do We Mean by "Culture"?

CULTURE is usually thought of as a knowledge of music, literature, painting, or other arts. Thus we say of persons having such knowledge that they are "cultured." Obviously culture in this sense is not something that everyone in a society has.

But culture may also be thought of as a set of beliefs expressed in behavior. Culture in this sense is not something consciously learned, like culture in the sense mentioned above. Rather, it is acquired by successive generations of a people through imitating the behaviors of their elders that express certain beliefs. Culture in this sense is the possession of a whole people.

The way a historical culture comes into being resembles the formation of a path. When someone first traverses a landscape, the terrain and the pathfinder's choices among plausible alternative routes determine the way he goes. Those who come after him follow the way he took because falling in with a discernible track is always easier than making independent explorations at every step of a journey. As time passes, successive travelers continuously make the track plainer and confirm it as the way to pass through that landscape until, eventually, the pathfinder's initial route acquires a compelling utility and rightness. Similarly, in the formation of a historical culture, successive generations of a people find before them—already laid out—the way of life of preceding generations; and as each generation imitates the belief-behaviors of that way of life, they make them ever more compelling and right for later generations. So too, just as the route taken by the pathfinder and his immediate followers is crucial to a path's formation, in the formation of a historical culture the belief-behaviors of the first generations of a people are crucial. Whoever wants to understand any historical culture will therefore pay special attention to its formative period. In the case of the United States of America, that period was the century and a half from 1610 to 1760, the colonial era of American history.

Historical cultures allow human beings to live in society with other human beings, something that requires a shared sense of a right way to live. Human beings have a "moral imagination," which is to say that we are capable of imagining right conduct and need to live with other human beings according to a right way of behaving.[1] A set of right belief-behaviors is as indispensable to human well-being as food and water. In many instances in history, ordinary men and women have preferred to suffer death rather than violate a belief-behavior of their culture.

A HISTORICAL CULTURE can be formally defined as a unique set of extremely simple beliefs, formed and communicated through behavior over more than three generations. Cultural beliefs thus differ from other kinds of ideas in having been acted on for longer than the lifetime of the oldest person in a society. That is why they must be extremely simple. If they were complicated they would not be sensible to many people, nor would they retain their coherence for many generations. Cultural beliefs have this order of simplicity: "Worship is a matter of conscience," "The emperor is divine," "We are God's chosen people." These are historical beliefs respectively of the American, the Japanese, and the Jewish peoples. Beliefs this simple can be acted on for thousands of years without losing their coherence, and can be understood by even the dullest-minded persons in a society.

The extreme simplicity of cultural beliefs also allows them to be expressed in varying behaviors over time. This is important because a people may have to alter their behavior if they find themselves living in altered circumstances. But while the behaviors that express cultural beliefs may change, the beliefs themselves remain the same. America, for example, was an almost entirely agricultural society during the century and a half when its culture formed in the 1600s and 1700s; then, beginning in the 1800s, America became a highly industrialized society. But that change, which was very great, involved no alteration in American beliefs regarding work—the beliefs I have designated "Primary Beliefs" in this book. Those beliefs remained the same whether the work that expressed them was performed outdoors in fields or indoors in factories.

It is the *set* of beliefs in a culture that makes it complex, not the individual beliefs—all of which must be extremely simple to retain their coherence over time. Similarly, each culture is unique because of its *set* of beliefs, not because each belief in the set is unique. Cultures are more or less alike depending on the number of their shared beliefs. Thus we can speak meaningfully of "Islamic cultures," "nomadic cultures," "Western cultures." And within any given culture, groups of persons may exist that share its belief-behaviors but have some belief-behaviors historically peculiar to themselves. To describe a particular culture is to claim a certain focus of attention and a comparative rather than an absolute uniqueness.

When the same belief is shared by several cultures, it is likely to be expressed by different behaviors in each of them. The Japanese belief in a divine emperor, for instance, has occurred in other cultures. But where the Japanese emperor was at times a mere puppet manipulated by a warlord, in the culture of the Incas in the pre-Columbian Andes of South America, where the same belief existed, the will of the emperor was an iron law of absolute authority. Mummies of all the Inca emperors were kept in a special room inside the imperial palace at Cusco to be brought forth to sit among the counselors of the living emperor whenever he had to make a decision of the gravest consequence to the empire—a behavior not found in Japan. In ancient Egypt, whose culture likewise included a belief in the divinity of the ruler, the corpses of Egyptian pharaohs were as carefully preserved as they were in the culture of the Incas; but their mummies were never brought forth and displayed. Quite the contrary. Great pains were taken to conceal the corpses of these rulers in places where, it was hoped, they would never be disturbed. A culture's particular set of beliefs, it appears, will cause a belief it may share with other cultures to be expressed in distinctive behavior.

The beliefs of a culture are transmitted in a more unerring and natural way than instruction and indoctrination. Since the beliefs that constitute a culture are expressed in behavior and acquired by imitating the behaviors that express them, historical cultures do not depend on literacy. They exist independent of conscious learning. Systems of education may reinforce or weaken a culture's beliefs, but they can neither produce a new culture nor guarantee the continuance of an existing one.[2] A historical culture is not a rational construction. For a person to change his historical culture, something acquired by participation in the historical way of life of a people, he must change his residence and acquire a new allegiance—among a people with a different history.

The illusion (one might well call it the disease) of revolutionaries is that they can cancel history and produce a new culture that will be a rational construction. They want a new set of belief-behaviors, which they will design. But historical cultures are highly resistant to willful change undertaken by political operatives. For a people with a historical culture, nothing justifies an attempt to deconstruct its beliefs and replace them with a different set of beliefs. Indeed, the beliefs of a culture determine a people's way of knowing whether something is justified. For this

what "
belief, culture

Debut

reason, cultures rarely change. History cannot be reversed and begun anew, the slate having been wiped clean, the way revolutionaries seem to think it can.

When a culture does change, it normally does so in piecemeal fashion over several generations of time. The change occurs by the addition of some new belief to a culture's set of beliefs, through acting on that belief for more than three continuous generations; or by the subtraction of a belief from the set by the gradual failure of successive generations to act on it. Such an addition or subtraction alters to some degree the dynamics of the whole set of beliefs by changing the relationships among them. True changes in a culture occur over so many generations that they are usually imperceptible until after they have been completed.

Why are more than three generations of behavior needed to establish, or enculturate, a belief? Because three generations are usually alive at any one moment in a society (children, parents, grandparents), for a belief to acquire historical validity for those in the youngest generation it must connect with an absent, fourth generation whom parents and grandparents knew but children did not. Seeing their parents and grandparents pay respect to the graves of the dead helps to establish in the minds of the youngest generation such a connection, as does hearing stories about their ancestors, holding dear the same symbols the dead held dear, listening to music associated with their cultural ancestors, preserving structures built or lived in by them, and receiving personal mementos or other possessions of their ancestors. In all these ways, a connection with the past is created in the young. It makes them feel that the way of life they see going on around them, which they are beginning to imitate, originated in and has been sanctioned by the past. (The respect for cultural ancestors need not, of course, be for a biological ancestor, or even for a person who really lived. It may be for a legendary or mythical ancestor, whose behavior embodies a belief of the culture. Only in the culture of a clan would one's biological and cultural ancestors be identical. In all nonclan societies, one's cultural ancestors always extend beyond one's biological ancestors.)

Another basic point about historical cultures is that they are organic. Not every person in every generation of a people acts on all the beliefs of that people's historical culture in exactly the same way. A historical culture has an organic, not a mechanical, conformity—like a forest in which there is always a certain amount of dead wood and downed timber, even when the forest as a whole is healthy. So, too, when the leaves of the deciduous trees in a forest change color in autumn and begin falling to the ground, not all leaves change color at the same moment or change to the same hue or fall from the trees at the same moment. Similarly, when the new leaves emerge from their bud cases in the spring, they do not do so uniformly. At no time in the life cycle of a forest is there a precise and total uniformity of process, or the same state of vitality in every tree. Yet the forest has a conformity, is healthy, and perpetuates itself. A culture's processes also have no total, precise uniformity, but rather a general organic character.

As with a forest, the features of a culture are best appreciated from an overview. Any attempt to comprehend all the details of a culture would be doomed to failure by the very nature of the attempt. One remembers in this regard the legend of the Spanish cartographer who wished to make a perfect map which would replicate every detail of the kingdom of Castile, on a scale of 1:1. He finally succeeded in making such a map—and, of course, it was as large as the entire kingdom. According to the legend, fragments of this wonderful map are still to be found moldering into the ground in remote and seldom-visited corners of Castile. To pretend to represent in full detail the organic wholeness of a historical culture would be a similar vanity.

In short, this book is based on the following propositions: that a people's culture consists of a particular set of simple beliefs learned and validated ("encultured") through behavior for many generations; that cultures satisfy an ineradicable human need for a shared sense of right behavior and make it possible for human beings to live together in society; that once a culture has formed, it tends to persist unchanged because it satisfies a deeply human need; and that every culture is the best culture to those who participate in it.

CHAPTER TWO

How American Culture Was Formed

THE UNITED STATES became independent of Europe 176 years after its first permanent settlement by Europeans. It took Brazil 290 years to achieve independence, and the mainland countries of Spanish America three centuries. (The island nations of Spanish America required four centuries.) Canada, settled by Europeans just one year after the United States, needed 374 years to achieve its independence, two centuries more than the United States.

In other words, America became independent of Europe much more rapidly than any other part of the New World. And it is still the only part of the Americas that has been fully sovereign for a longer period of time than it was a dependency of Europe (see the chart of comparisons on page 12). It will be early in the twenty-second century before the mainland countries of Spanish America and Brazil reach the point in their histories where they will have been independent longer than they were dependent; and Canada will not reach that point until the middle of the twenty-fourth century. The exceptional speed with which the United States achieved its independence is much more significant than the fact that it was the first of Europe's colonies in the New World to do so.

If only the United States among these nations became independent in less than two centuries after its first permanent settlement as a European colony, what accounts for this distinctive behavior? Was it the happenstance of the quarrel over taxation that occurred in the 1760s between England and her thirteen colonies? Undoubtedly that was the issue which brought these colonies to a war with England that resulted in their independence. But what made taxation without representation such a momentous issue that Americans would wage war over it? After all, most Englishmen in the 1700s were being taxed, and had always been taxed, without elected representation in the House of Commons. But they did not rise up against the legitimacy of England's government and fight an eight-year war over the issue, as Americans did when threatened for the first time in their history by taxation without representation. (Before the 1760s, Americans taxed themselves through their elected colonial assemblies.) Why did the inhabitants of these thirteen European colonies— nearly two-fifths of whom by the 1760s had ancestors from the Irish, Scotch, German (in 1760 about a third of Pennsylvania's population was of German stock), French, Welsh, Dutch, Finnish, Swedish, and other, non-English "races" of Europe— believe they deserved a right that few Englishmen held? Did they think that way because the ancestors of about half the colonial population of America had been born in England? Or was it because the conditions under which these colonists lived set them *apart* from most Englishmen and from other peoples of the New World? Certainly those conditions were unique in comparison with conditions in colonial Brazil, Canada, and Spanish America. They were also radically unlike conditions in England at any time in its history.

Perhaps a combination of an English inheritance and the influence of American conditions accelerated the will to independence among these colonials? But even if we adopt that view of

Comparison of Years of Dependence (light) and Independence (dark) of the United States, Brazil, Spanish America, and Canada

As of the year 2000

	Time to achieve independence	Independence compared to dependence
UNITED STATES (1607–1783 / 1783–2000)	176 years	41 years more of independence
BRAZIL (1532–1822 / 1822–2000)	290 years	112 years less of independence
SPANISH AMERICA* (1519–1825 / 1825–2000)	306 years	131 years less of independence
CANADA (1608–1982 / 1982–2000)	374 years	356 years less of independence

*Mainland countries only. (Spain's three island colonies, which were settled before 1519, remained under Spanish rule until 1898.)

the matter, we acknowledge that it was not a European cultural influence, operating alone, that accounts for the remarkably early will to independence observable in American history.

Had English culture been the determining factor in the formation of American culture, we ought to see in the history of England in the seventeenth, eighteenth, or nineteenth century some indication that republican government had strong roots in England. But there were no such roots. The development of democracy in England in the twentieth century has been influenced by America's democratic culture; the development of republican government in America in the eighteenth century was not brought about by the influence of England's aristocratic culture. True, a handful of Englishmen in the 1600s thought about and published works advocating the creation of a republic with a written constitution, such as Americans were to create in the 1700s. But these "Levellers," as they were derisively labeled, were so thoroughly suppressed in the seventeenth century by those in power in England that their ideas did not resurface for another two hundred years. Only with continual reluctance during the course of the nineteenth century was government "of the people, by the people, and for the people" imported into England and gradually implemented in the constitutional reforms of 1832, 1867, and 1884–1885. It was not until shortly before World War I—in 1911—that the power of the unelected House of Lords in the British parliament was finally broken and radically curbed. After that date the unelected lifetime members of the House of Lords could only delay the passage of laws; they could no longer, on their own authority acting independently of the elected House of Commons, prevent a bill's passage. The fact that English political culture has become more like that of the United States over the course of the last two centuries—and not the other way around—is perhaps the best proof of the primacy of American conditions in the development of American culture.

And the question of the origin of American culture really is one of primacy. Did it originate primarily in cultural beliefs brought over the Atlantic from England? A stoutly affirmative answer to that question can be found in *America's British Culture* (1993) by the late Russell Kirk; and David Hackett Fisher, in *Albion's Seed: Four British Folkways in America* (1989), has gone so far as to argue that America's regional cultures are offspring of Britain's regional cultures. But if one is interested chiefly in the *Americanness* of America's historical culture, primary attention must be paid to American conditions.

Before the political separation between America and England, there was a cultural separation that can be traced to American conditions; and the cultural separation was what led to the desire among Americans for political separation. The beliefs Americans had enculturated by 1760 made the issue of taxation without representation so momentous that they were willing to go to war over it. The king of England and majorities in the House of Lords and the House of Commons never believed Americans would do that, because they saw the issue from the perspective of their English culture. Americans saw it from the perspective of a culture that had formed in America during the preceding eight generations. It was not a series of ministerial blunders and political misjudgments in London that brought on the American Revolution. It was an irreconcilable cultural difference.

That Americans would fight over the issue of taxation without representation surprised the English upper class. But it was also surprising to most Americans to discover that they were determined to wage a war against England to secure rights that they had mistakenly referred to as "the rights of Englishmen." By the mid-1770s Americans discovered that they were not, after all, Englishmen living in America, but rather Americans with American interests and beliefs that were antithetical to the beliefs of England's aristocratic culture. Thomas Paine, a disgruntled Englishman with strong "Leveller" sentiments who was living in America in 1775, saw this clearly. In January 1776 he published an essay he titled "Common Sense," in which he informed Americans that they had no further need to defer to England's aristocratic culture, and should therefore no longer be subservient to a government dominated by titled lords and a king. "Common Sense" urged Americans to declare their independence, and it met with instant popularity. Paine's essay did much to make Americans *aware* of the non-English character of their belief about sovereignty. It did not create the cultural belief among Americans that the people are sovereign; the conditions of life in America during the previous century and a half had created that belief.

To look primarily to the peculiarities of life in America in the 1600s and early 1700s to explain the distinctiveness of American culture is not to deny an English influence or to claim that no beliefs exist in both American and English cultures. Rather, it is to insist that despite similarities, two cultures—one English and one American—already existed by the 1760s because America had a history that was radically different from England's.

The first agreement for government written in the future United states provides an opportunity for assessing whether American culture should be regarded primarily as an import from England or the result of American conditions. This brief document (the Mayflower Compact, as it is called) was drawn up and signed in 1620 by most of the adult males among the immigrants we know as the Pilgrims. At the time they were still living with their families aboard the ship they had hired to bring them to America, as it lay anchored off the Massachusetts coast. When they wrote it, they had looked upon the shores of America but had yet to make a home there and a living from its soil. Thus the simple statement these immigrants put their names to in 1620 in the main cabin of the *Mayflower*, pledging to combine themselves into "a civil Body Politick" for their "better Ordering and Preservation,"[1] can only be regarded as the work of Englishmen. But other facts are of greater moment. First, the Pilgrims were profoundly dissatisfied with life in England. They were disgruntled Englishmen. And rather than stay anywhere in Europe, they preferred making a home for themselves and their offspring in a Stone Age wilderness. What is more, the impetus for the Mayflower Compact lay not so much in the English culture of the men who wrote and signed it, but in their situation on the shores of a wilderness of unknown extent, full of bears, "panthers," and wolves, at the bleak onset of winter, with shelters against prowling beasts of prey and the biting frost still to be built. Under these circumstances their "Preservation" certainly did call for cooperation, or "better Ordering." This first-ever basis for government written in America, simple as it was, originated not in the culture of the country the Pilgrims had abandoned, but in the thinking of Englishmen who had turned their backs on Europe to embrace the peculiarities of life in America.

Everywhere on the Atlantic coastal plain of North America in the seventeenth century—in Massachusetts and Virginia and in all the other European colonies planted on this seaboard— conditions demanded from the earliest settlers and their American-born descendants, and all who came after them, voluntary unity, mutual aid, and government by consent. In a situation that required men to cooperate with one another for their survival, it was natural that behaviors such as these and the beliefs associated with them should become belief-behaviors imitated by successive generations. Neither the English social system, nor the English religious establishment, nor English institutions of government, nor English land distribution practices, nor England's historical beliefs regarding work—each of which was aristocratic—was brought across the Atlantic Ocean intact to become the basis for life in the twelve colonies authorized by the English crown during the 1600s on the mainland of North America. (Georgia, the thirteenth colony, was founded in the early 1700s.) Compared to life in England, these colonies enjoyed a great deal more social and geographic mobility, a significantly greater economic reward for the labor of common folk, and considerably more latitude for the exercise of religious and political freedom.

TO UNDERSTAND American culture, one must always bear in mind that it developed from the situation of civilized men and women living in a Stone Age wilderness. Almost nothing in the cultural memory of the initial European settlers on the Atlantic coastal plain of North America prepared them for living in such a place. New ways of acting together in society were necessary in order to survive and prosper in that immense tract of wild land on the western verge of the North Atlantic. Some idea of the immensity of this wilderness for the Englishmen who settled in it is conveyed by the fact that two of the present-day states whose territories lie mainly within the coastal plain (Georgia and North Carolina) each encompasses an area larger than England.

Approached from the sea, this great plain first appears as a thin line on the horizon, scarcely distinguishable from the distant waves. When Europeans made their first permanent settlement on it, shortly before the year 1610, it was in an almost entirely natural state.

So luxuriant was the growth of the ten-thousand-year-old forest that covered all but a few scattered portions of it—a forest that had developed after the retreat of the last Ice Age in North America—that mariners coming from Europe in the late spring or early summer were greeted while still at sea, far from the sight of land, by the mingled scent of sun-warmed resins from millions of pines and cedars and the fragrance of myriad flowering shrubs and trees. Forest trees in great variety—hickories, maples, sycamores, oaks, walnuts, ashes, poplars, cherries, elms, plum trees, crabapples, basswoods, sweet gums, locusts, butternuts, willows, chestnuts, beeches, tulip trees, birches, hemlocks, larches, firs, cedars, spruces, and many kinds of pines—among other species—grew on the northern portion of the twelve-hundred-mile-long plain; and on its southern reaches, besides many of the trees just named, were magnolias, palmettos, persimmons, mulberries, pecans, cottonwoods, cypresses, and other species peculiar to those more southerly latitudes. The two zones of forest growth intermingled around the Chesapeake, the immense bay in the middle of the plain's long coast. And everywhere, north and south, were wild grapevines, thick as a man's thigh, entwining the giant trees; thickets of rushes and thick-stemmed seaside grasses taller than a man; rich wild meadows,

The Atlantic Coastal Plain
of North America,
Birthplace of American Beliefs

tangles of swamp and marsh, ponds, big rivers, countless creeks and copiously flowing springs, broad sounds protected from the open ocean by elongated islands, and numerous bays and estuaries where a ship might find safe harbor.

But above all else were the forest trees, many centuries old, with trunks that four men with outstretched arms could not encircle. Their towering canopy of summer foliage, high above a would-be settler's head, was so thick and unbroken that it cast everything below it into a solemn gloom.

The fecundity of the animal life of this uncivilized land was astonishing. Concentrations of swans, ducks, and geese on the rivers, bays, and sounds during the seasons of migration were so enormous that when a whole flock took flight, it was sometimes half an hour before the last bird was airborne. Beds of oysters half as big as a man's forearm extended for miles, and there were even bigger abundant clams. Runs of spawning fish could fill the creeks from bank to bank. But the seasons and secrets of the land had to be discovered and the appropriate skills learned for harvesting its natural abundance, else a European in this Stone Age wilderness might starve to death at certain times of the year.

For Europeans the seemingly endless, ancient forest covering this plain was alien and dangerous, and repugnant to their sense of the right way to live. It had to be removed and a new civilization put in its place. The sunlight had to be let in, the trees felled (or killed where they stood by chopping a deep cut around their trunks to stop the flow of their vital juices); then the stumps of felled trees had to be pulled from the ground, or burned out, and the great branches and trunks manhandled into piles and burned (there was simply too great a volume of wood to be eliminated to do otherwise). Once the brutal work of removing the trees was accomplished and rudimentary fields for cultivation created, the ground had to be cleared of stones, plowed, and fenced, crops planted, homesteads built, towns laid out, marshes drained, wharfs and landings constructed, primitive "roads" hacked through the wilderness to connect the settlements in "the back country" with one another and with the seaports and anchorages on the coast, bridges built, fords located across creeks, and ferries established where creeks and rivers could neither be forded nor bridged. This work could be embraced wholeheartedly because for these Renaissance Europeans and their descendants, civilizing the wilderness they had chosen to make their home was an unequivocal good and an absolute necessity. The work proceeded quickly because there was much promise of "a land of milk and honey" in the interminable wilderness, once it had been transformed into pastures, orchards, croplands, and towns.

The continuous transformation of the great wilderness of forest, prairie, plains, mountains, and desert that once stretched across the entire center of the world's third-largest continent, from the immense coastal plain bordering the Atlantic to the precipitous, hilly coast bordering the distant Pacific Ocean, has been the principal event in the history of the American people. The behaviors and consequences associated with that transformation have, directly and indirectly, shaped many of the beliefs of American culture.

For ten generations after the first settlements along the Atlantic coast, no one knew for certain how far the continent extended beyond the "Endless Mountains"—as the Appalachian Mountains were designated on the earliest American maps—that formed the western perimeter of the plain, or what lay in the interior. Even after explorers began investigating some of the huge waterways of the continental plains in the center of North America, west of the Appalachians—the Ohio, the Mississippi, and the Missouri rivers which, together with their biggest tributaries and the five freshwater seas to the north of them, made a system of natural avenues of travel and transport surpassing anything in Europe—it would be another century before the extent and main features of all of that vast interior were truly known. By then—when the Lewis and Clark expedition of 1804–1806 reported on its round-trip journey across the center of the continent to the Pacific Ocean—a great deal of the ancient wilderness on the Atlantic coastal plain had been transformed into farmland, and beliefs linked to the improvement of the wilderness were already firmly enculturated among the American people.

HERE AND THERE on the Atlantic coastal plain, before the transformation of the wilderness began, were villages of semi-nomadic Stone Age hunters, gatherers, fishermen, and agriculturalists. Wearing garments sewn from the dressed skins of the wild animals they killed, and in the summer in some instances (according to the accounts of the first Europeans to meet them) going about naked or barely clad, these North American peoples kept no domesticated herd animals for meat and fiber or for carrying burdens. Apparently few of their villages contained more than a score or two of families; the largest seem to have had no more than a thousand inhabitants. Orchards of plum trees and fields of corn, where squash, beans, and other domesticated plants also grew, were adjacent to most of the villages, few of which were permanent settlements. Land was so abundant and population so sparse that whenever yields from agriculture began to decline due to depletion of the soil, it was usually easier for these peoples to resettle in another location and construct a new village, where fresh soil could be planted, than to fertilize old fields. The most populous tribes in the eastern part of central North America (such as the Iroquois, the Choctaws, and the Chickasaws) lived beyond the coastal plain, which may have had a native population of about 250,000 when Europeans began to settle it.[2] It is certain that before the end of the first century of European settlement on the Atlantic coastal plain, the descendants of these new settlers outnumbered the descendants of the migrating tribal bands from Asia that had settled on it tens of thousands of years earlier.

To the Renaissance Europeans who came to this thinly inhabited Stone Age wilderness in the 1600s, it was indeed a "New World"—being something totally unfamiliar to them. Historically and psychologically, however, it was *an immensely old world.* Sailing across the North Atlantic from Europe in the early 1600s was, for those colonists brave enough to commit themselves and their children to life in Stone Age North America, a regression through some six thousand years of time to a condition like that of Europe's deep past. It was a commitment to repeat the process of civilization all over again in as little time as possible. These emigrants boarded ships in a civilization undergoing a Renaissance and months later disembarked in a place like Europe had been around the year 4500 B.C. The "oldness" of the world they entered had to be redeemed from its condition of oldness, had to be made into something new. This journey backward in time to a primal geography gave the American-born descendants of the immigrants several non-European attitudes toward time: namely, that the past does not determine the future, that the actions of men can shape the future to a desired end, and, most of all, that time can be accelerated or "saved."

The seasonal extremes of heat and cold of that never-before-plowed coastal plain, its enormous forest, its seemingly inexhaustible plentitude of animal life, its maddening swarms of summer insects, its strange uncouth inhabitants, and its immensity of lonely coastline stretching away for hundreds and hundreds of miles to the west and south from its closest point to Europe, was quite unlike anything in Europe with its densely populated and civilized landscapes. Under these circumstances, mainly a certain kind of men and women chose to live in America, the kind who were deeply discontented with their lives in Europe; who were exceptionally brave and who could imagine a better future for themselves; who were willing to make personal sacrifices and take risks for the sake of the better future for themselves and their children they saw in their mind's eye; and who believed it was possible to improve their lives through their own efforts, no matter how insurmountable the obstacles to progress might seem. In Europe they had failed to find something important to their self-respect. They intended to pursue that something in America, and hoped to find it. They were essentially self-respecting failures bent on success: disgruntled Europeans who wanted to be freer and happier than it had been possible for them to be in Europe.

On the extensive coastal plain where they landed, they found themselves on the verge of a wilderness with continental depth. An explorer might travel inland for great distances without encountering any semblance of what had been discovered thousands of miles to the south and west, a century earlier, by other Europeans in their encounters with the great civilization of southern North America and western South America. In those parts of the American continents, city-building societies with dense concentrations of population in the tens of millions, and a civilized heritage going back twenty centuries, lived a completely settled existence. They relied entirely on large-scale agriculture and, in the central Andes, on the herding of hundreds of thousands of state-owned, domesticated animals that produced wool and meat and carried burdens. Those distant civilizations, with their mines of precious metals, their richly robed kings and courtiers, their glittering, crowded cities with massive temples, huge daily markets, monumental sculptures, fortresses of cut stone, palaces and administrative buildings, impressively engineered water systems, classes of skilled artisans, professional scribes, military orders, full-time merchants, and government officials, and ample agricultural production, represented to Europeans the familiar features of their own civilization. Those parts of the Americas resembled Europe as it had been during the Bronze Age. They were instantly recognized by the European powers for their imperial value, and were conquered soon after their discovery.

But on the Atlantic coastal plain of North America, Renaissance Europeans found nothing they considered to be of immediate value. All that existed there were hundreds of thousands of square miles of wild land having only a potential agricultural value, if enough people could be found to transform it into towns and cropland. From the perspective of European civilization, everything of value in central North America awaited creation.

THE NEW behaviors and beliefs regarding work, sovereignty, social relations, worship, and political rights that developed in America were contrary to England's imperial interests. Yet, to a great extent, the unique policies of colonial immigration, government, finance, and defense adopted by the English crown prompted the behaviors that enculturated these new beliefs.

Those policies were unusually permissive as compared with those of the kings of Portugal, France, and Spain in the Americas. But every European monarch who established colonies in the New World—including the kings of England—had the same purpose in mind: to enhance their wealth and power. No colony was founded anywhere in the Americas by any European monarch to be the seedbed of an independent country—and particularly not a republic that rejected monarchical government, as the United States did in 1776. In the imperial thinking of European kings, overseas colonies were permanently subordinate to the imperial interests of the throne that had authorized them. The king of Portugal who called Brazil his "milk cow" succinctly stated the basic European imperial attitude toward overseas colonies.

The reasons behind England's more permissive colonial policies had nothing to do with a more enlightened imperialism. England was racked by political strife during most of the century in which twelve of its thirteen colonies on the North American mainland were founded. These severe and prolonged upheavals diverted the crown's attention, allowing the subjects of the English king living in America more leeway in governing themselves than they would otherwise have had, and made it impossible to enforce every imperial order emanating from London. In short, the English civil war and the problems that preceded and followed it necessitated a great degree of self-responsibility in the colonies. Another factor peculiar to English settlement in North America was even more important: from the beginning the English kings made their colonists pay the cost of colonial administration, including the salaries of the governors appointed over them by the crown. (The policy was designed to minimize the expense of colonization to the royal treasury.) And in order to set the taxes that were needed to meet these expenses, the crown permitted the colonists to elect a legislature (an "assembly," as it was usually called) in each colony. This policy alone made England's colonists in America more self-sufficient and independent than any others in the New World. The colonial assemblies were each the equivalent of a House of Commons but with two important differences: they were elected by a much broader base of voters than elected the House of Commons in England, and there was no equivalent of a House of Lords, in which membership was for life, to balance the authority of the broadly elected colonial assemblies.

The effect of European circumstances on colonial policies may also be seen in the case of Canada. Conscious of the likelihood of wars with neighboring countries in Europe, the French crown refused to permit large-scale emigration to Canada, which would have diminished the pool of manpower available in France for military service. Consequently, although France had the largest population by far of any imperial power in western Europe, it sent the fewest colonists to the New World; and French Canada during the 150 years of its existence had the smallest population of any of the four major areas of European colonization on the mainlands of the Americas. Even Portugal, with only a tiny fraction of France's population, sent many more settlers to its colony of Brazil than France sent to Canada.

The differing geographies of the New World—both physical and human—also played an important role in determining imperial policies. The Spanish crown, for example, had no need for large-scale immigration to populate its American territories because they already contained a civilized population much larger than the population of Spain. All that was needed in Spanish America at the time of its conquest was a new, all-Spanish, all-Catholic governing class to replace the conquered native lords and to administer and defend the newly conquered "kingdom of New Spain" (i.e., Mexico and the rest of southern North

America) and the "kingdom of Peru" (western South America, from present-day Colombia to Chile). Hence the Spanish crown instituted strict controls over immigration to its American territories, and barred all Europeans who were not already subjects of the Spanish crown from taking up residence there. The tens of millions of native peoples brought under Spanish imperial rule by force of arms in southern North America and western South America immediately became taxpaying subjects of the king of Spain. But their new citizenship conferred no right to decide the amount and kinds of taxes they would pay. Their conquerors decided those matters for them. In the history of Spanish America, the culturally decisive event was the conquest of existing civilizations, not the creation of a new civilization from a Stone Age wilderness.

Geography also had an effect on immigration policies in Canada, where the commercially valuable products were the rich furs of its boreal forests and arctic tundra and the incredibly abundant catches of fish (principally cod) from its Atlantic fishing grounds. Exploitation of these natural resources required no large resident population of Europeans. Indian trappers expert in collecting and processing furs could gather the pelts of beaver, lynx, martin, otter, fox, mink, and ermine for French traders to ship to Europe. And fishing fleets based in Europe could harvest the fantastically productive fisheries off the coasts of Newfoundland, Labrador, and Nova Scotia and return with their catches to Europe with little need for their crews to go ashore in North America.

On the Atlantic coastal plain in central North America, however, there were no large populations of civilized peoples to conquer and rule for the benefit of a European crown, and no fabulous stores of fur and fish like Canada's for noncolonial workers to harvest as the basis of an imperial economy. What this temperate coastal plain mainly offered was a great deal of wild land for conversion to agriculture; therefore a large population of European farmers was needed, as quickly as possible, to transform its ancient forest into farms, a population that would also provide a market for the manufactured goods that English merchants would sell them. Consequently no restrictions on the number, religious affiliation, or nationality of immigrants were mandated by the English kings for their thirteen American colonies (the crowns of France, Spain, and Portugal all imposed such restrictions). Europeans of any nationality and religion could emigrate to these English colonies if they were willing to take an oath of allegiance to the English king.

Nowhere else in the Americas was such immigration allowed. It was a policy of self-selected (as opposed to governmentally screened) immigration. And more than any other single factor, this unique open-immigration policy distinguished the population that developed in the future United States from the other colonial populations in the Americas, and set Americans on a different path of cultural development. By the late 1600s the policy had given America an increasingly non-English, uniquely diverse European population. No country of Europe had ever had a self-selected population; nor did any other part of the New World have a population made up predominantly of the descendants of European immigrants who had chosen to live in it without being subject to governmental screening.[3]

As the Atlantic coastal plain was transformed into farms during the seventeenth and eighteenth centuries, land became owned by a larger portion of the population in the future United States than had ever been true in England or any other European country, or in any other European colony in the Americas. This general ownership of land proved fatal to the European conception of colonies as places that should remain subordinate to the interest of the monarchy that authorized them.

The colonial populations of Brazil, Canada, and Spanish America were very different. Historically in Brazil, some four-fifths of the colony's people were slaves. In Canada, where immigration was severely restricted and limited entirely to French Catholics, the population was quite small and completely homogeneous, being drawn from just one of Europe's many "races" and one Christian denomination. In Spanish America more than

80 percent of the population consisted of subjugated native peoples.

So mixed in European nationalities and Christian denominations did America's early population become, through self-selected immigration and intermarriage between descendants of different European "races," that such distinctions as Englishman and Frenchman began to lose their significance. That breakdown of European identities did not occur in Brazil, Canada, or Spanish America, where immigration was carefully prescribed and the practice of only one religion allowed.

The cultural consequences of the widespread ownership of property in America, and the rapid growth of a population of freemen from a mixture of the many "races" of Europe, could not be foreseen in England. Certainly by the mid-eighteenth century the European ancestry of most Americans was so mixed that they were no longer Englishmen or men of any European "race." They had become what the American poet Walt Whitman was to call "a race of races."

THE WAY European countries were historically populated differed from the way America was populated. England, for instance, the country from which the greatest portion of the self-selected emigrants to colonial America came, was populated between the fifth century B.C. and the eleventh century A.D. by successive invasions of already formed peoples: the Celts, the earliest known invaders; the Romans, who ruled England for five centuries; various Germanic tribes—the Jutes, the Saxons, and the Angles; the Vikings; and, most famously, in 1066 the Normans. Kings in England were simply the most successful military leaders; their "subjects" became those they had commanded or subdued in battle. Over the last two millennia, this pattern of invade, conquer, and rule has often been repeated in every part of the European continent.

A comparatively small continent attached to the world's largest continent and lying within sight of the second-largest continent, Europe has been entered from Asia and Africa over and over again by migrations of armed peoples looking for a new homeland to conquer. Such behavior set the pattern for European culture. The Roman Empire—the most successful example of the invade-conquer-rule pattern in European history—covered at its height all or parts of forty-four modern-day countries in southern and western Europe, North Africa, and the Middle East; and it was shattered by other peoples on the march, wielding greater military force, whose original homelands were in western Asia—the Huns, the Goths, the Vandals.[4] The augmentation of a settled population by an invading population, and the consequent imposition of lordship by the invaders' leaders, has constituted the sense of a historical past in Europe. From this experience emerged the class of persons known in European history as "noblemen" and the continent's historically aristocratic cultures, including that of England. (The claim of superior, or "noble," bloodlines had no other basis than the military prowess of an ancestor who had seized territory by force of arms and settled down to rule it, after rewarding his most important military subordinates with portions of the conquest.) The descendants of conquerors formed a hereditary governing caste of armed lords who enforced a behavior of subservience among the descendants of those whom their ancestors had conquered or commanded on the field of battle. Throughout Europe the subordination essential to military operations and the subordination required of a conquered people became a basis for social relations and cultural beliefs. The honorary military ranks held by Europe's ten reigning monarchs today, and the military dress they wear on occasions of state, are pale reflections of this history of invade, conquer, and rule.

America's demographic history was the reverse of Europe's tribal and group movements. It was a migration of individuals and families. While it is true that some organized groups (usually members of a religious community under the leadership of their pastor) did cross the Atlantic to live in America in the 1600s and 1700s, such groups amounted to only a small fraction of the total number of free immigrants who entered America. The bulk of the immigrants to America came as individuals and members of a family, and were strangers to one another when they arrived.

Nonetheless these self-selected immigrants had a strong bond with one another and with those who had come to America before them, all of whom had chosen to detach themselves from their native culture to seek personal advantage in America. That shared, common purpose provided a foundation for a new cultural identity. The need to cooperate with others in order to assure one's survival in America and improve one's chances for success was another basis for cultural identity. To civilize the Stone Age wilderness required consensual behaviors of cooperation because no class of hereditary nobility was present in colonial America to assert command. That authoritarian class, which the immigrants had deferred to culturally and obeyed while in Europe, remained in Europe. Persons of "rank and dignity," such as baronets and dukes, did not choose to live in a wilderness and suffer the deprivations involved in building a new civilization. Consequently the "commoners" from various parts of Europe who accumulated in increasing numbers in America in the seventeenth and eighteenth centuries were on their own and had to find new ways of ordering their society and protecting themselves. Their voluntary cooperation, especially in military matters, was fundamentally unlike the relations of subordination and command in the aristocratic cultures of Europe, with their differentiated social castes based on ancestry. Social distinctions among the self-selected immigrants to America and their descendants were based on something quite different: success in performing the tasks of developing a new civilization.

The demographic and social histories of the European colonies in Brazil, Canada, and Spanish America were also quite different from those of the future United States. The Spanish conquests in the 1500s of the four indigenous civilizations of North and South America reenacted the European pattern of invasion, conquest, and rule. (These were the Aztec Empire in Mexico, the remains of the Maya civilization in the Yucatan Peninsula and parts of present-day Central America, the Inca

Empire centering in Peru but extending from Ecuador to Bolivia and northern Chile, and the Chibcha civilization in the highlands of present-day Colombia.) After the conquest of these vast areas of the New World, and large areas between them inhabited by uncivilized Indians, two *reinos* (kingdoms) were organized, each governed by a powerful viceroy representing the person of the faraway Spanish king. These two viceroys presided over regal courts in Mexico City and Lima modeled on Spanish court life, and their authority was upheld by royal troops from the Spanish homeland. As in the greater part of European history, in the history of Spanish America the armed man on horseback, the professional soldier, has been the ultimate authority of the state, his military prowess associated with the idea of a conqueror's superior blood. By going to North or South America and subjugating indigenous civilized peoples, a Spanish captain of common lineage might receive a title from the Spanish king and acquire lordship over productive lands populated with skilled peasants long acculturated to paying tribute and rendering service to their native lords—peasants who would henceforth serve him. And he could look forward to his oldest son inheriting his lands, vassals, and privileges, and continuing the title and high estate he had won for himself through feats of arms. Such prospects were every bit as attractive as the possibility of discovering a horde of Indian gold or a rich mine of silver.

Throughout Spanish America, this reflection of the European pattern of making military prowess the basis for governmental authority and social rank may account for the difficulty the countries of Spanish America have had in establishing stable elected governments since their independence. An essay titled "Doctrina política del ejército" ("Political Doctrine of the Army"), published by a lieutenant colonel of the Argentine army in 1975, illustrates the problem in its statement: "La intervención política del Ejército ha sido invariable en la vida de la Nación, porque su participación es un hecho natural, dada la fundamental coexistencia de la Institución en el devenir histórico nacional." ("The intervention of the army in politics has been

constant in the life of the nation, because its participation in political life is natural, given the army's fundamental coexistence
with the ongoing historical development of national life.")[5] In
most countries of Spanish America before the late twentieth century, the army *was* "the nation." It was the only institution that
contained and the only authority that represented the idea of a
national existence. Exercising command over the army was
therefore the first priority for governing.

In colonizing Brazil the Portuguese did not conquer existing civilizations and rule them by force of arms as the Spanish
did in Mexico, Central America, Colombia, Peru, Ecuador, Bolivia, and northern Chile. But they repeated in another way the
European tradition of ruling subjugated races: they populated
Brazil primarily with slaves brought from West Africa, where
Portugal had long maintained trading posts for purchasing slaves
from local potentates. In Portugal's colony on the east coast of
South America, the slaves from Africa and their descendants,
who made up most of the population, lived and worked in permanent subjugation to the interests of their Portuguese masters.
And slavery was not abolished until 1888, three generations after
Brazil's independence from Portugal. In other words, slavery in
Brazil lasted for three and a half centuries—longer than in any
other part of the New World—and was the primary institution
and shaping influence of Brazilian culture.

In Canada the French established yet another kind of colonial population. Whereas tens of millions of conquered native
peoples comprised the bulk of the population of Spanish America, and hundreds of thousands of slaves made up four-fifths of
the population of Brazil, French Canada had the smallest population of any area of European colonization in the Americas. One
hundred and fifty years after the first permanent French settlement in Canada, it still numbered only about sixty thousand.
This comparatively tiny population consisted entirely of free
men and women from France and their descendants (except for a
few persons of mixed French and Indian ancestry), all of whom
were Roman Catholics. French Protestants could own property

in Canada and visit the colony to look after their property interests, but they were prohibited by law from wintering there—which has always been the true test of whether one is a Canadian. French Canada was a small piece of pre-Reformation France set down in northern North America: it was the most European, the most homogeneous, and the most conservative population (complete with feudal seignorial rights) of any American colony.

The function of this small, uniform population was to support the garrison of royal troops from France at the fortress of Quebec ("the Gibraltar of North America"), which controlled the only big river of North America that oceangoing ships could use to sail inland, directly off the Atlantic, for a thousand miles. France fortified the heights of Quebec that dominated passage on the St. Lawrence River in order to keep England, its great European rival, from gaining access to the North American interior. The raison d'être for the colony was to maintain that strong point and conduct the lucrative fur trade. Despite occasional military setbacks, France retained control over the St. Lawrence for a century and a half before Quebec finally fell to an English invasion force and the crucial event in the cultural history of Canada (usually referred to simply as "the Conquest") was accomplished. The military subjugation of French Canada in 1759–1760 was, like the Spanish conquests in the Americas, a repetition in the New World of the pattern of European history.

THE POPULATION of the thirteen colonies that became the United States of America in 1776 was distinct, then, in five basic ways from the colonial populations of Brazil, Canada, and Spanish America. First of all, it had a mix of Christian faiths because membership in one, state-approved-and-supported Christian church was not a requirement for emigrating to America.

Second, it was rapidly growing because, unlike the situation in Canada, government did not restrict the number of immigrants who could enter these colonies and because these colonists had an extraordinarily high birthrate. The large amount of affordable land available to them meant that families could be formed at an early age, thus prolonging the child-bearing years of married women.

Third, it was the only "racially" mixed European population in the Americas because immigration was not restricted to just one "race"of Europe and because there was continual intermarriage among its diverse European population. (There were also offspring from persons of European descent and the slaves of African descent, who may have averaged perhaps 12 to 14 percent of the population during the century and a half of the colonial era, as well as offspring born to persons of Indian and European descent and of Indian and African descent.)

Fourth, an overwhelming proportion of the people worked for themselves to their own direct benefit—the largest part of them as farmers on their own land—as opposed to the Indian trappers who were the main wealth-producing labor force in Canada (where a seignorial system of land tenure required the colony's freemen to render labor service to lords, or seigneurs), the multitudes of Indian peons who made up the basis of the economy of Spanish America, and the African-descended slaves who historically made up most of the population of Brazil.

Fifth, the majority of this population was not held in subjugation by force, like the slaves of Brazil, the Indians of Spanish America, and the French population of Canada after 1760. In short, the English-speaking colonies of North America at the time they declared their independence comprised the only colonial population in the Americas that was rapidly growing in numbers, constantly expanding its settled territories, and composed chiefly of self-selected immigrants and their descendants working for their own benefit.

Another singular feature of this colonial population was its military self-reliance. The kings of France, Portugal, and Spain all stationed troops from their homelands in their American possessions. The kings of England did not do this until after the conquest of Canada. Before that conquest, in order to minimize the cost of empire to the royal treasury, the English crown required the thirteen colonies on the Atlantic coastal plain to ex-

Comparative Synopsis of Conditions for Cultural Formation in Spanish America, Brazil, Canada, and the United States

During the first 150 years of their European colonization

Date of first settlement, rounded to nearest decade	Nature of settlement	Kind of European immigration allowed	Origin of 80% or more of the population	Principal wealth-producing labor force	Number of religions allowed	Government structure	Principal land defense	Rate of population growth
SPANISH AMERICA (1520–1670)*	Conquest of four populous civilizations, two of them imperial in scale	Only subjects from one European monarchy	North and South America	Civilized Indians serving their conquerors	One	Two kingdoms, each ruled by a viceroy	Royal troops from Europe	Slow, following massive die-off
BRAZIL (1530–1680)	Plantations along wilderness coast, little inland movement	Only subjects from one European monarchy	Africa	Slaves serving their masters	One	One appointed royal governor	Royal troops from Europe	Slow
CANADA (1610–1760)	Forts and trading posts restricted to wilderness river valley	Only subjects from one European monarchy	Europe	Indian trappers trading with colonists	One	One appointed royal governor	Royal troops from Europe	Extremely slow
UNITED STATES (1610–1760)	Plantations along a wilderness coast, steady movement inland	No restriction on country of origin	Europe	Citizens	No restriction	13 appointed governors and 13 elected legislatures	Colonial militias	Doubling every 20 years

*Mainland countries only. The first permanent settlement in Caribbean islands was in 1493; Spanish dominion in those islands did not end until 1898.

pend their own money and manpower in defense of their land frontiers. The taxes England tried to impose on these colonists in the 1760s were intended to make them pay for part of the cost of conquering Canada (for which Americans had provided some troops) and of the unavoidable new expense of garrisoning troops from England in Canada following its conquest.

In all these ways, then, the conditions under which the colonial population of the future United States lived were unique among the colonies of Europe in the Americas.

The chart on the preceding page compares and summarizes the conditions for cultural formation in the continental areas of European colonization in the Americas after Columbus's voyage of 1492–1493. It suggests that the future United States, during the formative period of its cultural history, had characteristics that made it the least European of Europe's four main areas of settlement on the continents of North and South America.

CHAPTER THREE

Primary Beliefs of American Culture

THE PRIMARY American cultural beliefs derive from the initial experience of European settlers in the future United States. They all relate to work, the first necessity for survival in a wilderness. It was the peculiar experiences of work—what kind was done, who did it, how much it was rewarded—that began the process of distinguishing American behavior from European behavior, which led during the next eight generations to the formation of a new American culture.

Primary Beliefs:

Everyone Must Work

People Must Benefit From Their Work

Manual Work Is Respectable

In December 1606, 144 Englishmen sailed from London aboard three ships to plant a colony in America. Four months later, in April 1607, when the ships dropped anchor in an estuary of the largest bay on the Atlantic coastal plain of North America, only 105 of the colonists were still alive. A little more than a fourth of those who had sailed down the Thames had died en route to America from the rigors of the prolonged voyage. By Christmas 1607, two-thirds of those who survived the voyage had perished in the wilderness of Virginia from malaria, dysentery, and other illnesses, from accidents and deadly quarrels among themselves, and from ambushes and attacks by natives living in the vicinity of the crude fort they had built and named Jamestown. But more than anything else, they died of starvation.

This was the fifth attempt by Europeans to colonize the Atlantic coastal plan. There had been Spanish settlements in South Carolina in 1526–1527 and 1566–1587, another Spanish settlement in Virginia in 1571, and in the 1580s an English settlement on an island off the North Carolina coast. All those attempts had sooner or later been swallowed up by the wilderness; and probably the Jamestown settlement too would have suffered that same fate within its first year except for the bold leadership of a twenty-seven-year-old English captain. His daring in commandeering food from the Indians in the vicinity of Jamestown kept thirty-eight of the colonists from starving their first winter in Virginia, until a relief ship carrying supplies and additional colonists arrived from England. But after an explosion of gunpowder tore open Captain John Smith's thigh, forcing his return to England for treatment of the terrible wound, the barely viable colony declined to the point of near extinction.

The commander of the relief ship that arrived at Jamestown in 1610 described the situation in the settlement three years after the first settlers had arrived. The colony appeared to him more like a ruin than an abode of civilized men: the fort's palisades had fallen over in several places, the gate into the fort was off its hinges, the small chapel was dilapidated and disused, and the huts the men had built as shelters stood empty and were being gradually dismantled for firewood. The handful of men still alive were sick and weak and living in the blockhouse, the only structure that was still sound, afraid to venture into the surrounding woods to gather fuel. What kept them huddled inside the block-house was plain to the newly arrived captain from the suffering he saw about him and from the colonists' reports of "the Indian as fast killing without as the famine and pestilence within."[1] Again, a ship bringing supplies from England had arrived just in time to save the colony from obliteration.

The fundamental problem at Jamestown was food. The Ad-venturers (as these colonists called themselves) depended on food supplies from England during the colony's first few years. The summers posed no problem for them because an abundance of spawning sturgeon could be caught from the James River; and in autumn and spring many migrating waterfowl were at hand. The winters were "the starving time," because not enough grain was planted, cultivated, and harvested during the rest of the year to get the Adventurers through this one season when Europeans could not gather enough food from the wilderness to keep up their strength and health. The hostility of the neighboring tribesmen posed a serious threat, to be sure. But the under-lying difficulty was a lack of locally grown food. The ocean sepa-rating Jamestown from its corporate backers in London, and the uncertainties of the Atlantic voyage in the seventeenth century, made delivery of supplies from England unreliable at best, and in any case prohibitively expensive for a colony that was supposed eventually to turn a profit for its investors. Unless a way could be found to make Virginia self-sufficient in food, this embryonic colony was doomed to vanish like the earlier European attempts to colonize the coastal plain of central North America.

It might seem that necessity and common sense would have forced these Englishmen to perform the agricultural work to as-sure an adequate supply of food. But the influence of culture can be stronger than common sense, and the Jamestown colonists had brought with them from Europe a culture unsuitable to the wilderness. Of course some of the settlers did clear patches of forest and cultivate them. But overall there were too many "Gentlemen" in the colony in relation to laborers; and gentlemen in Europe's aristocratic culture did no manual work. Just 12 of the 105 colonists on the colony's rolls were listed as "Laborers." This may have been a designation for persons skilled in agriculture, but more likely it identified workers with no particular skill, since twelve other men had a skill worth listing (one blacksmith, one barber, one bricklayer, four carpenters, one drummer, one mason, one sailor, one surgeon, and one tailor[2]), and surely a skill in gardening or husbandry would have been worth mentioning. These twenty-four men, then, out of a company numbering a little more than one hundred, constituted the colony's work force. The other eighty-one persons—three quarters of the colony— were listed as "Gentlemen" (fifty-four persons), "Boys," and "diverse others" (twenty-two persons, almost certainly the servants of the gentlemen, because not even their names were recorded). The fact that there were twice as many gentlemen as workers, and that the attendants to these gentlemen appear to have about equaled the number of workers in the colony, made for a disastrous imbalance. Local food production was essential to survival, but English gentlemen could not be expected to wield axes and spades to hack fields from a wilderness. They were accustomed to having their food raised and prepared and served to them by servants; they did not plant and cultivate it. Performing manual work of any kind was beneath their cultural dignity; yet gentlemen and their servants must eat.

This ratio of 3 to 1 of gentlemen and gentlemen's servants to workers was at the root of Jamestown's early history of misery and starvation. There were simply too many layabouts in relation to workers.

Captain Smith, writing about his experiences in Virginia, complained repeatedly about "slothfull and idle drones" who would rather go hungry than work. Only the willingness of "some few Gentlemen" to put aside their dignity and get their hands dirty in performing heavy labor, he noted, had given the settlement a chance of survival. In one forthright letter to the colony's backers in London, Smith urged that no more gentlemen be permitted to come to Virginia to consume its slender resources while they rested on their prerogative of having others wait on them and provide them with food and lodging. Rather than receive "a thousand such," he said, he would rather see "thirty Carpenters, husbandmen, gardiners, fisher men, blacksmiths, masons, and diggers up of trees" landed in Virginia. Indeed, it was Smith's general recommendation that no one be permitted into the colony who could not "well brooke labour." And in the book of instructions he prepared in London for the founders of future colonies, he emphasized that "Masters, Gentlemen, Gentlewomen, and children" should never be allowed to outnumber "men to worke." In settling a wilderness, idle persons were "very troublesome," and the effects of their idleness were "dangerous" to the colony's peace and harmony and a threat to its very existence. In his experience, "Gallants" did nothing but "complaine, curse, and despaire" and demand that people wait on them. He had had "much adoe," he said, to get food to maintain such clamorous "loyterers" at Jamestown.

The only kind of physical work that most of the gentlemen at Jamestown willingly performed was the search for gold, which they believed was to be found somewhere in Virginia. For a time, Smith recalled, "There was no talke, no hope, no worke, but dig gold, wash gold, refine gold, loade gold"; and a whole ship was actually freighted with fool's gold (Smith called it "guilded dirt") and sent back to London for assay by these gentlemen smitten by gold fever.[3]

The threat to Jamestown's survival was not resolved until the colony's "proprietors" in London, to whom the king of England had granted Virginia, decided to give most of the colonists three acres of land with the understanding that they would henceforth own it and feed themselves from the food they raised on it by their own labor. They would no longer depend on shipments of food from England. This new arrangement had an immediate effect and produced enough locally grown grain to supply the colony year-round.

The change brought about by private ownership of land in Virginia was described by one of the settlers as follows: "When our people were fed out of the common store, and laboured jointly together [on the company's land], glad was he [who] could slip from his labour, or slumber over his taske he cared not how, nay, the most honest among them would hardly take so much true paines in a weeke, as now for themselves they will doe in a day: neither cared they for the increase, presuming that howsoever the harvest prospered, the generall store must maintaine them, so that wee reaped not so much Corne from the labours of thirtie, as now three or foure doe provide for themselves."[4] Individual ownership of land and the opportunity to benefit from one's own labor, expended on one's own property, reversed the danger of starvation in Virginia. Labor would henceforth be rewarded in direct relation to the exertions of the laborer; those who did not work would not eat. There would be, John Smith said, "sufficient" reward when every man could "plant freely without limitation so much as hee can." He assured readers of his manual for colonies that in America whoever was industrious and diligent in his labors could expect to own in four to six years "for every acre he hath planted . . . twenty, thirty, forty, or an hundred" additional acres which he might pass down to "his heires for ever."[5] From his own labor, no worker anywhere in Europe in the 1600s could anticipate such benefits.

The original plan of the "proprietors" of Virginia was that their joint-stock company would retain ownership of all land, and everyone sent to Virginia to work the land would be in their employ. Under this arrangement, the work of laborers was intended for the profit and benefit of the company. But the Virginia proprietors allowed their friends, who were of course also gentlemen, to go to Virginia to see what riches they might turn up in the wilderness. These American wilds, however, contained no mines of gold or silver or rich civilizations to conquer, as Mexico and Peru had offered, and made no allowances for gentlemen. The culture of England, where land was owned by gentlemen and worked by peasants for the benefit of the owners, was a threat to survival in the Virginia wilderness. Not until the Virginia Company allowed workers to own land did the colony begin to be viable and attract an increasing population, as news of the availability of land in Virginia to common workers spread through Europe. Allowing common workers to own land saved Jamestown from extinction and assured the colony's survival and growth.

THE SAME LESSON had to be learned a few years later at Plymouth Plantation in Massachusetts. This second enduring English colony on the Atlantic coastal plain was quite unlike Jamestown in several respects. For one thing, it included women and children as well as men; for another, the motive of these colonists was not to show a profit but to practice their Puritan religion in a community of uniform orthodoxy, free from the harassment of other Christians having a different religious outlook. But in one important respect the men, women, and children who landed on the shores of Massachusetts Bay in 1620 resembled the Englishmen who had settled Jamestown thirteen years earlier: they started out working their land in common. And they met with the same dire results. The severity of the New England winter (compared to England's milder climate), the exhausting work of clearing wooded, stony land, and the weakness and illness caused by inadequate food resulted in the death of half the Pilgrims their first winter in America. The Massachusetts wilderness depressed the spirits of these settlers. It seemed to them "hidious and desolate," and the woods and thickets had in their eyes "a wild and savage" hue that made them feel cut off from "all the civill parts of the world."[6]

As at Jamestown, the Plymouth colonists also had to become hunters, fishermen, and gatherers of natural foodstuffs to stay alive; and, as at Jamestown, they depended on the local tribesmen for crucial supplementary supplies. In their relations with the Indians of Massachusetts Bay, however, the Pilgrims were luckier than the gentlemen adventurers who went ashore in Chesapeake Bay. The woods around Plymouth were strewn with the skeletal remains of natives who had died of a plague of some sort three years before the Pilgrims' arrival, in such large numbers that the survivors had been unable to bury all their dead.[7] Because of this die-off, the tribes in eastern Massachusetts in 1620 were not disposed to attack these settlers and willingly bartered with them.

The Pilgrims became so desperate for food that some of them bartered their bedding and clothes for a cup of Indian corn; in other instances they made themselves "servants" of the Indians in exchange for food. Even in the third year of the settlement, small bands of men, women, and children in tattered clothing were still scouring the woods and seashore for nuts, roots, and clams. So weak from lack of nourishment did they become that the Indians "contemned and scorned" them, one survivor remembered, and "begane greatly to insulte over them in a most insolente maner," stealing their pots of foraged food whenever they came upon them unattended. One adult male Pilgrim was found dead in a tidal flat where he had gotten stuck in the mud while clamming and had been too weak to extricate himself.[8]

During their third winter in New England, those Pilgrims who were still alive knew that without a fundamental change in their way of life, the entire colony would perish. "At length, after much debate of things, the Govr (with the advice of the cheefest amongest them) gave way that they should set corne every man for his own perticular, and in that regard trust to them selves; in all other things to go on in the generall way as before." So, every family was given "a parcell of land, according to the proportion of their number," and unmarried adults in the community were assigned to a family for this purpose. But the communal ownership of land and communal work for the common store, which had been practiced to that point, would be given up, it was decided, "only for [the] present." The land being allotted to families for private cultivation was intended only as an expedient, to see if it would increase food production; and "no devission for inheritance" was made. As in Virginia, private ownership of agricultural land made such an immediate improvement in food production that there was no question of reverting to communal ownership. Within a few years the initial land grants were recognized as permanent and as conveying the right to sell and bequeath them.

The change from communal to private ownership at Plymouth "made all hands very industrious," according to Governor William Bradford, who was in office when the division of land was made and who later wrote a history of the colony. Bradford's account of the effects of the change to private ownership of agricultural land continues:

> The women now wente willingly into the feild, and tooke their litle-ones with them to set corne, which before would aledg weaknes, and inabilitie; whom to have compelled would have bene thought great tiranie and oppression. The experience that was had in this commone course and condition, tried sundrie years, and that amongst godly and sober men, may well evince [the] vanitie of that conceite of Platos and other antients, applauded by some of later times; that the taking away of propertie, and bringing in communitie into a comone wealth, would make them happy and florishing; as if they were wiser then God. . . . For the yong-men that were most able and fitte for labour and service did repine that they should spend their time and streingth to worke for other mens wives and children, with out any recompence. The strong, or man of parts, had no more in devission of victails and cloaths, than he that was weake and not able to doe a quarter the other could; this was thought injuestice. The aged and graver men to be ranked and equalised in labours, and victails, cloaths, etc., with the meaner and yonger sorte, thought it some indignite and disrespect unto them. And for mens wives to be commanded to doe servise for other men, as dresing their meate, washing their cloaths, etc., they deemd it a kind of slaverie, neither could many husbands well brooke it.[9]

Edward Winslow, another Pilgrim leader who survived the starving time in Massachusetts, entirely agreed with Bradford's judgment, and gave two reasons why provision for individual ownership of land should be made in establishing colonies. First, because "every man in a measure more or less, loveth and preferreth his own good before his neighbor's"; second, because "the base disposition of some drones . . . is burdenous to the rest."[10]

As in Virginia, the allotment of private land in Massachusetts increased immigration; and the growth in population at Plymouth increased the demand for food, thus raising its price and the value of land under cultivation. In order to obtain cheaper land, newcomers to the colony and children of the earlier settlers who could not be accommodated on their fathers' acreage began moving into outlying districts where they organized new churches because they could no longer easily reach the church in Plymouth for worship. Once this process began, nothing short of the full exertion of the colony's governmental authority could have halted the settlement of new lands. That was not an option, however, since private ownership of land had proven of such benefit to food production and colonial prosperity. And both newcomers and descendants of the first settlers believed they deserved the same opportunity to own property that the original settlers had enjoyed.

According to Governor Bradford, as the people of Plymouth sought more land for cultivation and pasturage, "no man now thought he could live, except he had catle and a great deale of ground to keep them"; and settlers became "scatered all over the bay, quickly, and the towne, in which they lived compactly till now [Plymouth], was left very thine [thinly populated], and in a short time allmost desolate."[11]

Bradford tried to keep Plymouth from being depopulated. While recognizing the favorable results of private rather than communal ownership of land, he feared the desire for worldly gain would turn out to be "the ruine of New-England, at least of the churches of God ther, and will provock the Lords displeasure against them."[12] To prevent that, he decided to give from the colony's communally owned land "some good farms to spetiall persons, that would promise to live at Plimouth," and who might in that way be kept attached to the town and "helpfull to the church" there. But this strategy proved ineffectual. The special persons to whom he allotted land also became—*"within a few years"*—discontented because they too, though they had been given good land, "conceived them selves straitened, or to want accommodation . . . thinking their owne conceived necessitie" a reason to leave Plymouth in search of more and better land elsewhere in Massachusetts Bay. The lure of improving one's holdings was too strong to be checked by Governor Bradford and other Pilgrim leaders in a region where so much tillable land lay unoccupied.

TO GROW ENOUGH FOOD to make the colonies in Virginia and Massachusetts viable, everyone had to work, including gentlemen; and to motivate the colonists to work to their utmost capacity, their labor had to benefit themselves and their loved ones in a real way. The distribution of land in private plots satisfied both those requirements. And there was much potential farmland everywhere on the twelve-hundred-mile-long forested plain extending from eastern Massachusetts to the Florida peninsula, once the overburden of forest was removed. Arable land was its main asset, since there were no deposits of precious metals. In the thirteen colonies of the future United States, wilderness was made valuable by transforming it into farms. And in the 1600s and 1700s, small private landholdings were effected up and down the Atlantic coastal plain on a scale unlike anything in the history of England.

Unlike conditions in England, small farms worked by their owners were the prevailing mode of life in America. The big landholdings that a few families acquired in Virginia and along the Hudson River in New York were exceptions to that rule. What a historian of land distribution in early Virginia concluded, applied generally to the other colonies: ". . . whatever the variation in size, the small landholder constituted the major group in seventeenth-century Virginia." In 1764 the governor of Massachusetts reported that not more that 2 percent of farmers were renters, rather than proprietors, of the land they tilled. And throughout the colonies, the opportunities to acquire land or set up a shop put "the achievement of independence within the grasp of most able-bodied, active, and enterprising free men."[13] Landowners whose property was neither very small nor very large made up the majority in this colonial population; and they had a decisive effect on the formation of American culture. In England, farmers typically rented land from a great landlord; in America enough unoccupied land was available for farmers to own the farms they worked.

The three work-related beliefs—*Everyone Must Work, People Must Benefit From Their Work*, and *Manual Work Is Respectable*— began to be enculturated from the beginning of colonial settlement in America. Because agricultural work demands continual manual labor, and because the vast majority of workers in early America were engaged in agriculture, manual work of all kinds assumed a cultural respectability it did not have in the aristocratic culture of Europe, where almost all the land was owned by a few persons who considered themselves socially and morally superior to those who rented and worked their lands. In America, on the other hand, the performance of physical labor made no difference in one's class standing because people of all classes, even the highest, worked with their hands, fabricating and repairing things, plowing, cultivating crops, helping to bring in the harvests. To belong to the upper class of English society meant inheriting land and leading a life free from manual work. That was not the case in colonial America, where manual work was a common way of acquiring land and higher status.

Contrary to the belief-behaviors of English and other European cultures, in America manual labor carried no stigma of belonging to an inferior class. Landowners in colonial America and later periods of American history worked side by side in the fields with their hired help and ate with them at the same table when they came into the house for meals. European travelers to America often remarked on this behavior, which astonished them in being so different from the sharp class distinction in Europe between those who got their hands dirty and those who did not.

AMERICA WAS from the beginning, and remains to this day, a society of workers, most of whom may be said to begin life with little more than a willingness to work and an ambition to be at least self-supporting. Sooner or later they usually earn enough wherewithal to put them in comfortable circumstances and in many cases to allow them to bequeath to their children something of value. In exempting no social class from work, in rewarding common workers to the limit of their diligence, and in making little distinction between the worth of mental and physical work, the experience of Americans began to be differentiated from that of Europe. Because of the beliefs about work that developed in American culture, a plumber in twentieth-century America can make more money than a university professor and be just as truly a member of the middle class.

The development of a civilization from a wilderness made America, as Benjamin Franklin called it, a "Land of Labour."[14] As the identical experiences at Jamestown and Plymouth show, if men and women of European descent were to civilize the Stone Age wilderness of North America, the only way to bring a sufficient amount of labor to bear on that enormous task was to permit a greater reward to laborers (particularly ownership of land) than Europe's aristocratic culture allowed workers to have. The extraordinary labor of clearing the ancient forest from the Atlantic coastal plain required the possibility of extraordinary rewards to attract workers and call forth their best efforts.

The hope of gainful rather than subsistence employment, the chance to become a landowner, and the prospect of leaving some inheritance to one's children were the main incentives that drew workers to America from many countries of Europe. Those who left Europe were overwhelmingly from the lower and middling classes of the Old World—individuals who believed that in America they could better their lives materially through their own sweat. Almost no one of large fortune and high social rank left Europe to live in that great wilderness undergoing a transformation into farmland and towns. The conditions of life in

America and the kind of society that self-selected immigrants and their American-born offspring created required behaviors that enculturated beliefs about work and property ownership that did not exist in European culture. American culture had its genesis in the beliefs *Everyone Must Work*, *People Must Benefit From Their Work*, and *Manual Work Is Respectable*, which the behavior of Americans expressed early in the history of the future United States.

The material benefits to be gained from work in America were: an abundance of food at a cheaper price (including meat, which peasants in Europe rarely enjoyed); wages that were throughout the colonial era and down to the twentieth century double and triple the wages that were paid to hired laborers in Europe; and lower taxes compared to the rate of taxation in Europe. But the foundation of every other material and spiritual benefit of labor in American society was the opportunity to own a house or farm or shop and become free of lordly patronage. Europe offered comparatively few opportunities to accomplish such things. European peasants usually remained propertyless from one generation to the next because almost all the land was owned by the gentry and the great lords, who made every effort to pass their holdings intact to a single heir. In America the odds of earning more money for the same amount of work, of eating three "square" (i.e., substantial) meals a day, and of becoming a landowner or starting an enterprise of one's own to provide a commodity or service for others, were considerably better for an honest person of fairly sound judgment, steady habits, and some ability than they were in any of the countries of Europe that the immigrants had left.

The most striking result of workers in America benefiting more from their labor than workers did in Europe was the unprecedented speed with which they civilized an expanse of wilderness as large as the continent of Australia (the three million square miles of the contiguous forty-eight states of the United States). In some 275 years—from the time land first became available to common workers in Virginia, to the Census of

1890, which revealed that a frontier condition no longer existed anywhere in the contiguous territories of the United States (as defined by a certain density of population)—that enormous expanse of land was transformed into a single, unified nation by a rapidly growing population whose work in effecting the transformation benefited them. Civilizing the continent of Europe had taken twenty times longer than three centuries. The improvement of so much Stone Age space in so brief a time would not have been possible without an industriousness stimulated by material rewards.

The cultural beliefs that made manual work respectable, that provided workers an unusual level of benefit from their work, and that required every class of society to work, unleashed in America a focused human energy that operated with a rapidity and on a scale seldom, if ever, witnessed in human history. From two barely viable settlements in a wilderness in the first two decades of the 1600s, America had become by the first two decades of the 1900s one of the biggest, wealthiest, and most powerful nations in history; and is now, at the end of the 1900s, it is fair to say, the world's preeminent nation.

Never before in history has a society made up chiefly of self-determining, self-selected immigrants and their descendants come into being in a place that offered so much opportunity for gain for those who would work for it; never before in history has a unified nation of continental dimensions been created in less than three centuries by the work of millions of persons freely combining and organizing themselves politically and economically to their own best advantage. That exceptional accomplishment has been the principal historical experience of the American people. It is the principal fact of their cultural history. And it required ceaseless labor.

"We are all animated with the spirit of an industry which is unfettered and unrestrained," one European immigrant said about life in America before its independence from England, "because each person works for himself." This same immigrant called colonial America in the 1760s "the most perfect society now existing in the world"; another pronouncement on America in the mid-1700s proclaimed it "the best poor man's country."[15] And by 1774, the year before America's war for independence began, the people of colonial America already had a higher per capita wealth than the people of England[16]—though of course America's total wealth was still far less than that of England's. These statements describe the comparatively greater rewards to workers in America—regardless of whether they worked for wages, labored on their own land, or did business in their own shop—that distinguished life in America from life in Europe, both before and after American independence. In America work, not ancestry or class membership, was the basis of a person's dignity and personal identity. The primary importance of work in American culture is reflected in the question Americans typically put to someone they meet for the first time: "What do you do?" It is also reflected in an expression Americans often use in taking leave of each other: "Don't work too hard," and its variant, "Take it easy."

The settlement of the American wilderness produced a many-generations-long, noiseless revolution in the ownership of land. Never before had so large a proportion of a population become owners of private property and thereby gained a personal interest in upholding property rights. As Thomas Jefferson said in 1813, in a letter he wrote to John Adams, another former president of the United States, "Here every one may have land to labor for himself, if he chuses; or, preferring the exercise of any other industry, may exact for it such compensation as not only to afford a comfortable subsistence, but wherewith to provide for a cessation from labor in old age. Every one, by his property, or by his satisfactory situation, is interested in the support of law and order." A revolution in wages for those who worked with their hands also occurred, as they made several times what manual workers in Europe were paid for their labor. In the 1760s the average annual income of a landless American worker (thirty pounds sterling) was fifteen times greater than the income that qualified a man to vote in England (two pounds); around 1900 a

Hungarian mechanic could increase his wages fivefold by going to America.[17]

IN 1763 the king of England issued a proclamation forbidding his American subjects from taking up land west of the Appalachian Mountains; but a generation later the Congress of the United States passed an "Ordinance for ascertaining the mode of disposing of Lands in the Western Territory." That was in 1785, two years after the war that made America independent of English rule. After the American Revolution, the transfer to the national government of land the states had claimed west of the Appalachian Mountains, when they were colonies of England, opened an enormous territory to private ownership. And the land ordinance of 1785 provided for surveying those lands that lay north of the Ohio River into lots one mile square (640 acres), one-seventh of which were to be given to veterans of the Revolution in compensation for their services, one lot in every township to be used for "the maintenance of public schools," and most of the rest to be made available for sale to the public.[18] Nearly all this land became family farms.

Another manifestation of the American cultural belief that workers must benefit from their labor was the Homestead Act. Under the generous provisions of this 1863 federal law, which made nationally owned land west of the Mississippi River available for purchase by the public, any head of a family or person twenty-one years of age who was an American citizen, or who had filed a declaration of intent to become a citizen, could have a "quarter-section" of land (that is 160 acres, one-quarter of a square mile) simply by registering a claim to it, paying a ten-dollar registration fee, and residing on and cultivating it for five years. In contrast to this American land law, the "Lei de Terras" (land law) passed in 1850 in Brazil—a society in which slaves made up the vast majority of the population—favored great proprietors by establishing such high prices for undeveloped land that only the wealthiest Brazilians (the owners of the slaves) could afford to buy it; thus all but the wealthiest immigrants from Europe were prevented from becoming landowners. (The Homestead Act was repeatedly blocked in Congress by Southern slave-owning interests and was not enacted until the Civil War kept all representatives from the slave states out of Congress.)

One particularly notices in the Homestead Act the small size of each homestead (160 acres), which was designed to create a maximum number of privately owned family farms. One also notices the absence of any distinction between potential landowners who were native-born Americans and those who were foreign-born immigrants but wanted to become Americans. All that was required to homestead a quarter-section of land in the trans-Mississippi West in the latter half of the nineteenth century was ten dollars and a willingness to improve it by living and working on it—an investment that came to sixteen cents an acre plus the labor of making raw land into a productive farm.

Another piece of nineteenth-century federal legislation that reflects American cultural beliefs about work—the Morrill Act of 1862—set aside thirteen million acres of public land for sale at $1.25 per acre, the proceeds from which were to be used to establish at least one college in each state of the United States to teach "agriculture and the mechanical arts."[19]

PERHAPS THE TWO most influential conditions during the formative period of American cultural history were the scarcity of labor for hire and the availability of cheap raw land. These fundamental facts about life in early America were closely connected. The availability of cheap land throughout the colonial era and the century following American nationhood caused the scarcity of laborers for hire. Land being cheap, workers were constantly acquiring it, thus removing themselves from the pool of laborers for hire. Therefore hired labor was in chronic short supply, wages were high compared to those in Europe, and workers who were ambitious to acquire land could use their higher rate of pay to become independent proprietors. It was a benevolent circle for workers. In Europe, the circle of land, labor, and wages was vicious: land for sale was scarce and expensive, and the available supply of workers for hire was large; therefore wages were low.

The relation between land and labor peculiar to America during the formative period of its culture was certainly among the main motivations for immigration to America. It put American workers in a privileged position that workers had never occupied in Europe, with its governing class of aristocrats who monopolized the ownership of land.

The comparatively small number of paupers in America—another constant refrain of European travelers to America during the first three centuries of its history—was one sign that hired labor in America was historically scarce. In addition, the frequent moves and changes of jobs and occupations by workers, as they sought optimum wages and job satisfaction, likewise suggest the privileges of labor in America compared to Europe, where work was hard to get because of the oversupply of workers and where such mobility and changes of occupation were comparatively uncommon. (In countries where employment is difficult to come by, employed workers generally stay with what they are fortunate to have instead of seeking more satisfying work.) The famous American interest in labor-saving machines and efficient techniques of production also reflects the historical scarcity of labor for hire during most of American history. Likewise, the interest of colonial assemblies and, after American independence, state legislatures in promoting immigration testifies to the central role that workers have had in a country where historically there were never enough of them to do all that Americans wished to accomplish as quickly as possible.

The rapid growth of the American population—which in the fourth generation after the first settlements began to double every twenty years—was a direct result of the labor situation in America. By commanding higher wages and thereby often becoming the owners of farms, workers in America could form families sooner than was commonly done in Europe, thus lengthening the child-bearing years of married women and increasing the number of children born into families. (As early as

1784 Benjamin Franklin noticed that the abundance of cheap land encouraged "early marriages by the certainty of Subsistence in cultivating the Earth," and that these early marriages made "the Increase of inhabitants by natural generation . . . very rapid in America.") The abundance of food produced by numerous small farms also contributed, through better general nutrition, to the birth of more robust babies and thus a lower infant mortality rate and a greater average longevity in comparison to Europe. The longevity and low infant mortality rate that New England enjoyed in the 1600s, for instance, was not duplicated in England until more than two centuries later, in the 1890s.[20]

To ease the labor shortage in America, the proprietors of Virginia offered land to anyone who would pay the passage of an immigrant to Virginia—the so-called headright system. Another solution to the problem of labor scarcity put forward in Virginia was soon adopted by other colonies. It was termed "indentured servitude": a kind of contractual, voluntary slavery for a fixed period. In this system a recruiter in Europe would find a worker willing to go to America who could not pay his passage, and would have the man or woman sign an "indenture" (contract) by which he or she agreed to work in America without wages for a specified number of years (normally four to seven) for whomever owned the contract. In return, the indentured worker received passage to America and his or her food, clothing, and shelter from the owner of the indenture for the term of the contract. The recruiter, after arranging passage to America for the workers he had indentured, would either accompany them there to sell their indentures for a profit to someone in need of a worker, or would sell the indentures in Europe to someone going to America, who would resell them and the labor they represented in whatever American port he went to.

Once the system of indentured labor was in place, owners of ships and ship captains became the principal recruiters of contract labor to the English colonies on the North American mainland. The system benefited the poor of Europe who wanted to get to America to try to improve their lives but could not afford the passage money; the recruiter of indentured servants who profited from each laborer he recruited; the transatlantic carriers who had in indentured servants a new and highly profitable human cargo that was readily marketable in America; and those in need of hired hands in America who secured the services of a worker for a set period of years at a total cost much less than they would have had to pay a worker in wages on the open labor market of America. Because indentured servitude was to the advantage of everyone concerned, it quickly spread north and south from Virginia, throughout the colonies, and soon became the most common way of meeting the constantly escalating demand for labor in America.

Probably somewhat over half of all immigrants to America from Europe in the seventeenth and eighteenth centuries—the formative centuries of American culture—crossed the Atlantic as indentured servants. Success in becoming property owners was not uncommon among them after they worked off their contracted years of servitude and were free to labor for themselves. In the 1620s and 1630s, for instance, seven former indentured servants were elected representatives to the colonial assembly of Virginia and fifteen to the Maryland assembly.[21] And two of the members elected to the Continental Congress that authorized the writing of and approved the Declaration of Independence in 1776 were former indentured servants, as was the secretary of the Congress. All three of these men were signers of the Declaration.

Indentured servitude had one great flaw for employers: indentured servants frequently ran away from their masters before serving out the number of years specified in their contracts. In his *Autobiography* Benjamin Franklin mentions "a wild Irishman" who worked as an indentured servant in a printing shop in Philadelphia where Franklin was employed in the 1720s, and who "soon ran away" and was never apprehended. There were many such instances in colonial America of this understandable, albeit unlawful, behavior. If caught, runaway indentured servants were returned to their masters, and in punishment for having broken their indenture, years were added to the term of their servitude.

The frequency with which indentured servants ran away was to have far-reaching and unforeseen consequences in American history. The solution to the problem emerged in the 1600s and was recognized as law in Virginia by 1700: chattel slavery.

This new system of labor also spread quickly to other colonies because it was of even more advantage to employers than indentured servitude. And it offered traffickers in labor for America much greater profits. However, being a system of involuntary, lifelong servitude, it provided no gainful employment to workers; for them it was a system of labor with no hope of betterment. Chattel slavery had the added horror of being hereditary. Instead of the hope of perhaps leaving one's offspring some inheritance of property, as free workers might hope to do for their children, chattel slaves had to live with the shameful reality of passing on to their children a lifetime of personal abasement.

The year before the Pilgrims arrived in Massachusetts, the first workers of African descent arrived in Virginia. But they did not come from Africa, nor did they come in the condition of slaves. They were free men from the Caribbean islands, and they came as indentured servants. Like their white-skinned counterparts from Europe, these poor, dark-skinned workers sometimes became landowners after serving out their indentures. And like white indentured servants, they often broke their contracts by running away. But in a nearly all-white society like colonial America (as late as 1671 blacks made up only 5 percent of the population of Virginia[22]), runaway indentured servants with black skins were easier to trace and apprehend than runaway indentured servants who were white. Thus a black indentured servant who repeatedly ran away, and was repeatedly returned to the owner of his indenture for the punishment of added years of servitude, could end up working for the owner of his indenture for nearly his whole life. Consequently during the two generations following the introduction of indentured servants of African descent to Virginia in 1619, the system of indentured servitude for blacks gradually evolved into the legally recognized institution of chattel slavery—that is, the ownership of another person's body as "chattel," or movable property, and the ownership of their offspring as well.[23]

Chattel slavery provided the cheapest possible labor supply to employers: a lifetime of labor for one initial outlay of money, with the likelihood that from the investment would come generations of other workers also obliged by law to work for their owners all their lives. From a purely monetary point of view— setting aside the morality of "owning" the body of another human being created in the image of God—chattel slavery did much to ease the chronic shortage of labor for hire in America. And because the temptation to profit from slave labor was so great, it too, like the institution of indentured servitude, spread north and south from its point of origin in Virginia. By the early 1700s African-descended workers were being held in bondage as inheritable, saleable chattel in twelve of the thirteen colonies. (The founders of Georgia in 1732 prohibited chattel slavery but eventually gave in to the economic pressure to allow it.) As the institution of indentured servitude diminished in the late 1700s and in the early decades of the 1800s disappeared altogether, the number of slaves in America increased. Undoubtedly the rise of chattel slavery influenced the decline of indentured servitude.

Thus ironically—and, in regard to the development of American beliefs, perversely—chattel slavery evolved from the very opportunities for improvement that first attracted poor workers of both African and European ancestry to America as indentured servants. Chattel slavery was a perversion of American beliefs because it shamefully contradicted the American convictions that manual labor is respectable and that workers must benefit from their labor.

CHAPTER FOUR

Immigrant Beliefs

Improvement Is Possible
Opportunities Must Be Imagined
Freedom Of Movement Is Needed
For Success

MORE THAN 55 million immigrants have arrived in America in the last four centuries. This represents the largest movement of human beings to any one place in the history of mankind. And although restrictions on immigration to the United States have been in place for most of the twentieth century, a huge volume of migration to America has continued. (In 1980 more than 800,000 legal immigrants and refugees were permitted entry, a rate that exceeded the record decade 1901–1910; in the early 1980s between 3.5 and 5 million illegal immigrants were living in the United States.[1]) Since historically most Americans have been either immigrants themselves or descendants of immigrants, the belief-behaviors of immigrants have had a fundamental and determining influence on the formation of American culture.

During the first nine generations of American cultural history (1610–1790), almost every immigrant was from Europe; in the second nine generations of that history (1790–1970), increasing numbers from Asia, Africa, and countries in the Americas also emigrated to the United States. Wherever they came from, and regardless of the century in which they came, these millions of immigrants brought with them to America three simple beliefs which their behavior as immigrants demonstrated: *Improvement Is Possible, Opportunities Must Be Imagined*, and *Freedom Of Movement Is Needed For Success*. These convictions of the immigrants became American beliefs because they were passed down through the example of behavior, in a continual transmission from one generation to the next.

IMMIGRATION TO AMERICA has been extremely diverse throughout the nation's history. Even in the 1600s, the first century of settlement in America, many persons from the British Isles—Irishmen, Welshmen, and Scotsmen—came to America with little or no knowledge of the English language. That continued to be true of immigration from the British Isles in the 1700s and well into the 1800s. Various countries and languages of the European mainland were also represented in the emigration to America from the 1600s on. The diversity of American immigration during the formative centuries of American culture was pointed out long ago by Thomas Paine in his essay "Common Sense" (1776), when he said, "Europe, and not England, is the parent country of America."

In fact, the population of America was from England alone only for the seventeen years between 1607, when the first permanent English settlement was founded, and 1624, the year the Dutch settled the island of Manhattan and began colonizing the valley of the Hudson River. In 1664, when an English naval expedition seized these Dutch settlements and made them part of

England's territories in the New World, a dozen European languages were already being spoken in the hamlet at the southern tip of Manhattan, which the Dutch had named New Amsterdam and the English renamed New York. When the English Quaker William Penn led colonists from England to Pennsylvania in 1682, the best sites along the lower reaches of the Delaware River had already been occupied for two generations by Finns and Swedes; and a few generations after that date, one-third of Pennsylvania's population was of German extraction. From 1624 on, therefore, the proportion of English stock in the American population declined, and it has declined ever since. By the beginning of the American Revolution in 1775, perhaps only half the American population was of English ancestry.[2]

More important demographically were the frequent marriages in America between persons from the various "races" of Europe. As one immigrant noted in the 1700s, "the name of Englishman, Frenchman, and European is lost" and a new "race" is created: "They are a mixture of English, Scotch, Irish, French, Dutch, Germans, and Swedes. From this promiscuous breed, that race now called Americans have arisen. . . . I could point out to you a family whose grandfather was an Englishman, whose wife was Dutch, whose son married a French woman, and whose present four sons have now four wives of different nations." In no other place of European settlement in the New World was there such a "strange mixture of blood" among a rapidly growing population of free men and free women whose ancestors were "once scattered all over Europe."[3] And families of mixed ancestry have continued to be commonplace in America down to the present. An American woman writing in 1993 offers some typical cases:

> My husband and I are middle-class whites (German, Swedish, Danish, French, English, etc.). Many of the children of our white friends, relatives and neighbors have married into other races and ethnic groups. A few of these spouses are: a male medical student of Chinese descent, a Turkish woman doctor, a

Hawaiian man, a woman born in Japan, a gorgeous, dark-skinned Brazilian woman. . . . One of my cousins married a woman of Chinese descent, and one of my sons married a third-generation American of Japanese descent. She says about 60% of Americans of Japanese extraction marry outside their race. The son of our white/American Indian friends married a blond woman of Irish extraction. Another of their sons married a Chicana. The son of one of our black neighbors married a Cuban woman. His sister married a black man for a while, then divorced and married a white German-American.[4]

The mixing of European "races" in America in the 1600s and 1700s produced a people distinct from any single nation of Europe, including England. When Americans declared their independence in 1776, they "already differed from our kinsmen of Britain in blood as well as in name" and were members of "the English race only in the sense in which Englishmen belong to the German."[5] (The American historian, politician, and man of affairs who made this comment was to be the twenty-sixth president of the United States, Theodore Roosevelt.) After the loss of their thirteen American colonies, Englishmen sometimes soothed their injured feelings by dismissing those who had thrown off English rule as a "mongrel" breed.

Regardless of their "racial" and national origins, the immigrants who have come to America during the four centuries of its history have shared the conviction that going to America would improve their lives. This conviction, *Improvement Is Possible*, is what made them potential immigrants, whatever the country of their birth. Acting on that conviction made them immigrants. And it made them Americans before they ever laid eyes on America.

In the cultures the immigrants left behind, not everyone believed in improvement through emigration. Only a portion of those who were dissatisfied with their lives in Europe acted on that dissatisfaction by leaving their homelands for America. Most stayed where they were, afraid to make a change that, although it might improve their lives, might bring hardship and failure. Consequently those who did not truly believe that improvement was possible stayed at home and put up with their dissatisfaction or deprivation instead of risking emigration. A few of those who were dissatisfied and stayed behind became agitators for reform. The immigrants were those who were dissatisfied and who believed in an immediate, radical reformation in their own lives, which they would determine for themselves. They were not interested in revolutionary changes to European society or culture. They were interested in improving their own lives by removing themselves to a place where a new world was in the making.

That willingness to act on the possibility of a radical improvement in their own lives was a fundamental outlook they shared regardless of their "race" or nationality, the language they spoke, or the religion they practiced. Closely tied to their willingness to act on the possibility of improvement was their ability to "see" a better future in their mind's eye, to imagine opportunities. In moving to the place where they hoped those imagined opportunities would be realized, they showed a conviction that freedom of movement was necessary to success. After their arrival in America, they continued to act on the beliefs that had compelled them to cross the ocean to a new continent: *Improvement Is Possible, Opportunities Must Be Imagined, Freedom Of Movement Is Needed For Success.* When they set foot on American soil, these beliefs gave them a nucleus of convictions with other Americans, whose immigrant ancestors had passed down to them these same beliefs through the example of their own behavior.

Because the immigrants believed they could better their lives, and because of their commitment to the pursuit of an imagined, future happiness, even those who arrived in America speaking no English had a stronger bond to one another and to the immigrants who had preceded them, and to the American-born offspring of those immigrants, than they had to their compatriots left behind in their native land. Having chosen to emigrate to a new homeland rather than suffer deprivation in their native land, they showed a self-respect at odds with their native culture and a willingness to risk being part of a new way of life that most of their compatriots lacked. Regardless of their country of origin or "race," they were discontented persons in search of self-improvement; each of them had made the same momentous choice of abandoning everything familiar in favor of an imagined future.

They were committed to success in America; they expected their move to America to result eventually in success. To fail meant a retreat to their native land in defeat. Such a retreat would have been an admission that their decision to emigrate had been a fool's dream. Some of them, of course, did fail to make a better life for themselves in America; and of those who failed, some did return to their old homeland. But most stayed. And even if they did not begin soon after their arrival in America to realize their imagined opportunities, they persisted in trying to find the happiness they had imagined for themselves, so as to retain their self-respect. If they finally gave up all hope of success for themselves, they fell back on the hope that their offspring would succeed where they had failed, and thus justify their decision to emigrate to America.

Happiness and success are not amenable to statistical analysis. Yet it would be safe to say, on general grounds, that many more immigrants or their descendants succeeded in America than failed. Otherwise the volume of immigration to this one place in the world would not have continued to increase from one century to the next as it did. Streets in America might not be paved with gold, and much loneliness, hard work, and not a little suffering might be the lot of most immigrants involved in the struggle to make a new life in America; but sufficient numbers of immigrants were able to send enough money from their earnings in America to persons left behind in the old homelands to pay for the passage of friends and family members (and sometimes even strangers) to come to America—thus convincing more and more Europeans that going to America was worthwhile. Perhaps more than anything else, that sure evidence of success in America—the money sent back to the countries of origin by the immigrants—

increased the volume of immigration to America from villages, farms, and cities all over Europe and, later on, from villages, farms, and cities in Asia, Africa, and other parts of the Americas.

The pre-emigration beliefs of immigrants explain why America has historically been able to assimilate into one nationhood so many persons of diverse languages, religions, and "races"—a phenomenon so well established by the mid-1700s that one immigrant who arrived in America in 1759 was already saying that in America "individuals of all nations are melted into a new race of men."[6] Whether one uses the now familiar metaphor of the melting pot or some other figure of speech to describe it, the assimilation in America of diverse immigrants into one nationality is a fact of primary importance in American history. The process began long before the American Revolution and continues to the present. The "potent digestion" of America—as one native-born American writer called the phenomenon in 1866—is one of the distinguishing features of American culture.[7] This merger of individuals from many nations into a new cultural identity originated in large measure in the traits of mind, character, and behavior that distinguish immigrants from other types of persons. America was the only part of the New World whose population was made up predominantly of self-selected immigrants and their descendants. And throughout American history, the convictions of immigrants about improvement, opportunity, and movement have periodically been refreshed by new waves of immigrants. More important, the behavior of the self-selected immigrants after their arrival in America has been a model for their offspring to imitate in enculturating belief in improvement, opportunity, and freedom of movement.

Sociologists explain immigration in terms of "push and pull"—the push of conditions in the immigrant's place of origin, and the pull of conditions in the contemplated destination. They ignore the mentality that disposes only some persons in a distressed population to emigrate, even though the entire population is subjected to the same "push and pull." Certain character traits and beliefs decide which persons among a distressed population will in fact emigrate. The many persons who may be dissatisfied with conditions in one place, and who may have heard reports of satisfactory conditions in some other place, do not all leave their homeland. Only some will actually be moved by such circumstances and reports to undergo the trauma of emigrating to the place where conditions are supposedly better. What overcomes the strong natural attachment to one's birthplace and the inertia of the familiar that keeps most human beings fixed in their native culture, is a personal belief in the possibility of improvement through emigration and a personal belief in opportunities "seen" only in the mind's eye. When one finds a society made up mostly of persons having such beliefs, and the descendants of such persons, one has the makings of a new culture.

The hopeful visionary, whose self-respect is appreciably greater than his respect for the established way of life of his native place, is the person who will emigrate to a distant shore. The emigrant is the person with enough bravery to act on what he sees only in his mind's eye. There can be no mistake on this important point. It requires both extraordinary vision and extraordinary courage to uproot oneself from one's native culture, cross an ocean, and begin a new life on another continent in a place where conditions are bound to be unfamiliar and where one may not even understand the language being spoken. That is a daunting prospect, and it keeps most persons from being emigrants.

America has attracted persons from every nation on earth who have presented this profile; for that reason, more than any other, America has enjoyed remarkable success in assimilating Finns and Englishmen and Colombians and Germans and Koreans and Frenchmen and Palestinians and Ukrainians and Welshmen and Lithuanians and Angolans and Norwegians and Jamaicans and Egyptians and Canadians and Turks and Mexicans and Italians and Scotsmen and Japanese and Russians and Brazilians and Iranians and Irishmen and Lebanese and Poles and Chinese and Ethiopians and Zairians—and individuals from many other peoples on every inhabited continent of the world. It is interesting to note in this regard that one of every five recipients of the Medal of Honor—the nation's highest military award for valor in battle—has been an immigrant. A Mexican immigrant, who was not yet a U.S. citizen when he won his Medal of Honor during the Vietnam War, when asked why he had felt compelled to fight so bravely for a country of which he was not a citizen, said simply: "I was always an American in my heart."[8]

The pre-emigration beliefs of the immigrants to America— *Improvement Is Possible, Opportunities Must Be Imagined,* and *Freedom Of Movement Is Needed For Success*—were the mold by which their diversities of nationality, language, and religion could be amalgamated into a new American identity. Each immigrant and immigrant group (that is, persons coming from the same country) has had a peculiar experience in America, distinctive to that individual or group; but they have generally shared, as immigrants, belief in the possibility of improvement, a capacity for imagining an improved future for themselves, and a commitment to movement as part of the search for improvement. Those were the beliefs they acted on in leaving their native places, and they shared those beliefs with the American-born descendants of the immigrants who had preceded them and had passed them on to their descendants through the example of their behavior.

George Santayana, who was brought to America from Spain as a child in 1872 and became a professor at Harvard University, remarked in his book *Character and Opinion in the United States* (1920) that being an American is "almost a moral condition, an education, and a career." The observation contains much truth. The opportunities for success in America for anyone with the imagination to see them have, to an extraordinary degree, made life in this nation a matter of choices (a moral condition); and, in trying out various paths to success in America, a person learns things that could not be learned in a more restrictive society (life in America as an education); and, living in America, one cannot avoid recognizing that achieving and maintaining a certain level of success is not only possible but required to retain one's self-respect (being an American as a career). Perhaps no other culture has ever made participation in it "a moral condition, an education, and a career."

THE CHOICES and opportunities for self-determination that have been basic to American life have not figured prominently in the life of European countries. The culture of England, for example, historically has placed great importance on knowing one's "place" in society and respectfully staying in it; on paying deference to "one's betters" in a hierarchy of classes having different social responsibilities and comparatively little upward mobility. Americans, because of their immigrant-derived beliefs in the importance of freedom of movement and self-improvement, have difficulty accepting the notion of social "betters" and of occupying a fixed position on a social scale, which may be why few American servicemen stationed in England during World War II felt "at home socially." England was "a society which worked by deference," and "the Americans [stationed in England] did not defer; that was the first and strongest impression they made" on Englishmen.[9]

One twentieth-century historian of American social behavior, in identifying "extreme mobility" as one of the characteristics of American life, said: "People move up and down in the social scale [in the United States] and round about the country like bubbles in a boiling kettle. Social life everywhere is . . . in a constant flux."[10] The reason for this phenomenon is that society in America involves a competition to improve. And the competition is never-ending because there is no definition of ultimate improvement. Consequently no one's social status in America is ever fully assured, and in American culture no social class has ever deserved or received the sort of deference that members of the uppermost class of English society have historically received from the social classes "beneath them." In its history, America has had no hereditary aristocrats like England's, whose status was assured and remained stable for many generations. Freedom of movement in America has meant social mobility both up and down. Therefore the idea of "one's betters" is repugnant to an American; and it is culturally difficult, if not impossible, for Americans to show a heartfelt deference to another human being.

The difference between English and American beliefs in this regard was well illustrated during the 1991 visit to the United States of the queen of England. Elizabeth II, then age sixty-five, was taken on a tour of a housing project and introduced to one of the householders, a Mrs. Alice Frazier, age sixty-seven, who, by way of welcoming her distinguished visitor, said (according to reporters covering the queen's activities), "How are you doin'!?" and enfolded the royal personage in a full hug.[11] By the standards of English culture, this should never have happened. Although acting in the best of goodwill, Mrs. Frazier was guilty of a breach of English decorum of shocking proportions, namely not knowing her place and minding her manners in the presence of one of her "betters." No "commoner" in England, as Mrs. Frazier would naturally have considered herself had she been born and raised there, would ever have hugged Her Royal Majesty on first acquaintance—or on any subsequent acquaintance either, for that matter. But, being an American, Mrs. Frazier regarded the queen as just another woman of about the same age as herself who deserved a friendly welcome.

Is it any wonder, then—given the recurrence of such behavior on the part of Americans over the years—that some Englishmen who have traveled in America have reported that Americans have no manners? What these English observers mean, of course, is that Americans are culturally incapable of the sort of deference that the people of England have historically shown members of England's "ruling class."

According to English cultural beliefs, Americans are deficient in this regard; but only because they have a democratic culture, incorporating social mobility and the pursuit of improvements, rather than an aristocratic culture, incorporating deference to a governing class and a deep-seated acceptance of social tradition. The difference has a long history. One English visitor to Pennsylvania when it was a colony of England lamented that the lowliest inhabitant of the province acted as though he had "a right to Civility from the greatest"; and an English administrator serving in America shortly before the outbreak of the war that separated America from England complained that all "distinctions of rank" had been lost in America because "wealth and preferment are alike open to all men."[12] Conversely the American writer Ralph Waldo Emerson in the nineteenth century found the "social barriers" between classes that he observed in England disagreeable to his American sentiments and deplored "the submissive ideas pervading these people." About the relations between classes in England he went on to say, "An Englishman shows no mercy to those below him in the social scale, as he looks for none from those above him: any forbearance from his superiors surprises him, and they suffer in his good opinion."[13] Although Emerson was a great admirer of England, as an American he did not feel at home in the presence of the English caste system any more than did the American GIs stationed there during World War II.

THE TENS OF MILLIONS of immigrants to America during the past four centuries have invariably sought improvement of some sort. But improvement was also demanded by the reality of the Stone Age wilderness, an encounter that lies at the heart of American history. For both these reasons, the status quo has been culturally unacceptable to Americans. Entire campaigns for the presidency of the United States have been successfully waged by a candidate invoking the slogan that "change" is needed and making the pitch that he can "get the country moving again." These terms of discourse touch a responsive cultural chord in Americans when put forward with apparent sincerity and conviction. Americans like movement and change because their cultural ancestors were immigrants who chose a change of residence to improve their lives. Whether voters really think that a candidate who invokes these cultural beliefs would, if he became president, "get the country moving again" (whatever that means) is beside the point—which is that most Americans culturally believe that it would be a good thing to do. Any candidate for the presidency who can convince voters that he is for change and movement will receive a great many votes he would otherwise not have gotten.

The first settlers in America began improvements on the wilderness soon after they stepped ashore and organized themselves. This meant destroying and replacing the wilderness. But the process of improvement did not stop with the creation of civilized structures and landscapes. The radical transition from wilderness to farmland began a way of life in which continual betterments became a norm of behavior. Thus when Noah Webster published his first dictionary of the American language, two hundred years after the founding of Jamestown—*A Compendious Dictionary of the English Language* (1806)—he defined the word *improvements* as "additions to or meliorations of a farm, as buildings, fences, clearings, &c."; and in his monumental *American Dictionary of the English Language*, published in 1828—the first great lexicographical accomplishment by an American and the basis for all subsequent dictionaries of American English—he defined *improvement* as "a making or growing better, or more valuable; as the *improvement* of the roads; the *improvement* of the breed of horses or cattle," and gave as the definition of the plural of the word (*improvements*), as he had done in his first dictionary: "valuable additions or melioration, as buildings, clearings, drains, fences &c., on a farm."

The first stand of trees felled and burned by Englishmen at Jamestown, in order to clear a field for planting a crop, was the beginning of a new way of life. It was a way of life that led Samuel Clemens, writing under the pen name Mark Twain, to say in 1867: "To find a new planet, to invent a new hinge, to find the way to make the lightnings carry your messages. To be the *first*—that is the idea. To do something, say something, see something, before *anybody* else—these are the things that confer a pleasure compared with which other pleasures are tame and commonplace, other ecstasies cheap and trivial."[14] The fascina-

tion of Americans with "firsts" is a sign of their historically com-
petitive commitment to constant improvement.

Making improvements—whether to a farm or to the sum of
human knowledge—is an unending process because what is better is always a comparative judgment, as in the American exchange of greetings: "How're things?" "They could be better."
The European claim that Americans lack a sense of the past
and are oriented to the future has some truth to it. But Americans are future-oriented only in the sense that their culture is
improvement-oriented. They believe the future will be better
than the past because their cultural ancestors, who were immigrants, held that belief and acted on it. And of course things can
always by made better if you culturally believe, as Americans do,
that improvements are both possible and required.

Americans are mindful of the past as a starting point for
measuring improvement. They compete among themselves to
make things better, but they are also competing with previous
generations. They act to make their own lives better, but they
also hope to leave an improved world for future generations and
to have the good opinion of generations yet unborn. Hence they
are interested in being the "first" to do something, and they have
a passion for statistics as a way of measuring progress. (The
American Statistical Association was founded in 1839.) The
fondness for improvements on a grand scale is also reflected in
the popularity of stories about exaggerated accomplishments in
the performance of work that transforms (improves) the landscape, such as in the doings of heroes like Paul Bunyan and John
Henry.

Because of the rapidity with which Americans improve their
homeland from one generation to another, things grow old fast
in America. New improvements are made at a rate that guaran-
tees constant obsolescence. An "old" family, an "old" church, an
"old" city does not have the same meaning in America as those
same expressions have in Europe, not just because the span of
American history (four centuries) is a great deal shorter than that
of European history, but also because Americans want things to

be "new and improved." Their sense of history is that of having rapidly brought forth a new civilization directly from a terribly old reality: the Stone Age. That sense of the past simply does not exist in European culture. The Stone Age has faded from European consciousness during the much longer course of European history.

Wilderness represents what is truly old for Americans. At least in part, the motive behind creating Yellowstone Park, the first nature preserve in the world—which Americans did in 1872 when the Far West was still being settled—was to keep intact an example of the ancient wilderness that represented their country's past. The Wilderness Act of 1964 preserved from improvement tracts of "wilderness" throughout the United States totaling the combined areas of the states of Connecticut, Iowa, and Michigan (96 million acres), in order that Americans in all parts of the country might have a sense of their nation's past.

America's history of creating in just a few centuries a single nation nearly the size of all of Europe stands in stark contrast to the history of that continent. Disunity and warfare have characterized the history of Europeans. One has only to compare the stable state boundaries of the United States with the fluctuating borders of European countries during the past two centuries to see the remarkable difference between the histories of Europe and America. For most Americans, history has been a foundation for further improvements. For Europeans, the past has been a source of grievance and conflict, a justification for retaliation in the present for the wrongs done to one's self or one's ancestors.

Although interested in the past as a way of measuring progress, Americans do not brood over past wrongs nor allow their lives to be determined by past events. Rather they are, as a people, hopeful and forward-looking because their cultural ancestors were immigrants who believed in the possibilities of "starting over again" in a new place. For Europeans, however, the past is never quite over. Woodrow Wilson as president of the United States learned this fact when in 1919 he attended the Paris Peace Conference that ended World War I and discovered that his European allies were intent on exacting vindictive, ruinous reparations from their defeated foes, and that his American attitude of making a "soft" peace was considered naive and unacceptable to victorious Europeans. Europeans keep score about what their ancestors did to each other. Americans keep score about their progress.

To most Americans, it hardly matters what one nation may have done to another in the past, or what someone's great-grandfather may have done to theirs. While the past is not insignificant to the American people, it is the present and the future, where improvements can be made, that matter most. The 1963 "I Have a Dream" speech of Martin Luther King, Jr., illustrates very well this American characteristic. For an American, the imagined future is more culturally relevant than whatever horrors may have transpired in the past.

THE BELIEFS *Improvement Is Possible, Opportunities Must Be Imagined,* and *Freedom Of Movement Is Needed For Success* are classically illustrated in *Giants in the Earth,* a novel by the Norwegian immigrant Ole Edvart Rölvaag about Norwegian immigrants homesteading the Dakota prairies in the 1870s. Rölvaag emphasized the imagination that motivates his central character, Per Hansa, a Norwegian fisherman turned American farmer:

> But dearest to him of all, and most delectable, was the thought of the royal mansion which he had already erected in his mind. There would be houses for both chickens and pigs, roomy stables, a magnificent storehouse and barn . . . and then the splendid palace itself! The royal mansion would shine in the sun—it would stand out far and wide! The palace itself would be white, with green cornices; but the big barn would be red as blood, with cornices of driven snow. Wouldn't it be beautiful— wasn't it going to be great fun! . . . And he and his boys would build it all![15]

This immigrant also imagines a white picket fence around "a big, big garden" with fruit trees set out in it, as well as many other things he and his sons will create on the Dakota prairie. Per Hansa's visions of the future typify the mentality of Rölvaag's pioneers, who are "more interested in visualizing how things were going to turn out than in making a bare statement of how they actually were."[16] Imagining the future sustained them in their work to make their visions come true, and provided meaning and direction to their daily efforts.

Per Hansa's wife is the exception who proves the rule that the homesteaders are inspired and comforted by their visions of the future. She is constantly brooding on the past, yearning for the old way of life left behind in Norway. The wilderness of grass in the center of North America to which her husband's vision has brought them is too strange, too intimidating to her. She is indifferent to the purpose of building a better future that has drawn him and their Norwegian neighbors to the Dakota Territory. She longs to return to the familiar security and traditional ways of her parents' farm in the old country. The primitive vastness of the Great Plains weighs on her spirit. She lacks the imagination that would allow her to see this wild solitude one day filled, all the way to the Rocky Mountains, with farms and towns, the way her husband and the others can. Lacking their imagination of the future to give her hope, she suffers a mental breakdown; and Per Hansa is overcome by guilt as he realizes that his compelling dream of owning a farm of 160 acres has destroyed the mind of his beloved Beret. In his anguish he exclaims to the Lutheran minister of the settlement about the wrong he has done his wife: "She has never felt at home here in America. . . . There are some people, I know now, who never should emigrate, because, you see, they can't take pleasure in that which is to come—they simply can't see it!"[17]

Rölvaag demonstrates that the pioneers had to be able to see opportunities for an as-yet-unrealized future in order to sustain their backbreaking labors and their forlorn lives on the prairie:

> [The trips to town] were the jolliest days, said some; no, they were the worst of all, said the others. It may be that both were

right. . . . The oxen moved slowly—whether the distance was thirty miles or ninety miles made little difference. In the sod house back there, somewhere along the horizon, life got on your nerves at times. There sat a wife with a flock of starving children; she had grown very pale of late, and the mouths of the children were always open—always crying for food. . . . But in the town it was cheerful and pleasant. There one could get a drink; there one could talk with people who spoke with enthusiasm and certainty about the future. This was the land of promise, they said. Sometimes one met these people in the saloons; and then it was more fascinating to listen to them than to any talk about the millennium. Their words lay like embers in the mind during the whole of the interminable, jolting journey homeward, and made it less long. . . . It helps so much to have something pleasant to think about, . . . the unknown, the untried, the unheard-of, was in the air; people caught it, were intoxicated by it, threw themselves away, and laughed at the cost. Of course it was possible—everything was possible out here. There was no such thing as the Impossible any more. The human race has not known such faith and such self-confidence since history began. . . . And so had been the Spirit since the day the first settlers landed on the eastern shores; it would rise and fall at intervals, would swell and surge on again with every new wave of settlers that rolled westward into the unbroken solitude.[18]

Without faith in what they saw in their mind's eye, many more of the homesteaders would have broken down under the strain of their struggle with loneliness, blizzards, drought, prairie fires, and locust plagues. One has only to fly across the continent in a commercial airliner today and look down from the plane's altitude at the Great Plains below to see the wonderful reality of the accomplishments of the pioneers Rölvaag described and celebrated in his novel—the vast quilt of farms stretching from horizon to horizon for a thousand miles, which are the most abundantly productive agricultural lands on the planet.

An earlier American writer, James Fenimore Cooper, in his novel *The Pioneers*, describing the settlement of upstate New York in the 1790s, also portrays the importance of vision. The frontier judge and land developer in this novel selected the site for a town from a hill in the wilderness which he named "Mount Vision." And we are told: "The mind of Judge Temple, at all times comprehensive, had received, from his peculiar occupations, a bias to look far into futurity, in his speculations on the improvements that posterity were to make in his lands. To his eye, where others saw nothing but a wilderness, towns, manufactories, bridges, canals, mines, and all the other resources of an old country, were constantly presenting themselves, though his good sense suppressed, in some degree, the exhibition of these expectations."[19]

In one scene in Cooper's story, one of the pioneers takes a cousin who has been absent from the settlement for several years to see the "improvements" he has made since her last visit. Their talk goes like this: "Where are the beauties and improvements which you were to show me?" "Where! why every where. Here I have laid out some new streets; and when they are opened, and the trees felled, and they are all built up, will they not make a fine town?" "I see no streets in the direction of our walk, unless you call the short avenues through these pine bushes by that name. Surely you do not contemplate building houses, very soon, in that forest before us, and in those swamps." "We must run our streets by the compass, coz, and disregard trees, hills, ponds, stumps, or, in fact, any thing but posterity."[20] The future improvements which this person sees in his mind's eye move him and the other pioneers of Templeton to be active in fulfilling them, and give them the determination they need to overcome obstacles.

In a book the American poet Stephen Vincent Benét wrote during World War II, he said something quite similar about the pioneer mind. "When an American showed a European a few log cabins in a malarious swamp and called the result a great city, the European didn't know whether to laugh in his guide's face or to make the soothing remarks that one makes to the insane. But the American was not seeing what was in front of his eyes—the sharp-nosed pigs in the street, the agued and sallow people. He was seeing what ought to be there in fifty years' time—and he was perfectly willing to call the place New Athens or Palmyra or Eden, and find nothing absurd in the name."[21]

The cultural significance of such historical novels as *Giants in the Earth* and *The Pioneers*, and the remarks of Stephen Vincent Benét, is that they correspond to the reality of American history. The Stone Age wilderness of central North America *was* transformed into farms and towns by the labors, sacrifices, and suffering of generations of immigrants and their American-born descendants. They had in mind an imagined future, first on the Atlantic coastal plain and then on the trans-Appalachian hill country and the Great Plains of the middle of the continent, and finally in the series of mountain ranges, valleys, and basins farther west, all the way to the Pacific Ocean. Seeing the future was necessary at every step of that progress across the continent. Had millions of individuals not imagined opportunities generation after generation, America could never have grown in the brief span of four centuries from the tiny seed of Jamestown, a settlement of one hundred Englishmen, into a mighty nation that will soon reach a population of 300 million.

BUT AMERICANS have not been just dreamers. They have been doers, achievers of dreams. As heirs of cultural ancestors who were immigrants, they have had a hopeful and potent imagination which has stimulated them to sustained action. And their accomplishments have continually attracted more and more immigrants having the same kind of character—persons from all over the world who were Americans at heart before leaving for America, persons who were able to see with their mind's eye opportunities for a better future for themselves and their posterity and who were determined enough and brave enough to act on what they imagined and willing to tackle almost any obstacle to try to realize what they imagined.

One American who between 1790 and 1810 traveled eighteen thousand miles through the backwoods of New England and New York said this in 1803:

> A person who has extensively seen the efforts of the New England people in colonizing new countries cannot fail of being forcibly struck by their enterprise, industry, and perseverance. In Maine, in New Hampshire, in Vermont, in Massachusetts, and in New York, I have passed the dwellings of several hundred thousands of these people, erected on grounds which in 1760 were an absolute wilderness. A large part of these tracts they have already converted into fruitful fields, covered it with productive farms, surrounded it with enclosures, planted on it orchards, and beautified it with comfortable and in many places with handsome houses. Considerable tracts I have traced through their whole progress from a desert to a garden, and have literally beheld the wilderness blossom as the rose.[22]

This same observer—Timothy Dwight, president of Yale University from 1795 to 1817, who year after year when Yale was not in session made extensive journeys on horseback through New England and New York for his health—called the American "colonization of a wilderness" a process that Europe and "the records of past ages" did not contain. This was why for more than twenty years he kept records of his annual journeys on horseback in the northeastern United States.

Based on what he saw during his travels, Dwight confidently and accurately imagined in 1804 that "at no great distance of time" Americans would be settling on the shores of the Pacific Ocean.[23] Within two generations his prophecy was fulfilled: the first wagon train of Americans left Missouri for the Pacific Coast on May 11, 1841, and arrived in California on November 1 that year. Dwight had been certain in 1804 that Americans would not only settle California (then a province of the Spanish Empire) but also colonize the entire western drainage of the Mississippi called "Louisiana," the immense area of the southern Great Plains vaguely referred to as "Texas" (which also belonged to

Spain at that time), and all the lands in between California, "Louisiana," and "Texas." And he was sure of his prediction because he had seen the large-scale, rapid improvements accomplished during his lifetime in the northeastern United States.

Around the same time Dwight made his prediction, Noah Webster began work on his great dictionary of American English. As he said in the preface of the published work when he finished it twenty-two years later, "a standard" was needed for the language that he believed would one day be spoken by the *"three hundred millions of people"* destined to occupy the United States of America[24] (a prediction that stands an excellent chance of being fulfilled before the two hundredth anniversary, in the year 2028, of the first edition of his *American Dictionary of the English Language*). Like countless other Americans in all walks of life over the past four centuries, Noah Webster was a visionary who foresaw a great future for America and labored mightily to make his particular contribution to the realization of that vision. He was inspired to apply himself to the production of the first great dictionary of American English by what he imagined was going to happen in the United States of America. To carry out his intention of tracing the meanings of English words to their roots, he taught himself to read nineteen ancient and modern languages. The monumental achievement of this self-taught lexicographer—one of the great accomplishments of American civilization—would not have been possible without his commitment to his vision of a future nation of 300 million *at a time when the population of the United States was only 4 percent of that predicted total.*

WHAT KINDS OF THINGS have Americans imagined and worked to achieve? Historically they have enjoyed for the most part what the immigrants lacked in the countries where most of them had been "peasants" or members of the "lower orders" of society: the opportunity to live in a good house or to own a piece of ground; the opportunity to eat better food; the opportunity to rise in social station; the opportunity to move about freely over hundreds, and even thousands, of miles of territory without having to seek authorization from a government official; the opportunity to get an education and have access to books; the opportunity to participate in choosing who would govern, and to criticize freely their government without fear of reprisal; the opportunity to worship God without having to pay taxes to support the priests or ministers of a state-approved church; the opportunity to be free of lordly dominance and patronage and the obsequiousness that is unavoidably a part of such a relationship; and the opportunity to be whatever one might aspire to be, and had the capacity for being, regardless of who one's parents had been or what they might have done in their lives. To the hero of Rölvaag's novel *Giants in the Earth*, who had been a fisherman in Norway, owning 160 acres of good wheatland and having a two-story farmhouse with a picket fence around it and a big red barn with white trim was, in his imagination, like being a king and living in a palace.

Rölvaag himself was an immigrant. The difference between his life in Norway and his life in America exemplifies the realization of one immigrant's vision. When he left his native Norway for America he was a twenty-two-year-old fisherman, born and raised in an impoverished community of fishermen near the Arctic Circle. Early in his life his fisherman father had told him that the son of a fisherman was not worth educating beyond elementary school. In America he went to work on the farm of the uncle in South Dakota who had sent him the money to come to America, and after several years of toil there he had enough savings to pay for two years of study at a preparatory school, where he learned to speak and write English, and four years at St. Olaf College in Minnesota, where he got as an adult the education that his father had informed him he was unworthy of having. His academic performance as a student was so impressive that upon his graduation the college officials offered him a position on the faculty. He accepted the offer, and on the strength of it borrowed five hundred dollars which he used to pay for a year of postgraduate study in Norway before taking up the post. In time this son of an impoverished Norwegian fisherman became chairman of his department at his alma mater and the author of a novel about the lives of Norwegian immigrants on the Dakota prairie.

THE IMMIGRANTS and their descendants who between 1600 and 1900 transformed the Stone Age wilderness of central North America from ocean to ocean and melded themselves into a new cultural identity created a distinctive national space, unlike any other in the post-1492 Americas. Its distinguishing features are its continental unity and extraordinary provisions for freedom of movement.

Because of the preponderance of slaves in Brazil, freedom of movement there was forbidden to most of the population during the crucial formative centuries of its cultural history. Slaves are not free to work for themselves, and their residence is fixed wherever their master decides to use them for his benefit. Furthermore the geography of the Amazon Basin, which covers most of Brazil's territory, inhibited large-scale movement of settlers inland. There are hundreds of species of insects in the Amazon, for instance, whose bites are harmful to human beings. Even now, almost five centuries after the Portuguese colonized the coast of Brazil, most Brazilians still live within 150 miles of the Atlantic. Up to twelve feet of rain a year fall in the Amazon Basin, which contains the planet's largest rain forest and largest "river." The term used by the Brazilians for the Amazon is more accurate: "*O rio mar*," the river-sea. The designation is no exaggeration, for the discharge of this "river" creates a bore of fresh water so powerful that it pushes the ocean aside for a hundred miles out into the Atlantic. At its mouth, the banks of the Amazon are so far apart that they are invisible from mid-channel because the curvature of the earth hides them from view. Twice a year this unbelievably huge river-sea (whose undredged main channel is 150 feet deep throughout most of its 3,000-mile length) and the tributaries that feed it inundate an area larger than the Mediterranean Sea, the world's largest inland body of salt water. To say that the Amazon Basin is uninviting to large-scale human settlement and development is an understatement.

The situation in French Canada—for somewhat different reasons—also kept most of its colonial population stationary. Again, geography—in this instance the freezing arctic and sub-arctic climates of Canada and the amazing saturation of its interior with ponds, lakes, and bogs—discouraged the colonial population of Canada from leaving the St. Lawrence River valley and steadily spreading inland, though Canadian *coureurs de bois* (woods runners) showed extraordinary skill and enterprise as long-distance explorers and far-ranging fur-traders during the few months of the year when the watery interior of Canada was not locked in ice and could be traversed by canoe. More important than the influence of geography, however, was the policy of the French government in keeping the population of French Canada small and concentrated in the valley of the St. Lawrence River. All these factors—the forbidding geography of most of Canada, its small population, and the firm control of Canadian affairs exercised from France by the French crown—dampened the self-determination, freedom of movement, and expansiveness of Canadian settlers. The world's second largest nation in size, Canada still ranks only thirty-fifth among the nations of the world in population, and most of that population remains concentrated near Canada's southern border.

An interesting fact about this continent-size nation is that the right of its citizens to move freely from one Canadian province to another, without authorization from the government of the province into which the citizen wanted to move, was not recognized until 1982. The Constitution Act of that year stated: "Every citizen of Canada and every person who has the status of a permanent resident of Canada has the right to move to and take up residence in any province and to pursue the gaining of a living in any province." The pamphlet *The Constitution and You* issued by the government of Canada to explain to Canadian citizens the 1982 act says, in reference to this provision (under the heading "The right to move about the country"): "You have probably taken it for granted that you're free to move anywhere in Canada to seek a new job and a better life. But that hasn't exactly been the case, because some provinces have denied employment in certain industries to workers from other provinces. The Charter protects your right to mobility by declaring that every Canadian and every permanent resident is free to move or to look for work anywhere in Canada, without discrimination based on province of residence or previous residence. However, where the provincial employment rate is lower than the national average, a province or the federal government may take measures to favour residents who may be economically or socially disadvantaged."

Freedom of movement and unity of space in Spanish America have also been restricted by geography and culture. Going from one end of Spanish America to the other—that is, from Mexico's northernmost border to the southernmost extreme of Chile—is like traveling across the United States at its widest part, returning to the starting point, and then going two-thirds of the way back again across the country—a distance of some eight thousand miles. The geography of most of this elongated territory is dominated by the world's longest chain of great mountains, including thirty-one peaks that exceed twenty thousand feet. (The highest peaks in the contiguous states of the United States are just over fourteen thousand feet.) Communications in this great *cordillera* of mountains, which dominates the geography of Spanish America, are, to say the least, difficult. And this rugged, soaring terrain has much to do with why Spanish America is divided into sixteen different countries, with all of the inhibiting barriers to freedom of movement that borders between nations involve.

But cultural history has also played a large role in restricting physical and social mobility in Spanish America. The Spanish conquest of the civilizations in the Americas gave the resulting empire a peasant-master social structure which limited the freedom of movement of most of its people. The descendants of the millions of civilized Indians who had been subjugated by conquest were kept in a perpetual state of servile subordination and dependence on their Spanish masters. Naturally this social status militated against their freedom of movement and was similar in effect to the master-slave society in Brazil. As with slaves, the free movement of the "peons" who historically made up the greatest part of the population of Spanish America was not desirable to those who controlled their lives.

Even before the coming of the Spaniards, the cultures that existed in this part of the Americas were unconducive to freedom of movement. And Spanish-American culture developed from those indigenous foundations. Pre-Columbian Mexico and Peru too were organized around a peasant-master relationship: a small minority of powerful, armed lords and a mass of subordinate peasants. Those pre-conquest Indian civilizations, as much as the post-conquest society of Spanish America that supplanted them, were ruled by castes based on noble blood. In the Inca Empire—the most rigidly hierarchical of the civilizations the Spaniards conquered—an emperor who was believed to be divine ruled with an authority whose absoluteness has seldom been seen in history; and no one moved throughout his vast empire (which was as large as western Europe) without authorization from one of his officials.

In no part of the Americas but the future United States, which had a rapidly increasing population descended from self-selected immigrants, did a post-1492 culture develop that favored freedom of movement, self-determination, and unification of a continental geography. And these processes of freedom of movement and self-determination were dynamically related: self-determination presupposes a freedom to move about without government control.

America's unilingualism is another crucial feature of the cultural unity of American space. English did not develop as the national language of the United States because it was imposed by the thirteen governments of the thirteen colonies; rather, the utility of speaking a common language was embraced by non-English-speaking immigrants as a way to enhance their mobility and chances for success in America. Here too one sees the effect of the pre-emigration belief of immigrants in imagining opportunities for improvement and in freedom of movement.

American geography was eminently suited to the belief in freedom of movement of the immigrants and their descendants. The coastal plain stretching from eastern New England through Georgia posed no serious geographical barrier throughout its length except rivers, and those could be crossed by establishing ferries at various points. Indeed, the larger rivers intersecting this 1,200-mile-long plain were natural highways for movement off the coast. In the northern part of the plain, the Connecticut River, the Hudson River (navigable by oceangoing ships of the seventeenth and eighteenth centuries for 130 miles), the Delaware River, and the Susquehanna River all allowed the movement of goods and people by barge, boat, and ship, while in the southern portion of the plain the Potomac, the James, the Neuse, the Santee, the Savannah, and the Altamaha rivers provided further avenues for inland movement. In the center of the plain the 200-mile length of Chesapeake Bay—into which the Susquehanna, the Potomac, and the James empty—furnished another important means of communication. Most of the early settlements in America were along these waterways and the shores of Massachusetts Bay, Long Island Sound, and Pamlico Sound. Ships could also navigate from place to place up and down the coast, and from early on Americans were enterprising shipbuilders.

The behavior of no other people manifests the level of individual mobility American history displays. Each year from 1960 to 1994 among the American people there were on average 41 million changes of address.[25] And this has been going on for a long time. During the ten years of the 1830s, more than half the population of Boston (56 percent) were new arrivals (those who were no longer there in 1840 having died or relocated).The same degree of movement persists today in American cities: "40 to 60 percent of the inhabitants depart every decade."[26] Even in the 1700s there is evidence that Americans were frequent movers. Of the 56 signers of the Declaration of Independence, 15 (27 percent) were born in a state of the United States other than the one they were representing in the Continental Congress, and another 8 (14 percent) were immigrants, so that a total of 41 percent of these founders of the nation had made at least one major move during their lives.

EARLY IN their history Americans set about improving their internal communications to make the movement of goods and people within their nation easier, faster, and cheaper. They improved communications along the Atlantic Coast by digging canals across the big neck of land between the lower Delaware River and the upper part of Chesapeake Bay and the wide peninsula separating the Delaware from the Hudson River, which shortened coastwise travel between New York, Philadelphia, and Baltimore by hundreds of miles. These were the first of many projects to speed interstate transportation. In the construction of a great canal across the length of the state of New York in 1825, the behavior of Americans made even plainer their interest in freedom of movement and the unification of their national territory through improved communications between states and regions. The completion of the Erie Canal—360 miles long with a vertical lift of 571 feet—connected four of the five freshwater seas in the center of North America called the Great Lakes with the Atlantic Ocean via the head of navigation on the Hudson River. The Great Lakes served by the Erie Canal have more than 3,000 miles of shoreline within United States territory.

A potential for movement and unity of communication also existed in the network of huge rivers in the middle of the country. These rivers were navigable by shallow-draft boats of various kinds from the Appalachian Mountains to the Rocky Mountains, and from the latitude of Lake Superior to the Gulf of Mexico. The principal waterways of this continental system of interconnected rivers—the north-south oriented Mississippi and its two main tributaries, the Ohio coming in from the east and the Missouri from the northwest—have a combined length of almost six thousand miles. The lesser tributaries of these three main streams (the Allegheny, Cumberland, Tennessee, and Wabash rivers; the Arkansas, Illinois, Republican, St. Francis, White, and Wisconsin rivers; and the James, Little Missouri, Platte, Osage, and Yellowstone rivers) afforded sixteen thousand miles of additional waterways. Because of this potential for communication by rivers and lakes, American inventors early on were interested in the development of steam propulsion for boats. By 1840 steam-powered boats were in service on eastern waterways, the Great Lakes, and the Ohio-Mississippi-Missouri network of rivers.

American geography offered tremendous advantages for the movement of people and goods. But it took vision, inventiveness, immense investments of work and money, and a keen cultural interest in freedom of movement to seize upon those advantages and create a unified space. The truth of that generalization can be seen in the history of the Pampas, the coastal plain bordering the Atlantic in southern South America. The size of Texas, this South American coastal plain offered far greater opportunities for agricultural development than the Atlantic coastal plain of North America. Anyone who has ever traveled the Pampas— from the southern states of Brazil through Uruguay to the Andes of Argentina—can testify that these plains equal the best agricultural land of the North American Great Plains. Furthermore the Pampas had no covering of heavy forest to be removed before it could be transformed into farmland; and the three rivers (the Uruguay, the Paraguay, and the Parana) which empty into the great estuary in the middle of this coastal plain are far larger and go much farther into the interior of South America than any river on the Atlantic coastal plain of North America. Despite these attractive natural advantages, the Pampas were not settled by large numbers of Spaniards and developed into the highly productive agricultural lands they have become since Spanish rule ended in South America.

Understandably, the potential agricultural riches of the Pampas held less attraction for sixteenth-century Spaniards than the actual riches found in Mexico, Central America, and the uplands of Colombia, Ecuador, Bolivia, and Peru, where already there were productive agricultural landscapes worked by millions of civilized Indian peasants and fabulous mines of precious metal. Hence the Pampas remained a place of only marginal settlement until the nineteenth century; and nothing like what happened in the north, in the future United States of America, happened there for half a century after the independence of this part of the New World from Spanish rule. Only in the second half of the nineteenth century did the Pampas begin to receive the sort of large influx of immigrants that the Atlantic coastal plain of North America had received from early in its European settlement.

As the American people acted on the immigrant belief in freedom of movement, they did not rely entirely on the use of natural waterways and man-made canals. In 1775 Daniel Boone established a horse trail across the Appalachian Mountains into Kentucky. By 1792 it had been improved into a wagon road traversing the length of Virginia before crossing over to the west through the pass in the Appalachians called the Cumberland Gap, at a point almost exactly midway between the Atlantic Coast and the Mississippi River. Much of the initial movement of Americans into the trans-Appalachian West passed over this Wilderness Road, as it came to be called. By 1818 a second trans-Appalachian wagon road called the National Road, this one paved with crushed stone, had been completed farther to the north. It connected the headwaters of the Potomac River on the coastal plain with the great rivers in the center of North America. By 1832 this second east-west road had been extended through the states of Ohio, Indiana, and Illinois to the Mississippi across from St. Louis, Missouri. And by that same year, 1832, American settlers were also using a much longer wagon route called the Oregon Trail, from Missouri across the central plains of the continent and through the Rocky Mountains and the Great Basin into the country called Oregon—the present northwest corner of the contiguous forty-eight states. (In the first decades of the 1800s, Americans also built a series of north-south canals linking the Great Lakes with tributaries of the Ohio and the Mississippi.) By 1855 the first bridge had been constructed across the Mississippi; by 1869 American engineers completed the world's first transcontinental railroad, linking railroad systems already built in the eastern, southern, and middle United States with the Pacific Coast. At the end of the nineteenth century the United States had more miles of railroad track than all the other principal railroad-building nations of the world combined (Britain, France, Germany, Russia, and India), even though those countries contained three times as much territory as the United States and many times its population.

Americans likewise took the lead in the nineteenth century in inventing and building systems of telegraph and telephone communication; and in the early twentieth century created the world's first mass-produced automobiles, a national system of dealerships for selling them, extensive paved roads for their travel, and nationwide systems of gasoline production and distribution and service stations to keep them in running order. Because of the cultural belief of Americans in freedom of movement, the United States now has more privately owned motor vehicles than any other part of the world, more than one and a half for every man, woman, and child in the country, and more paved roads (over three million miles) than any other country. Although a good deal of the technology for automobiles was developed in Europe, it was America, because of its culture, that made the automobile a means of mass public transportation. More than any other mode of transportation, the automobile appeals culturally to Americans because of the freedom of individual movement and choice of travel it affords.

In the early decades of the twentieth century, Americans pioneered the technology of airplanes. In the final decades of the century, American inventors have led the world in developing personal computers as a means of instant communication and instant access to knowledge.

These various historical behaviors of Americans, in developing networks of communication to unify their national space, gave individuals maximum freedom of movement and made possible the mass transportation of goods about the country and rapid communication of information, all of which reflect the immigrant's belief in the importance of free movement in pursuing imagined opportunities for improvement. Because of this aspect of American culture, no other big country in the world (the United States is the fourth largest in size after Russia, Canada, and China) has ever been so effectively united by so many frequently used systems of communication. The progressive unification of American space and the American consensus to speak the same language have been among the principal distinguishing characteristics of the historical behavior of the American people.

DESPITE THE late-twentieth-century idea that modern communications systems have shrunk the world and made it smaller (the "global village" idea), the truth of the matter is that the world is now a much, much larger place for its inhabitants than it has ever been before. Hundreds of millions of people in the late twentieth century have experienced intercontinental travel, and many more than that have used instant intercontinental telecommunications. Never before in history has mankind been able to travel and communicate so easily across such vast distances. Modern technologies have created an ampler—not smaller—space by making the whole globe accessible to a growing number of persons.

The culture of the United States has had a marked influence in this development. As Americans built their systems of mass communication over the last two centuries, uniting their big country, they created a model for the rest of the world of the prosperity that the free movement of goods and people and information can help to produce. The kind of space Americans created—as a consequence of the immigrant beliefs of their culture and the desire of the immigrants to speak the same language—has begun to influence the world to move toward the creation of the same kind of unified space.

CHAPTER FIVE

Frontier Beliefs

What Has To Be Done Will Teach You
How To Do It

Each Person Is Responsible For
His Own Well-Being

Helping Others Helps Yourself

Progress Requires Organization

THESE FOUR American beliefs, derived from experiences during the first century and a half of settlement in the wilderness of the Atlantic coastal plain as it was transformed into farms and towns, represent often-noted characteristics of American behavior and belief: a tendency to inventiveness and admiration for "hands-on" learning and the "can do" spirit; a preference for self-reliance and independence; a dutiful adherence to generosity; and an enthusiasm for forming and belonging to organizations.

But how is the independence of individuals to be reconciled with a fondness for forming organizations? And how can helping others be consistent with self-reliance? The seeming contradiction in these related beliefs of American culture is more an appearance than a reality. Life in the wilderness of central North

America and in the rural communities and small towns into which the wilderness was transformed required behaviors that may appear contradictory but were in fact complementary ways of accomplishing what Americans refer to as "getting ahead." (The phrase "to get ahead," defined as "to advance; to prosper," appeared in Noah Webster's 1828 *Dictionary of American English* and had to have been in common use in America well before that date to be included in the dictionary.) "Getting ahead" has applied, and still applies, to an individual's improvement of his life; but it likewise applies to social advancement, to the development of a new civilization where before 1600 there had been only wilderness. In America both self-reliance and cooperative social behavior were needed because the progress of individuals and the progress of society were mutually beneficial, indeed synonymous.

Immigrants left Europe for colonial America in order to "get ahead." They wanted to make a better life for themselves, but for individuals to "get ahead" in America required the creation of a new society and its advancement. During the formative period of American culture, to improve one's lot in life—and at times just to survive—demanded learning by doing and forming organizations that would not only benefit the lives of individuals directly but also strengthen communities, and in that way indirectly benefit individuals. What benefited the individual in America was a measure of what benefited society; what benefited society was a measure of what benefited individuals, because improvements to the moral, economic, and political order increased the chance for self-improvement. The voluntary organization of associations and institutions of many kinds contributed to the general welfare of American society. In the wilderness, individuals in a settlement had to behave responsibly toward one another and contribute voluntarily to the general welfare of their community in order to make self-improvement and a viable community possible. As one of the great historians of the American frontier said in summarizing the situation of persons on that frontier: "The first lesson the backwoodsmen learnt was the necessity of self-help; the next, that such a community could only thrive if all joined in helping one another."[1]

For three centuries, once the frontier of crude domestication of wild land had passed westward, land development and other forms of progress continued in the recently civilized new settlements. The advance of the frontier and subsequent improvements to post-frontier society depended on every person being responsible for his own well-being as he worked cooperatively with others to improve the economic, political, and religious institutions necessary to both society and to individual lives. Progress that did not benefit both society and individual lives was not real progress. This identification of the good of society with the good of individuals—which in America was not a philosophical proposition but a daily reality—lay at the heart of the frontier experience and America's remarkably rapid progression from a condition of wilderness to the world's fourth-largest nation in size and the world's largest national economy.

IN PLACES where few people live—such as a frontier or the rural communities and small towns that replace a frontier—mutual reliance is as practical as self-reliance; and extending a helping hand to one's neighbor is no less important than taking responsibility for one's own well-being. On roads I have driven in rural Texas, when cars pass each other going in opposite directions it is customary for each driver to greet the other by raising a hand from the steering wheel—in continued acknowledgment, it seems to me, of the sense of mutual dependence their cultural ancestors felt during the days of the Texas frontier. (The drivers who do this greet strangers as readily as acquaintances, because in the days of the frontier in Texas a mutual interest automatically existed between strangers.) I have also been the recipient of such greetings on rural roads in Cochise County, Arizona, a county considerably larger than the state of Connecticut but with a population only the size of the Connecticut town of Waterbury. In 1954, while working for the summer in Sublette County, Wyoming, one of the least densely populated counties in the United States outside of Alaska, I learned that passing up a stranger whose car had broken down was simply not done.

Having been born and raised in a town of a thousand people on the Allegheny River in western Pennsylvania, I know what neighborliness is like in a small town—what happens when there is illness or a death in a family, or someone's car gets stuck in a snowdrift, or a house catches fire.[2] My lifelong friend George Thomas, a community leader in the South End neighborhood of Boston, finally succeeded in convincing me before his death in 1996 that things are not all that different in America's big cities; that neighborhoods still exist in urban areas where people look out for each other.

As Americans say, giving someone a helping hand is just a recognition of the truth that "What goes around, comes around," that the person you help today will help someone else tomorrow; so you are likely one day to have the help you gave to some stranger returned to you by another stranger. As a cultural behavior, helping others is a kind of community insurance policy. The beliefs *Helping Others Helps Yourself* and *Each Person Is Responsible For His Own Well-Being* are, in American culture, both essential to personal well-being.

During World War II when President Franklin D. Roosevelt wanted to aid the countries who were fighting Nazi Germany, before America's entry into the war, he explained his plan of sending war material to Britain as being the same as lending a next-door neighbor a garden hose to put out a fire in his house, lest it spread to yours. He invoked this idea of rendering timely help to a neighbor in a mutually threatening situation, which he called Lend-Lease, because the belief that helping others will help yourself had been acted upon by the American people from early in their history. By using that particular figure of speech, he was able to win the support of the American people and the approval of Congress for his Lend-Lease program.

The best example, however, of the American belief-behavior *Helping Others Helps Yourself* is the Marshall Plan of 1949–1951, named for President Harry S Truman's secretary of state George C. Marshall. The Marshall Plan was a massive foreign aid program to relieve the misery existing in Europe after World War II, which Marshall described in 1947 in announcing the need for such a program. The economies of European countries at the time were either dislocated or shattered, and increasing numbers of Europeans were going hungry. It seemed likely that chaos, followed by some sort of continent-wide authoritarian takeover, was inevitable if something was not done to restore normal production of food and goods in Europe. Secretary Marshall concluded his summary of the desperate situation by saying: "The truth of the matter is that Europe's requirements for the next 3 or 4 years of foreign food and other essential products—principally from America—are so much greater than her present ability to pay that she must have substantial additional help, or face economic, social, and political deterioration of a very grave character." The United States government therefore proposed to give the countries of Europe the money they would need to restore their ruined economies. The Soviet Union rejected the offer of Marshall Plan aid, and would not allow the countries its armies occupied in central Europe, such as Poland, to accept it either. In the fourteen European countries that did accept American help, the turnaround in their economies was dramatic. After three years of Marshall Plain aid, their production of food and goods exceeded prewar levels.

The key to the success of the Marshall Plan was the decision by Washington to allow the governments of the countries who accepted the aid to decide how to use it. As Secretary Marshall said in his speech outlining the plan, it would be "neither fitting nor efficacious" for Americans to tell Europeans how to spend the money. They knew what their most urgent priorities were; therefore they should choose how to apply the billions of dollars they were to receive from the United States. The American cultural belief *What Has To Be Done Will Teach You How To Do It* is as much in evidence in the Marshall Plan as the belief *Helping Others Helps Yourself.*

This amazingly effective aid program was not motivated,

however, only by sympathy for human suffering. It also helped America. As Marshall said in proposing the program:

Aside from the demoralizing effect on the world at large and the possibilities of disturbances arising as a result of the desperation of the people concerned, the consequences to the economy of the United States [of the further deterioration of Europe's economy] should be apparent to all. It is logical that the United States should do whatever it is able to do to assist in the return of normal economic health in the world, without which there can be no political stability and no assured peace. Our policy is directed not against any country or doctrine but against hunger, poverty, desperation, and chaos. Its purpose should be the revival of a working economy in the world so as to permit the emergence of political and social conditions in which free institutions can exist.[3]

Under the Marshall Plan the American people gave Europeans (in terms of 1992–1995 dollars) $108 billion annually in 1949, 1950, and 1951, a total gift of well over $300 billion. But this enormous donation of money to Europeans made it possible for them to purchase millions of tons of corn and coal and wheat from American farmers and miners, and to buy billions of dollars of capital goods from American manufacturers—none of which they would have been able to afford without the aid. In the late 1940s and early 1950s the United States was the only country in the world capable of supplying raw materials and manufactured goods on that scale; so not only was the economy of Europe restored by the Marshall Plan, but the American people enjoyed a more booming economy.

In keeping with the American belief *Helping Others Helps Yourself*, an extraordinary proportion of Americans of all ages, from teens to octogenarians, volunteer each year to help strangers and neighbors through nongovernmental organizations. Americans have "the highest volunteer rate" in the Western world, according to a sociologist who has made a comparative study of sixteen countries of Europe and North

America. (In 1990 it was nearly four times the volunteer rate of Britain.) The rate of volunteering in the United States has in fact increased in the last decade and a half. Computed at the average hourly wage paid to nonagricultural workers, the more than fifteen billion hours of volunteer work performed by Americans in 1992 had a dollar value of $176 billion.[4]

In donating money to charitable causes, the behavior of Americans is also extraordinary. In the eleven years 1985 through 1995, giving to charitable causes in the United States by individual Americans averaged nearly $89 billion a year; corporations, foundations, and bequests contributed another $20 billion on average in each of those years. Thus the total annual funds donated by individuals and corporations in America during the decade 1985–1995 came to an average of $109.4 billion a year. In 1996 donations of money by individuals—which make up four-fifths of all philanthropic giving in the United States—was a whopping $150.7 billion.[5] Here too, as in their increasing donation of time to help others, the trend among Americans is toward increased giving.

To an American these facts may not seem unusual. But it is unusual, compared with behavior in other nations, that about half the American population eighteen years of age and older should be doing some sort of volunteer work and giving more than $325 billion a year in time and money to their fellow Americans—$150 billion in money and $176 billion in donated time. Such conduct has distinguished the culturally normative behavior of the American people from that of other peoples.

Americans even seem to want to compete with one another to see who can give and do more for the needy. Two generations before America's political separation from England, Benjamin Franklin was raising money for community improvement projects such as a hospital that would treat indigent sick people free of charge; and as part of his fund-raising activities he devised the concept of matching funds to increase contributions. The challenge to match the contributions of others was effective in Franklin's day because even in the early eighteenth century

Americans did not wish to think of themselves as deficient in generosity.[6] Long before anyone began to speak of an American culture or analyze it, Benjamin Franklin in the 1730s knew as well as Franklin Roosevelt in the 1940s how to appeal to the cultural beliefs of his fellow Americans.

To civilize the wilderness required every member of American society to show initiative and self-reliance. Society had no responsibility for assuring the happiness or well-being of any of its members. That could be achieved only by each member of society taking responsibility for his own well-being and by lending a helping hand on occasion to those in need. The exciting reality of American life was that everyone was making something of his own life and contributing to the making of a new civilization. It was that way at the beginning of colonial settlement; it is that way still. America continues to be a work in progress. After four centuries of American history, Americans still believe as a people that each person should try to "get ahead" and that American society should also be improved. The engine for getting ahead remains the willingness of individual Americans to assume responsibility for their own well-being and for helping others when self-reliance becomes, at least for a time, impossible for them.

The American term "booming"—meaning to go forward very fast—comes from the days of sailing ships, when it referred to the rapid progress of a ship through the water under full sail and with a good wind astern. It has become part of the general vocabulary of Americans because as a people we have always been interested in rapid progress. The word "boomtown," as a reference to a town in a new mining region or oil field where production is increasing rapidly, is a variant of "booming." To be part of an exciting, phenomenal advancement has been a constant wish of Americans.

SETTLING the wilderness of central North America posed problems for the pioneers that their ancestors in Europe had never faced in recorded history. An inventive, positive spirit—what

Americans call a "can do" attitude—was required to solve those problems and achieve progress in the immense task of civilizing a continental wilderness. One lesson the settlers quickly learned in the wilderness, and passed on through their behavior, was the need for organization to initiate and sustain progress. Such associations had to be formed by ordinary people; their organization could not wait for the impetus of a "higher authority."

This recognition seems to have been widespread among the American people even in colonial times, for by the mid-1700s there were already "numerous voluntary organizations" in America.[7] Tocqueville in 1835, reporting on his trip to America in 1831–1832, noted that he had found an "immense assemblage of associations":

> Americans of all ages, all conditions, and all dispositions constantly form associations. They have not only commercial and manufacturing companies, in which all take part, but associations of a thousand other kinds, religious, moral, serious, futile, general or restricted, enormous or diminutive. The Americans make associations to give entertainments, to found seminaries, to build inns, to construct churches, to diffuse books, to send missionaries to the antipodes; in this manner they found hospitals, prisons, and schools. If it is proposed to inculcate some truth or to foster some feeling by the encouragement of a great example, they form a society.

This was not, Tocqueville noted, the way things were done in his native France or in England. In France the government took the initiative in founding organizations and institutions; in England the initiator and organizer of any association would be "a man of rank."[8]

Once a civilization had been created, with the help of organizations, Americans wanted to make things still better. Continual progress became a way of life for them. They were constantly on the lookout for what could be done or might be done, constantly experimenting with quicker, better ways of accomplishing whatever it was they decided should be done. They learned how to do things by sizing up what they had decided to do, then thinking through how to accomplish that particular goal. They learned how to do things by attempting to do them, and from their successes and failures learned how to do things better. The measure of improvement was always the purpose that something was supposed to serve. For immigrants and their American-born descendants, the novelty of life in America opened their minds to the necessity and possibility of doing things that had never been tried before. Nothing was taken for granted as a final stage of development. Tradition as a justification for continuing to do something in a particular way lost for Americans much of its cultural relevance. Constant, rapid improvement was their goal.

Formal schooling and book learning were one means by which improvement and success might be accomplished, and therefore education was respected. But the person who discovered something in the "school of hard knocks" through "hands-on" learning, or who created something new and useful as a result of what he had learned on his own by trial-and-error experimentation or independent study, was more greatly respected and admired than the man of book learning. His discovery or creation was more in keeping with the American frontier experience. The "self-made man" was the most admired American type. He was "an American original." Benjamin Franklin was an example of it; so was Nathaniel Bowditch (1773–1838), the self-taught American mathematician, navigator, and actuary; so was Thomas Edison (1847–1931), the inventor of the light bulb and other basic apparatuses of modern life; so too were the inventors of the first self-powered aircraft, the brothers Wilbur (1867–1912) and Orville (1871–1948) Wright. Every generation of Americans has had numerous examples of the self-made man, because life in the wilderness demanded a "can do" spirit.

Their situation taught the American people that individual efforts were most effective in organizations. This may seem to contradict the model of the "self-made man" and self-reliance. But, after all, Benjamin Franklin, one of the great examples in American history of the self-made man, usually embodied his ideas for civic improvement in an institution; and many of the institutions he organized in eighteenth-century Philadelphia have endured and continue to serve good purposes. One of the associations Franklin organized, with other ambitious young mechanics, was a reading and debating club. They called it the Junto, a name that suggests moving ahead together. Franklin was also active in founding schools in Philadelphia and took the lead in organizing the American Philosophical Society to develop basic research and scientific knowledge. Likewise Edison, at his laboratory in Menlo Park, New Jersey, worked with a team of assistants to test his ideas. The genius of America has in large part been a penchant for efficient organization, because an institution or formal association of persons magnifies individual ability and assures faster, more enduring progress. If it is efficiently organized, an association can make maximum use of average talent.

The behavior expressing the American belief *Progress Requires Organization* is reflected in the twelve double-columned pages of "Associations and Societies" in the *World Almanac and Book of Facts* listing organizations in the United States having national memberships. A random alphabetical sampling from these pages gives some idea of the range of associations Americans have formed (most of these in the twentieth century, though some date from the nineteenth): the Acoustical Society of America, the Society of Biblical Literature, the American Association of Cereal Chemists, the National Cooperative Business Association, the Descendants of the Signers of the Declaration of Independence, the Institute for International Education, the Forest History Society, the Government Finance Officers Association, the American Helicopter Society, the American Association of Inventors, the Lewis and Clark Trail Heritage Foundation, the Lighter Than Air Society, the Institute of Mathematical Statistics, the National Muzzle Loading Rifle Association, the Independent Order of Odd Fellows, Parents Without Partners, the American Society for Personnel Administration, the Portuguese-American Federation, the Public Relations Society of America, the National Recreation and Park Association, the U.S. Revolver

Association, the American Running and Fitness Association, the National Sculpture Society, the Soil Science Society of America, the National Women's Christian Temperance Union, the United Way of America, the Catholic War Veterans of the U.S.A., the American Zoo and Aquarium Association. Of course the listing of national organizations from which this sampling is taken is nowhere near complete. The directories of just the organizations devoted to combating disease, poverty, ignorance, and crime in the United States in the 1880s ran to hundreds of pages.[9] And for every national organization that has ever existed in America, there have been many more associations and societies at regional, state, and local levels.

So many organizations in America serve the same purpose that we have national organizations of organizations, such as the American Public Transit Association (1,100 organizations) and the National Council of Women of the United States (33 affiliates) and the U.S. Golf Association (8,631 clubs) and the Council of Jewish Federations (200 agencies) and the American Council of Learned Societies (56 societies) and the National Federation of State High School Associations (51 associations) and the Child Welfare League of America (800-plus agencies) and the Federation of Egalitarian Communities (250 plus) and the National Association and Affiliates Credit Union (51 credit union leagues) and the Amateur Baseball Congress (1,300 leagues) and the United States Cerebral Palsy Associations (155 affiliates) and the National Federation of Grandmothers Clubs of America (number of member organizations not given).[10] Sometimes there is more than one national organization of organizations serving the same interest. Inevitably, in a country with such a plethora of organizations and a fondness for forming associations, an American Society of Association Executives has been organized, which reported in 1997 a national membership of 18,000.

Perhaps nothing reflects the American genius for organization better than the American invention of the constitutional convention, by which Americans produced a workable national government and the governments in each of their many states.

The constitutional convention is a special-use organization. No country of Europe had ever devised such a limited, temporary institution for the creation of a government.[11]

Usefulness was one measurement of progress in America. But another was how many persons an invention or innovation might benefit. From about 1660 on, each generation of Americans was born into a population twice as large as the one their parents had been born into. This doubling of population every twenty years during most of America's history made usefulness to the greatest number of persons one of the principal aims of American inventiveness and productivity, and one of the main causes of American prosperity. But as the population burgeoned and the increase required the production of more food, goods, and services, the territory of the United States also increased, mainly through diplomatic negotiations and purchase. (Even the war with Mexico [1846–1848] ended with the United States paying Mexico for the land it had already taken by force—an unheard-of act in the history of Europe.) Thus America's rapid population growth brought none of the problems that would have been caused by a constant and remarkable growth of population in a European country with fixed boundaries, or whose expansion into neighboring territory was opposed by powerful peoples on its borders. Quite the reverse was true in America: rapid population growth and territorial expansion augmented opportunities for further improvements and increased the internal marketplace for profitable enterprise. From the late 1700s on, Americans showed an interest in the mass production of goods and uniform standards of production because they were interested in making as many things of high quality as possible, useful to as many people as possible, in a rapidly increasing population. There was more profit and prosperity—more "getting ahead"—for everyone in doing things that way.

THE ADVANCEMENT of individuals and the advancement of society have been complementary components of American history. An association hostile to the interests of some other association would be, culturally speaking, un-American. In the long run it could not advance either the well-being of the Americans who belonged to it or the well-being of American society as a whole. The Ku Klux Klan—or any other group whose reason for being was hatred for another segment of society—would be a good example of such a counterproductive association. Organizations devoted to increasing opportunities of various kinds for their members are consistent with the history of American culture; organizations that aim to restrict the opportunities of other people or to regulate other people's freedom of advancement may truly be said to be un-American.

When one group's interest is seen by those who belong to it to be all-important, transcending and excluding the interests of every other part of society, that group becomes what might be called anti-social. The well-being of its members and of society then must both suffer, no matter how plausibly argued or how righteous the group's interest may seem to be. The slave owners of the antebellum South, in the decades leading to the Civil War, were such a group. They made their interest paramount, without regard to any other interest. The self-proclaimed spokesmen of various segments ("minorities") of the American population sometimes act in a way similar to that behavior by advocating exclusive interests without restraint; business corporations that conspire to eliminate competition from other corporations or from small entrepreneurs also fit this profile of behavior.

No group within a society has a moral right to claim an interest that is paramount. To accept such a claim would mean that the owners of slaves in America in the 1840s and 1850s were correct in insisting that their right to own such "property" was justified by history, law, custom, and (some of them said) genetic superiority, regardless of any interest or consideration put forward by any other segment of society, including most Americans, whose state governments had abolished slavery in their states well before 1840. If a society can afford to accommodate everyone's special, self-defined interest regardless of cost (a decision that rests with the majority in a democratic society), well and good. If not, priority must be given to the needs of those whose interests can be accommodated, which are just as legitimate as any other.

CHAPTER SIX

Religious and Moral Beliefs

God Created Nature And Human Beings

God Created A Law Of Right And Wrong

Doing What Is Right Is Necessary
For Happiness

God Gave Men The Same Birthrights

America Is A Chosen Country

THE BELIEF *God Created Nature And Human Beings* is the main cultural belief of the American people about religion. Apparently the "big bang" theory of twentieth-century science—that the earth and human beings evolved following a unique explosion of matter into a universe—has not appreciably weakened the belief among Americans in God the Creator. In opinion polls conducted in the United States between 1982 and 1993 on the question of how human beings came into existence, a consistently large proportion of Americans—a minimum of 82 percent and a maximum of 87 percent—chose from the various explanations presented to them either the response "God created the human race about 10,000 years ago" or "An evolutionary process with God." (The former response was preferred by margins of 6 to 12 percent over the latter.) During the twelve consecutive years of this survey, only 7 to 9 percent of Americans chose "An evolutionary process without God," and between 4 and 11 percent made no choice from the options presented.[1] Thus more than four of five Americans (82 to 87 percent) in the 1980s and early 1990s believed that God created human beings, either in progressive stages or in a single creative act.

Multiyear polls of Americans about prayer and the Bible—in Western cultures the most widely read book expressing the belief *God Created Nature And Human Beings*—corroborate the polls just cited. The results of this survey also found a 4 to 1 ratio of belief in God the Creator among Americans. Published in *An American Profile: Opinions and Behavior, 1972–1989*, the findings show that between 1984 (the year questions on the Bible were first asked) and 1989, 79 to 89 percent of Americans consistently responded that they believed the Bible to be either "the actual word of God" or "the inspired word of God."[2]

Another survey of American views regarding the Bible conducted in 1993 and published in *Index to International Public Opinion Survey, 1993–1994* shows the same result: 15 percent of Americans chose the characterization of the Bible as an "ancient book of fables, legends, history and moral precepts recorded by men"; 3 percent had no opinion on the Bible's authority; and 82 percent chose the descriptions "the actual word of God" (33 percent) and "the inspired word of God" (49 percent). This same 1993 poll also found that 55 percent of Americans prayed on a daily basis. (Only 2 percent responded "Never" in answering the question "About how often do you pray?" And just 1 percent chose to make no response to the question.) The same sampling of opinion in 1993 found that when presented with eight choices regarding belief in God, 64 percent of Americans chose the response "I know God really exists and I have no doubt about it." Another 14 percent chose the response "While I have doubts, I feel that I do believe in God." Thus almost four-fifths of Americans (78 percent) had either a quite firm belief in God (64 percent) or a confident belief in God's existence (14 percent).[3]

A poll conducted for and published in *U.S. News & World Report* (April 4, 1994) found that "68 percent of Americans are members of a church or synagogue," and "46 percent of Americans describe themselves as born again," with 13 percent of these saying their conversion was "sudden." This same survey found that four of five Americans (including 71 percent of college graduates) believe the Bible is "the actual word of God to be taken literally word for word" (34 percent) or "the inspired word of God, but not everything in it can be taken literally" (46 percent). A poll commissioned by and published in *Newsweek* (March 31, 1997) found that a little more than half of adult Americans—54 percent—pray at least once a day and 29 percent more than once a day.

Compared to the peoples of western Europe—the part of the world to which cultural historians most often link the culture of the United States—belief in God among Americans is exceptionally strong. A 1990–1991 international survey commissioned by the United Nations Economic and Social Council (UNESCO) and published under the title "The Decline of Religious Beliefs in Western Europe" found that while 78 percent of the population of Great Britain believed in God, only 19 percent of believers felt that God was "very important" in their lives; in France, 62 percent believed in God and 13 percent considered God "very important" in their lives. In the United States, on the other hand, 89 percent believed in God, and more than half of them—58 percent—felt that God was "very important" to them. Some poll results put the portion of the American population that believes in "some sort of Supreme Being" at 95 percent.[4]

Tocqueville had this to say about his first impression of America in the 1830s: "On my arrival in the United States the religious aspect of the country was the first thing that struck my attention; and the longer I stayed there, the more I perceived the great political consequences resulting from this new state of things. In France I had almost always seen the spirit of religion and the spirit of freedom marching in opposite directions. But in America I found they were intimately united and that they reigned in common over the same country."[5]

The belief *God Created Nature And Human Beings* contains three propositions which satisfy three distinct questions: Does God exist? How does God make himself known? and, Are human beings just a part of nature? The belief affirms that God does exist and that he makes his existence known through his power to create. In believing that God created nature and human beings, another proposition is likewise affirmed: that human beings are not just another part of God's creation but a unique part of it, deserving separate mention. This in turn suggests that human beings have characteristics that distinguish them from the rest of nature, and that as a consequence human beings stand in a unique relationship to God.

As a people, Americans have continued to believe—though of course not every American in every generation has believed— in God the Almighty, Maker of Heaven and Earth, including human beings who have a personal relationship to their Creator. This is the Judeo-Christian conception of a personal God. While the belief *God Created Nature And Human Beings* is by no means unique to the historical culture of the United States, it appears stronger among Americans than in other Western countries. (It occurs also, of course, in Israel and in the many nations around the world that practice Islam, the revealed religion and way of life whose prophet is Muhammad. Like Christianity, Islam shares more than one of its beliefs with the revealed religion of Judaism.)

While no one can claim to have an indisputable answer to the question of why God is "very important" to more than half the population of the United States, several kinds of experience seem to have combined for Americans in their history to enliven the faith in God that the self-selected immigrants brought from Europe.

The knowledge of nature in its primeval condition was one

such experience. Living as they did amidst the awesome natural forces and dangers of a Stone Age wilderness, the cultural ancestors of Americans knew firsthand, as it were, the living God who created nature and human beings. And they experienced a vivid daily sense of their dependence on God's providence in their lives. These generations were, of necessity, continuously involved in securing their livelihoods by the sweat of their brows in the midst of nature, mainly as fishermen and seafarers, tillers of the soil, fellers of trees, or as occasional hunters, fishers, and trappers. Through these activities they gained an awareness of nature that strengthened their belief in God the Creator, which, in most cases, either they or their immigrant forebears had brought with them to America out of Christian Europe in the seventeenth and eighteenth centuries. For Americans during those centuries, the presence of God was continuously evident in his creation. In going to and living in America, they experienced an uncivilized world quite unlike Europe, a world in which the Creator had spread before them a richly endowed, primordial continent whose harvests they could gather with their labor.

As late as the nineteenth century the great poet of American democracy, Walt Whitman, rightly called Americans "an outdoor people." Even today, at the end of the fourth century of American history, hiking, hunting, camping, fishing, and boating are common recreational activities among Americans, both old and young, because the American people have a deep cultural affinity for the outdoors. In 1990 more than 282 million visits were made to the 47 million acres in the 50 national parks of the United States; another 90 million visits were made to the 27 million acres of the 54 nature preserves that have been set aside as national seashores, national lake shores, national rivers, national trails, and national recreation areas.[6] State forests, municipal parks, and private nature preserves received millions of additional visits.

Before most of the American people began living in urban and semi-urban landscapes in the twentieth century, insulated from day-to-day contact with an intact natural world, most

Americans had direct personal experience of the power of the God of nature. They knew too, as an outdoor people, that the laws of nature's God could not be trifled with or ignored. This nature, which Americans as a people experienced in the seventeenth and eighteenth centuries and the first half of the nineteenth, differed appreciably from the nature that Europeans experienced in most parts of their long-civilized continent during the same period. Although most Europeans in that time also were engaged in outdoor activities such as farming, which put them in direct contact with the land and the laws of nature, it was not for the most part the primal nature that Americans knew. Twentieth-century European visitors to the American West find it strange that deadly attacks by wild animals are still possible; but Americans have long known, as Ralph Waldo Emerson said in the nineteenth century, that "Nature is no sentimentalist." To survive in a wilderness, a person must thoroughly appreciate that fact.

In early America, nature consisted still of glorious prairies of grassland extending hundreds and hundreds of miles, lonesome forests larger than whole countries of Europe, pristine wild rivers, five sealike blue lakes that together formed the largest connected body of fresh water on earth, and great expanses of both deserts and wetlands. Even in the urban and semi-urban landscapes that most Americans now inhabit, an experience of some semblance of that kind of primal, beautiful nature is often only a few hours' drive away. And a sense of wide-open spaces continues to be part of the historical consciousness of Americans.

Even now Americans are continually reminded of the ultimate power of nature in the wildfires that every "fire season" in the American West endanger communities (sometimes even the suburbs of Los Angeles); in the tornados that every "tornado season" rip through landscapes and communities in the Midwestern states,[7] and in the hurricanes that every "hurricane season" can destroy property and lives along the southern and eastern coasts of America from Texas to New England. These kinds of regularly recurring exhibitions of nature's irresistible forces are not part of life in Europe, a continent where wildfires are rare and the devastating storms known as tornados and hurricanes never occur. Perhaps, therefore, one factor in making the God of nature so important in the lives of Americans, and in inclining almost all Americans to communicate with God in prayer (a majority of them every day), has been the experience of successive generations of Americans of both the splendor and power of unmediated nature.

Nature in that part of North America inhabited by the early settlers inspired awe; but it was not forbidding. In being both temperate and inviting, central North America differed basically from the tropical, the subarctic, and the high-mountain geographies that characterize Brazil, Canada, and Spanish America, where the world's largest tropical river basin and forest, the world's largest subarctic inland sea, and the world's longest chain of towering mountains have limited the efforts of civilized men and women to transform nature to suit their purposes. The nature that the cultural ancestors of Americans knew was primal and wild; but it was also transformable across the center of a whole continent, from one ocean to another, as no other part of the Americas was—given sufficient numbers of highly motivated and cooperative workers with the imagination to see what they wanted to make for themselves and their posterity.

All of central North America was eventually transformed by such people. But at every stage of that great transformation, Americans felt that their accomplishments as a people had been performed with God's leave, blessing, and guidance. It has been part of their experience as a people to humble themselves before God in prayer in facing the daunting tasks that have confronted them and to offer thanks to God for their successes and the blessings of their homeland.

In American history, the need to rely on God in facing the fearsome forces of nature began with the ordeal of crossing the Atlantic Ocean, at least until the mid-nineteenth century. Indeed, in the era of wooden sailing ships when American culture originated, those who chose to cross the Atlantic and became emigrants needed faith in God's help just to have the courage to undertake the voyage. Accounts by immigrants from the seventeenth to the nineteenth centuries regularly contain invocations to the God of nature in describing their feelings before, during, and after the ordeal of crossing the great Atlantic to America.

Sometimes faith in God was decisive. Although the circumstances of emigration varied, the story of one emigrant family who faced the ordeal of an Atlantic crossing in the early nineteenth century illustrates the lively faith in a living God that often played a part in deciding who would go to America.

Hours before the scheduled sailing of this English tenant farmer, his wife, and their minor children for America, his courage faltered. He went to his wife and declared that after spending a sleepless night imagining the perils that lay before them, he had thought better of his decision to go to America and now wished to stay in England. (His wife recorded the episode many years after their emigration, in a memoir that one of her sons, a journalist, helped her write.) He particularly feared, he said, that should anything happen to him "on the stormy ocean, or in a strange land and among pathless woods," some terrible fate might befall her and the children. Consequently he proposed to go down into the ship's hold, retrieve their bundles, and return home. After listening to this, his wife raised her eyes "to Him 'who sitteth above the water-floods'" and reminded her fearful husband that it was too late now to go back, that they had sold the bulk of their possessions to raise their passage money to America and had given up the lease on the farm they had been renting and therefore had no place to which they might return. Besides, she told him, he should remember that God, in his almighty providence, could "preserve us and our children across the seas or in America as . . . in England." She advised that they proceed as arranged and "look to Providence for success."

These encouraging words, affirming a simple and sincere faith in God's providence, so heartened the man that he once more determined to risk the voyage to America. A few hours later he and his family were embarked on the ocean bound for America, having "previously confided ourselves," the wife recalled in her memoir, "to the care of Him 'whom earth and seas are ready to obey.'" When they arrived at their destination in Illinois, after a trying passage across the Atlantic and through the Gulf of Mexico to New Orleans, and a long steamboat trip up the Mississippi River, they heard for the first time in their lives the cries of wolf packs and learned the meaning of the phrase "howling wilderness." Soon afterward, when the blizzards of the American heartland descended on them out of the Canadian arctic, they experienced a ferocious cold unlike any they had known in England's, milder, maritime climate, and against which the clothes and bedding they had brought from England scarcely protected them. But their fearful trials of the spirit had a satisfactory ending. A few years after taking up land in Illinois, they were acclimatized to their new homeland and had become, through unremitting labor and the exercise of prudence, the owners of a farm far grander and far more productive than any they had ever dreamed of owning while they lived in England, where they had rented a small acreage of another man's land.[8]

Courage and an ability to imagine a better way of life than the way of life in Europe were, as a matter of course, prerequisites to undertaking the emigration to America. But it appears that faith in God's protection was also needed to reinforce the would-be emigrant's courage and vision of a better way of life, particularly in taking the initial step of committing oneself, and often one's entire family, to the ordeal and uncertainties of an Atlantic crossing. Besides the landsman's fear of the ocean's vastness, and of drowning in a storm at sea, there was also apprehension of the well-known miseries of shipboard life in a wooden sailing vessel. Not uncommonly, it had to be continually pumped to stay ahead of leaks to the hull, during a voyage that usually lasted two to three months. The immigrants had to endure crowded compartments, stifling air, a stench from inadequate sanitary facilities, vomiting from motion sickness, bed lice, the constant dampness of clothing and bedding, hunger and thirst if rations ran low during a voyage, as they frequently did if the ship encountered adverse wind or foul weather (passengers on the early immigrant ships were responsible for their own provisions), and the very real danger of contagious diseases (before the twentieth century the death rate on immigrant ships often ran to 10 percent, whether or not a contagious disease spread through the ship's company). One eighteenth-century voyage counted thirty-two deaths among just the children of the immigrants; and the author of this report observed matter-of-factly that those below the age of seven "seldom survive the sea voyage."[9] Some ships simply disappeared on the Atlantic and were never heard from again, their whole company perishing from storms or, occasionally, pirates who left no trace of their crimes.

Those who lacked the imagination to appreciate the dangers they faced by embarking on the Atlantic in the days of wooden sailing ships would probably also have lacked sufficient imagination to have conceived of departing for an unknown, faraway continent in order to better their lives. Those who boarded the ships for America were willing to trust in God and put their lives in his hands. While one could not say that only persons of faith emigrated to America from Europe, belief in nature's God, the Creator of heaven and earth and human beings, certainly prevailed in the American population during the formation of its culture. Benjamin Franklin, at the age of seventy-eight, remarked that one could "live to a great Age" in America without encountering "either an Atheist or an Infidel."[10]

CONSCIOUSNESS of God's blessings, and the desire to give thanks to God for them, have also been fundamental to the American experience. Americans in their development as a people had much to be thankful for. Certainly as the forest that had covered the Atlantic coastal plain was cleared away, and in the nineteenth century the densely matted grasses of the vast trans-Appalachian prairies and plains were plowed and converted into croplands and cattle ranges, the former wilderness of central

North America began to yield abundant harvest. Even before Americans moved from the coastal plain into the plains of the mid-continent, a European visitor to the colony of Pennsylvania observed that "in the humblest or poorest homes, no meals are served without a meat course; and no one eats bread without butter or cheese." This same observer reported an abundance of vegetables and fruit "cheaply sold." One traveler from Spanish America who came to the United States shortly after its independence was "amazed at the abundance and magnificence" of the meals that mechanics and common laborers were able to eat.[11] This historical bountifulness of agricultural products in America, which made food cheaper and more widely available than it was in Europe, gave an especially strong impulse to the sense of thankfulness among Americans for God's blessings.

The gifts of uncultivated nature were also unusually abundant during the formative centuries of American culture. In the rivers and great inland lakes of America and on the offshore Atlantic fishing grounds were prolific concentrations of heavy-bodied, succulent salmon, bass, trout, shad, cod, bluefish, and sturgeon. Many freshwater and saltwater turtles could be found, and many kinds of shellfish—lobsters, crabs, crayfish, scallops, oysters, clams, mussels—as well as big rookeries of nesting seabirds where eggs could be collected. Nuts, wild plums, wild grapes, and various wild berries could be gathered in their seasons. Deer, bison, elk, bear, moose, antelope, wild sheep, and other big-game animals inhabited the forests, prairies, and mountains; and savory game birds such as turkey, grouse, quail, and prairie chicken—the property of no man—could be had for the shooting. (In Europe such fine food as venison and salmon was available only to the great landlords; it was worth the life of a poor man to be caught taking a salmon or a deer on a nobleman's estate.) In the spring and autumn, the skies along the bays, lake shores, and big rivers of central North America swarmed with fabulous numbers of migrating ducks, cranes, geese, and swans. Flocks of migrating wild pigeon were so dense and so huge that even the firing of a cannon into the swiftly passing cloud of birds caused it to swerve only momentarily.[12] Good building materials for constructing houses and barns and other buildings—the finest timber, the most durable stone, deposits of sand and shells for mortar and stucco—were widely available and could be had at low cost, or for just the labor of collecting them. Long-burning hardwoods were so plentiful for firewood in America that even persons of humble means could keep as warm in winter before roaring fires as only the high and mighty could in Europe. This great profusion of the natural productions of the earth and waters of central North America gave common Americans much satisfaction and cause for thanking God, who had seen them, or their ancestors, safely across the ocean to partake of the abundance America had to offer.

Most of all, however, as a cause for thanksgiving, there was available to common folk in central North America the blessing of unoccupied tillable land. Because there was so much of it, it could be had cheaply, or sometimes simply by "squatting" on it and "improving" it—that is, by cutting down some trees on a tract of wilderness and building a crude dwelling in the clearing. "Certainly in the 1760s and 1770s, as earlier, the most impressive aspect of the free population of Britain's American colonies was the extraordinarily large number of families of independent middling status, which was proportionately substantially more numerous than in any other contemporary Western society."[13]

The essay Benjamin Franklin wrote in 1784 to inform would-be European emigrants on what to expect in America provides an insight into the belief-behaviors of Americans not long after American culture became fully formed. In his essay this son of an English immigrant emphasized that though his native land was "the Land of Labour, and by no means what the English call *Lubberland*, and the French *Pays de Cocagne*, where the Streets are said to be pav'd with half-peck Loaves, the Houses til'd with Pancakes, and where the Fowls fly about ready roasted, crying, *Come eat me!*," it was just as surely a country that "the Divine Being . . . has been pleased to favour" with a "remarkable Prosperity."[14]

And in telling in his autobiography of his rise from humble origins as the youngest son of a candle maker to affluence as the publisher of a newspaper and a highly popular almanac in America's largest city, and international fame as a scientist, Franklin attributed his many and varied accomplishments to "the Blessing of God" and, from the perspective of his middle age, wrote: "And now I speak of thanking God, I desire with all Humility to acknowledge, that I owe the mention'd Happiness of my past Life to his kind Providence, which led me to the Means I us'd & gave them Success.—My Belief of This, induces me to *hope*; tho' I must not *presume*, that the same Goodness will still be exercis'd towards me in continuing that Happiness, or in enabling me to bear a fatal Reverse, which I may experience as others have done, the Complexion of my future Fortune being known to him only: and in whose Power it is to bless to us even our Afflictions."[15] The patience with which Franklin bore years of pain from bladder stones before his death proves the sincerity of these words.

A wholesome fear of God's power as manifested in nature, a trust in his providence, a faith in his goodness, and a thankfulness for his blessings—all these religious emotions were intensified by life in America. They deepened among the American people the belief that *God Created Nature And Human Beings*.

AS A PEOPLE, Americans have also believed that *God Created A Law Of Right And Wrong*. Again, the conditions of life they experienced in America in transforming a primordial continent enlivened this belief of Judeo-Christian religion and made it a part of American culture.

The belief in a God-created law of right and wrong for human beings incorporated the Ten Commandments, which in the spread of Christianity throughout Europe had become the moral foundation of European civilization and which were brought to the Americas to become the moral basis of new civilizations on these continents. But the moral law inherent in God's creation that Americans came to believe in was revealed in the nature of things as well as in scripture. Rather than commanding resistance to specific temptations, such as worshiping false gods, committing adultery, bearing false witness, committing murder, envying the possessions of another person, or treating parents with disrespect, this law posited that there is a right and a wrong in doing *anything*, whether physical or moral, and that the rightness or wrongness of an action will be revealed in its results.

This highly pragmatic, natural law did not replace the Ten Commandments; it expanded them. It was a generalized revelation of right conduct through effect, which included the injunctions of the Commandments and went beyond them. In this view of right and wrong, an inherent similarity exists between physical and moral realities, and wrong or right conduct toward other persons has consequences as inescapable as actions of an entirely physical kind—even if in some cases the effect of a personal action is not as immediate as a physical action. However difficult it is to foresee the consequences of one's choices, the operation of God's moral law is unerring. It is the law the nineteenth-century American writer Henry David Thoreau referred to in "Higher Laws," a chapter in his autobiographical book *Walden*: "Our whole life is startlingly moral. There is never an instant's truce between virtue and vice. Goodness is the only investment that never fails."[16] Walt Whitman stated the law in these terms in a poem he titled "To Think of Time":

> The law of the past cannot be eluded,
> The law of the present and future cannot be eluded,
> The law of the living cannot be eluded, it is eternal,
> The law of promotion and transformation cannot be eluded,
> The law of heroes and good-doers cannot be eluded,
> The law of drunkards, informers, mean persons, not one iota
>   thereof can be eluded.

Only one moral law has been, is, and always will be at work in the universe. Its operations are certain in promoting the good. They are precise and unavoidable. The law determines the results of the unselfish behavior of "heroes and good-doers"; it determines also the results of the behavior of "drunkards and informers" and other persons who are "mean" in their treatment of others and themselves.

As Americans believed in and acted on it, God's natural law of right and wrong embraces every human concern and activity, including political affairs. So in 1776, when elected representatives of the thirteen colonies declared their independence from England, it was the *necessity*—the term occurs three times in the Declaration of Independence—imposed by "the Laws of Nature and of Nature's God" that was cited to justify the separation of the United States from England.[17] As Thomas Paine observed in his popular pamphlet "Common Sense," urging Americans to declare their independence: "Even the distance at which the Almighty hath placed England and America is a strong and natural proof, that the authority of the one over the other, was never the design of Heaven. . . . there is something very absurd, in supposing a Continent to be perpetually governed by an island. In no instance hath nature made the satellite larger than its primary planet, and as England and America with respect to each other reverse the common order of nature, it is evident they belong to different systems. England to Europe: America to itself."[18] It was right and natural—in the nature of things as God had created them—that America should be independent of Eng-land, Paine argued; and the elected delegates to the Second Continental Congress agreed in asserting in the Declaration that the United States was entitled by "the Laws of Nature and of Nature's God" to a "separate and equal station" "among the Powers of the earth."

This belief, that the Creator had revealed to mankind a law of right and wrong in the nature of things, is illustrated in other writings by leaders of the American revolution in government. Thomas Jefferson consistently referred to his belief in such a law in both public writings and private letters. In "A Summary View of the Rights of British America," for instance, a pamphlet he wrote a year before the American Revolution began, he stated that "The great principles of right and wrong are legible to every reader"; that "a free people [claim] their rights as derived from the laws of nature, and not as the gift of their chief magistrate"; and that "The God who gave us life gave us liberty at the same time."[19] In "Query XVIII" of his *Notes on the State of Virginia* (1784), Jefferson identified as the "only firm basis" for a nation's liberties "a conviction in the minds of the people that these liberties are of the gift of God." (The motto Jefferson chose for his personal seal was: "Resistance to Tyrants Is Obedience to God.") George Washington manifested his belief in a God-given, innate law of right and wrong in his "Farewell Address" to his fellow Americans, in which he declared that his forty-five years of public service had convinced him that "Providence has . . . connected the permanent felicity of a nation with its virtue."[20]

In the case of Benjamin Franklin, we know not only that he believed in an innate, God-given law of right and wrong, but also when and why he came to believe in it. Franklin tells us in his *Autobiography* that when he was twenty-two and contemplating going into business on his own, he was highly dissatisfied with himself. In his teens he had concluded that "Vice & Virtue" were "empty Distinctions" and had become "a Freethinker" who rationalized moral relativism with the sophistry that since God was both all-powerful and all-good, nothing that occurred could ever be wrong—a line of reasoning that ignored the fact that human beings have free will and are not, therefore, automatons of virtue controlled at every moment by God's will. At age twenty-two, however, Franklin's recollection of his shabby treatment of several people troubled him; and he also recalled offenses he had suffered at the hands of persons who were, like himself, "freethinkers." He began therefore to doubt the cleverness of his youthful reasoning, and to see that although "certain Actions might not be bad *because* they were forbidden by [the Bible], or good *because* it commanded them; yet probably those Actions might be forbidden *because* they were bad for us, or commanded *because* they were beneficial to us, in their own Natures, all the Circumstances of things considered."[21] At the time he came of age, Franklin discovered that, *in the nature of things*, he should do to others what he would have them do to him, that this principle, which encompassed the Ten Commandments, was the moral law inherent in Creation.

After reaching this conclusion about the operation of a natural law of right and wrong in God's creation—that good conduct is neither a matter of biblical revelation nor of personal judgment, but rather that what is good and bad for human beings exists in the nature of things as God has created them—Franklin as a young man wrote out a simple religious creed, containing "the Essentials of every known Religion." This creed (also recorded in his *Autobiography*) affirmed "one God who made all things"; God's government of the world "by his Providence"; the obligation of worshiping God "by Adoration, Prayer & Thanksgiving" and most important by "doing Good to Man"; the existence and immortality of the soul; and the certainty that God will "reward Virtue and punish Vice either here or hereafter."[22]

The emphasis on conduct in this creed is an essential component of the belief *God Created A Law Of Right And Wrong*, which presumes that human beings have the freedom to choose between conduct that is, in the nature of things, right and conduct that is, in the nature of things, wrong, as judged by the effects of the conduct on our and others' peace of mind. Furthermore the belief implies that human beings have the understanding to discern (if not infallibly in all cases, at least ordinarily) the difference between what is right and what is wrong. The principal assumption, however, is that human beings have a relationship to their Creator which requires them, if they are to be happy with themselves, to do what is right. Because of Franklin's experience as a youth—his unhappiness with his own freethinking conduct toward others and the conduct of other freethinkers toward him—he realized that *Doing What Is Right Is Necessary For Happiness*. These two beliefs—*God Created A Law Of Right And Wrong* and *Doing What Is Right Is Necessary For Happiness*—are reciprocal truths.

Two years after he formulated his religious creed, Franklin

published an essay "On the Providence of God in the Government of the World," discussing the relationship between God and human beings. Providence, this essay maintains, is the concept that God governs by his free will the world he created by his free will. Franklin also states that God in making human beings in his image has given them "in some Degree" free will, power, and goodness. Although human beings naturally do not have God's limitless free will, power, and goodness, to the degree they have these qualities they are "accountable for their Actions." The essay concludes that it is "unreasonable to suppose it out of the Power of the Deity to help and favour us particularly or that we are out of his Hearing or Notice or that Good Actions do not procure more of his Favour than ill Ones." Therefore God's power and freedom to act in the world is "the Foundation of all true Religion; for we should love and revere that Deity for his Goodness and thank him for his Benefits; we should adore him for his Wisdom, fear him for his Power, and pray to him for his Favour and Protection; and this Religion will be a Powerful Regulator of our Actions; give us Peace and Tranquility within our own Minds, and render us Benevolent, Useful and Beneficial to others."[23]

The relationship between God and human beings that Franklin outlines in his essay on God's providence is that between a Person of infinite, limitless capacity and persons of a finite degree of understanding, power, goodness, and freedom. Despite their lesser capacities, God intends human beings to use their capacities to understand and obey the moral law he has created for their happiness. He has given human beings his own attributes, though in lesser degree, so that we can achieve happiness; he has not made human beings automatically obedient to his law. Whether human beings like it or not, the moral law God created has imposed moral responsibility on them; and that responsibility is the basis of their personal relationship to their Creator and their relationships to one another.

The twentieth-century American novelist William Faulkner also spoke of living under this kind of moral necessity. Late in his life, in discussing with university students the meaning of the stories that had won him international fame, including a Nobel Prize, Faulkner said he believed that moral truths were inscribed on the human heart. A person had to be honest, for instance, not because telling the truth was virtuous "but because that's the only way to get along. . . . If people lied constantly to one another you would never know where you were, you would never know what was going on." Compassion in one's relationship with others was also a necessity because "if people didn't practice compassion there would be nothing to defend the weak until they got enough strength to stand for themselves." These "verities of the human heart" must be practiced, Faulkner reasoned, in the same way Benjamin Franklin had reasoned two hundred years earlier, "not because they are virtues" but because the practice of them is "the best way to live in peace with yourself and your fellows."[24] In the speech he made when he accepted the Nobel Prize in 1950, Faulkner affirmed his belief in the "old verities and truths of the heart, the old universal truths [of] . . . love and honor and pity and pride and compassion and sacrifice." From that podium offering worldwide attention, he declared his conviction that "[man is] immortal, not because he, alone among creatures, has an inexhaustible voice but because he has a soul, a spirit, capable of compassion and sacrifice and endurance."[25] Both the young eighteenth-century Pennsylvania printer and the mature twentieth-century Mississippi novelist believed as Americans that human beings must obey an inherent moral necessity for the sake of their souls' tranquility.

Franklin in 1728, at age twenty-two, awakened to God's law of right and wrong for human beings. Around the same time, in 1730, a religious fervor known as the Great Awakening began stirring among the American people. This general, intercolonial religious revival spread during the 1730s and 1740s through all thirteen colonies and may well have contributed to the unity manifested a few decades later, in the 1760s and 1770s, in the struggle for American independence. Certainly the Great Awakening in America contributed to a distinct shift away from the European cultural belief in government-instituted-and-enforced religious orthodoxy toward a belief in the authority of individual conversion and churches controlled by the worshipers who organize them.

Religious authority in England was vested in an established national church, financed by the state, membership in which was required as a qualification for participating in government. This was not a suitable structure for America, and the European belief in a state religion that was part of government began breaking down soon after the first permanent English settlements in Virginia and Massachusetts. In New England from the 1640s on, one can see a steady decline in the orthodoxy and the centralized ecclesiastical authority the Puritans had originally instituted. By the early 1700s church membership in the thirteen colonies was at its historic low: only about one-eighth of the New England population, one-fifteenth of the inhabitants of the middle colonies, and one-twentieth of the population of the Southern colonies had a "formal religious affiliation."[26] The Great Awakening radically changed all that. In the 1730s and 1740s church memberships soared; so did the number of churches. As a direct consequence of this religious awakening, four new colleges— Princeton, Rutgers, Brown, and Dartmouth—were founded in America to train ministers. Today something approaching three-quarters of the American population (nearly 70 percent in the early 1990s, and increasing) are members of churches; and some of the fastest-growing denominations (Mormon churches and Assembly of God churches) are among the most demanding in their doctrines and practices.[27]

The Great Awakening stressed emotion over reason, conduct over theology, and autonomous church government over authoritarian ecclesiastic hierarchies. It made the way one lived one's life more important than the catechism one repeated. And when the preachers of the Great Awakening exhorted Americans to experience the sanctifying power of Christ as their personal savior, America had at last found a religious outlook suited to a culture that made the individual, not classes, the unit of society. This awakening of personal religious convictions in America strengthened the beliefs *God Created A Law Of Right And Wrong* and *Doing What Is Right Is Necessary For Happiness*. By "democratizing" religion, the Great Awakening made religion primarily a matter of personal conviction and moral conduct: an effort to please God and gain peace of mind through obedience to his moral law by (as the young Benjamin Franklin said in his religious creed) "doing Good to Man." The Great Awakening was the final step for the American people in removing religion from the realm of government, as in European culture, and making it a matter of individual necessity and conviction.

Good works may not guarantee happiness or salvation, but being "born again" in the spirit does require an effort to reform one's bad conduct. The spiritual revival of the early eighteenth century, and other revivals that have periodically appeared since, have given vitality to the religious beliefs of Americans, no matter which Christian denomination they belonged to. These revivals have been Christian movements, since the population of the United States has historically been overwhelmingly Christian; and all of them have stressed the importance of conduct toward others, the emotion of a personal commitment to Christ, and the concept of a church as a vessel from which God's living spirit may be poured into the hearts of men and women.

The Great Awakening forged a unity of religious sentiments even while the number of churches and Christian denominations in America grew. This diversity, which European travelers regularly noticed and which many of them found shocking, indicated the seriousness that religion had in American culture from the 1730s on—a seriousness that led individuals to organize churches having forms of worship they truly believed in. The diversity manifested personal seriousness about religion and the peculiar strength of religious faith in America. The belief *God Created A Law Of Right And Wrong*—which is part of a spiritual conversion because of its emphasis on conduct as a sign of love for and thanks to God—strengthened belief in equality among Americans by making all persons equal before the moral law that God had created. What has been important in America is that persons having a belief in God demonstrate that belief in their conduct toward others; having a single, uniform theology has not been historically important in American culture.

A society almost wholly constituted by self-selected immigrants and their American-born descendants gave importance to the belief *Doing What Is Right Is Necessary For Happiness*. For the only hope of satisfying the desire for happiness that motivated this society, whose immigrant ancestors had all been seeking happiness, lay in voluntary cooperation—which demanded that one do the right thing in one's relations with others. It was in everyone's self-interest to treat other persons with respect so long as they too were doing the right thing by contributing to the common good.

Doing the right thing in this society was an attempt to ensure God's continued favor and to pay back the blessings one received from living in America. A passage from a personal letter by Benjamin Franklin in 1753 expresses, with more clarity and exactness than any other passage of early American writing I am aware of, the religious character of paying back to others the blessings one receives in America:

> As to the Kindness you mention, I wish it could have been of more Service to you. But if it had, the only Thanks I should desire is, that you would always be equally ready to serve any other Person that may need your Assistance, and so let good Offices go round, for Mankind are all of a Family.
>
> For my own Part, when I am employed in serving others, I do not look upon my self as conferring Favours, but as paying Debts. In my Travels and since my Settlement I have received much Kindness from Men, to whom I shall never have any Opportunity of making the least direct Return. And numberless Mercies from God, who is infinitely above being benefited by our Services. These Kindnesses from Men I can therefore

only return on their Fellow-Men; and I can only show my Gratitude for those Mercies from God, by a Readiness to help his other Children and my Brethren. For I do not think that Thanks and Compliments, tho' repeated Weekly, can discharge our real Obligations to each other, and much less those to our Creator.

You will see in this my Notion of Good Works, that I am far from expecting (as you suppose) that I shall merit Heaven by them. By Heaven we understand a State of Happiness, infinite in Degree, and eternal in Duration: I can do nothing to deserve such Reward: He that for giving a Draught of Water to a thirsty Person should expect to be paid with a good Plantation, would be modest in his Demands, compar'd with those who think they deserve Heaven for the little Good they do on Earth. Even the mix'd imperfect Pleasures we enjoy in this World are rather from God's Goodness than our Merit; how much more such Happiness of Heaven. For my own part, I have not the Vanity to think I deserve it, the Folly to expect it, nor the Ambition to desire it; but content myself in submitting to the Will and Disposal of that God who made me, who has hitherto preserv'd and bless'd me, and in whose fatherly Goodness I may well confide, that he will never make me miserable, and that even the Afflictions I may at any time suffer shall tend to my Benefit.[28]

In the seventeenth and eighteenth centuries in Europe, members of a ruling class conferred favor and benefits on one another and on persons they considered to be "beneath" them as human beings. In America, society had been voluntarily constituted by self-selected immigrants, and persons pursued happiness on their own and in company with others who also strived toward that goal. Given the unanimity of their common purpose, Americans in helping others were able to count on the help of others who had, in their turn, benefited from someone's help. To do the right thing in such a society was not so much a matter of righteousness as practical self-interest and gratitude to God for living in a place where so much freedom to pursue happiness existed and where one could count on the respect and help of others in pursuing the common goal.

In *Letters from an American Farmer* (1782), Michel-Guillaume-Saint-Jean de Crèvecoeur, himself an immigrant, tells the story of an immigrant named Andrew whose career in America illustrates "the happy effects which constantly flow, in this country, from sobriety and industry, when united with good land and freedom." Andrew is from the notoriously poor Hebrides islands off the coast of Scotland. Upon arriving in Philadelphia, he, his wife, and their young son are noticed by an American farmer who gives them good advice and goes out of his way to arrange for jobs for all of them. By Hebridean standards, the wages Andrew receives for his work are so high he can scarcely believe he is to be paid so much. During four years in Pennsylvania this honest European "peasant," as he is called by Crèvecoeur, increases by twentyfold the small life savings he brought to America, acquires ownership of land, and develops a sense of civic responsibility he never had in his former homeland. As he serves on juries and oversees the maintenance of roads near his farm, he loses what Crèvecoeur calls the "European prejudices" of subordination and servility. As the years passed and Andrew's prosperity, independence, and civic responsibilities increased, we are told, he "helped others as generously as others had helped him."

A TWENTIETH-CENTURY Scottish historian, who lived at different times in several regions of America and spent a lifetime studying the United States, has observed that "deep in the American mind is a belief that his is God's Country, and that the phrase is no mere booster's boast, but the statement of a sacred truth."[29] The United States of America *is* God's country in the sense that Americans for many generations have felt that their nation has been especially blessed by God, that it could never have been established and endured so successfully without God's favor and protection. The belief is also true in the sense that, as a people, Americans have believed that God has wanted to use America as part of a divine plan for the redemption of mankind—by the creation of a new nation modeled on new principles of behavior. America is also a "chosen country" in the sense that those who created it were mostly those who chose to emigrate to it and their descendants. In all three of these ways— as a country especially blessed and sanctioned by God, as a country used by God to communicate to mankind a new way of life, and as a country chosen by millions of self-selected immigrants as their preferred residence—Americans believe *America Is A Chosen Country*. In making real the sovereignty of the people, in creating and widely distributing unprecedented wealth, and in achieving astonishing social unity in a population of such diverse origins, the United States has seemed to generations of Americans to have God's favor and approval.

The men the American people have elected to the presidency of the United States have consistently expressed in their inaugural addresses a belief in God's special care for America. These pronouncements are chiefly concerned with the state of the nation at the moment the new president assumes office. But inaugural speeches have always included some perspective on the nation's past and thoughts about its future, and these comments have frequently alluded to God.

Some presidents have made surprisingly personal public testaments to their faith. The first words of President Dwight D. Eisenhower, for instance, to the great crowd assembled in front of the Capitol in 1953 to witness his inauguration as president were these:

> My friends, before I begin the expression of those thoughts that I deem appropriate to this moment, would you permit me the privilege of uttering a little private prayer of my own. And I ask that you bow your heads.
>
> Almighty God, as we stand here at this moment my future associates in the executive branch of government join me in beseeching that Thou will make full and complete our dedica-

tion to the service of the people in this throng, and their fellow citizens everywhere.

Give us, we pray, the power to discern clearly right from wrong, and allow all our words and actions to be governed thereby, and by the laws of this land. Especially we pray that our concern shall be for all the people regardless of station, race, or calling.

May cooperation be permitted and be the mutual aim of those who, under the concepts of our Constitution, hold to differing political faiths; so that all may work for the good of our beloved country and Thy glory. Amen.[30]

Forty-six years later, in 1989, another veteran of World War II who became president of the United States, George Bush, in taking his oath of office used the same Bible that George Washington had used two hundred years before. Bush also prefaced his first speech as president with a prayer, which likewise appears to have been his own composition:

. . . my first act as President is a prayer—I ask you to bow your heads. Heavenly Father, we bow our heads and thank You for Your love. Accept our thanks for the peace that yields this day and the shared faith that makes its continuance likely. Make us strong to do Your work, willing to heed and hear Your will, and write on our hearts these words: "Use power to help people." For we are given power not to advance our own purposes nor to make a great show in the world, nor a name. There is but one just use of power and it is to serve people. Help us remember, Lord. Amen.[31]

President Jimmy Carter in 1977 laid the Washington Bible on the podium but took his oath of office on a Bible his mother had given him, opened to this passage in the Old Testament: "He hath showed thee, O man, what is good; and what doth the Lord require of thee, but to do justly, and to love mercy, and to walk humbly with thy God" (Micah 6:8). He quoted the passage in his address and referred to it a second time.[32] President William

McKinley, in his inaugural in 1897, paraphrased the same passage, and President Warren G. Harding likewise quoted it in 1921.

In the first inaugural address by an American president, George Washington referred to God repeatedly as "that Almighty Being who rules over the universe," "the Great Author of every public and private good," "the Invisible Hand which conducts the affairs of men," and "the benign Parent of the Human Race." Washington also referred to God's "benediction" and "providential agency" and to "the propitious smiles of Heaven," "the eternal rules of order and right which Heaven itself has ordained," and to God having favored the American people with "unparalleled unanimity on a form of government for the security of their union and the advancement of their happiness." He ended his speech with a "humble supplication" to God that "His divine blessing" might foster "the enlarged views, the temperate consultations, and the wise measures on which the success of this Government must depend."[33] No one knew better than this first president that the United States of America would not have won the American Revolution if military might had been the only factor. Against all odds, America had defeated the most powerful European imperial power of the age, and Washington was convinced that victory had been gained with God's aid and guidance. As the man elected in 1787 to preside over the convention that produced the Constitution of the United States, he knew full well the seemingly irreconcilable political differences that had been brought into agreement during that summer of debate in Philadelphia—again, he believed, with God's help. He had ample reason, therefore, to feel that America enjoyed God's special blessing.

During Washington's first administration, one of the first acts of the First Congress was to establish an office of chaplains to begin each meeting of the Senate and the House of Representatives with a prayer by an ordained minister—a practice that is still followed. The First Congress also established a chaplain service of the military forces of the United States. And on the reverse side of the Great Seal of the United States, approved by the First Congress on September 16, 1789, were these symbols: a disembodied eye surrounded by a burst of light at the apex of a pyramid having thirteen courses of stone, representing the Eternal Eye of God watching over the then thirteen states of the United States; and above these symbols the Latin motto *Annuit Coeptis*, meaning, in reference to God, He Has Favored Our Undertaking. The statement "In God We Trust," which began appearing on U.S. coins during the Civil War, was made the nation's official motto by act of Congress in 1956 and is affixed above the speaker's chair in the House of Representatives. Similarly the popular poem written by Francis Scott Key in 1814 in celebration of a crucial victory during America's second war with England, which was made the national anthem in 1916, has as its concluding lines before the refrain: ". . . may the heav'n rescued land/ Praise the Power that had made and preserved us a nation./ Then conquer we must, when our cause it is just,/ And this be our motto: 'In God is our trust.' "

The lengthy invocations of God in the second inaugural of Thomas Jefferson (1805) and the fourth of Franklin D. Roosevelt (1945) are especially interesting when compared with the much briefer invocations in the earlier inaugural addresses of these presidents—a fact which leads one to wonder whether the trials of this office bring even the most self-assured men to "walk humbly" with God.

Jefferson in his first inaugural alluded to God as "that Infinite Power which rules the destinies of the universe" and referred to the American people "acknowledging and adoring an overruling Providence." In his second inaugural address, however, Jefferson expressed himself in terms one might have expected to hear in a sermon by a seventeenth-century Puritan divine. "I shall need, too," Jefferson said in 1805, "the favor of that Being in whose hands we are, who led our fathers, as Israel of old, from their native land and planted them in a country flowing with all the necessaries and comforts of life; who has covered our infancy with His providence and our riper years with His wisdom and power, and to whose goodness I ask you to join in supplications with me that He will so enlighten the minds of your servants, guide their councils, and prosper their measures that whatsoever they do shall result in your good, and shall secure to you the peace, friendship, and approbation of all nations."[34]

When Franklin D. Roosevelt first took office as president in 1933 and dedicated the nation to solving the problems of the Great Depression, he said merely: ". . . we humbly ask the blessing of God. May He protect each and every one of us. May He guide me in the days to come." But in 1945, in his fourth inaugural, after more than three years of a world war fought by the largest military forces any American president had ever commanded, and after the deaths of many tens of thousands of Americans on battlefields around the world, a careworn Roosevelt remarked—as he had not done in any of his three previous inaugurals—that he had taken his oath of office "in the presence of our God." And he concluded the address with a heartfelt reference to God that was longer than all of his previous inaugurals' references, saying: "The Almighty God has blessed our land in many ways. He has given our people stout hearts and strong arms with which to strike mighty blows for freedom and truth. He has given to our country a faith which has become the hope of all peoples in an anguished world. So we pray to Him now for the vision to see our way clearly—to see the way that leads to a better life for ourselves and for all our fellow men—to the achievement of His will, to peace on earth."[35] Four months later this longest-serving U.S. president was dead, having exhausted himself in defending the American freedoms he had come to believe God wanted all of humanity to have.

The lengthiest comment by any American president on God's providential relation to America was pronounced by the man who served in the office during the Union's greatest crisis. Abraham Lincoln took office as president for the second time in 1865 during the final weeks of the Civil War. In his second inaugural he quoted and paraphrased five biblical passages, and said of the war which had been ravaging the land for four years:

> Both [sides in this war] read the same Bible, and pray to the same God; and each invokes His aid against the other. It may seem strange that any men should dare to ask a just God's assistance in wringing their bread from the sweat of other men's faces; but let us judge not that we be not judged. The prayers of both could not be answered; that of neither has been answered fully. The Almighty has His own purposes. "Woe unto the world because of offences! for it must needs be that offences come; but woe to that man by whom the offence cometh!" If we shall suppose that American Slavery is one of those offences which, in the providence of God, must needs come, but which, having continued through His appointed time, He now wills to remove, and that He gives to both North and South, this terrible war, as the woe due to those by whom the offence came, shall we discern therein any departure from those divine attributes which the believers in a Living God always ascribe to Him? Fondly do we hope—fervently do we pray—that this mighty scourge of war may speedily pass away. Yet, if God wills that it continue, until all the wealth piled by the bond-man's two hundred and fifty years of unrequited toil shall be sunk, and until every drop of blood drawn with the lash, shall be paid by another drawn with the sword, as was said three thousand years ago, so still must it be said "the judgments of the Lord are true and righteous altogether."
>
> With malice toward none; with charity for all; with firmness in the right, as God gives us to see the right, let us strive on to finish the work we are in; to bind up the nation's wounds; to care for him who shall have borne the battle, and for his widow, and orphan—to do all which may achieve and cherish a just, and lasting peace, among ourselves, and with all nations.[36]

In thus expressing his inmost feeling that the Civil War was God's judgment on the American people for their sinfulness in having enslaved their fellow man, Abraham Lincoln seems to have been addressing himself to God in humble prayer as much as he was addressing the men and women assembled to witness his second inauguration. He was praying that he and they would obey God's will as Christ had taught it to mankind during his lifetime on earth: that the victorious North would forgive its enemies in the South and be charitable toward them; remember its own sinfulness (slavery in the United States was, in Lincoln's mind, "American Slavery," not Southern slavery); accept the severe punishment of the war as God's justice on them as a people for the sinfulness of having permitted slavery; and judge not their defeated adversaries, lest their own sins be judged by God.

In 1862, the second year of the war, Abraham Lincoln had recorded on a slip of paper, found among his papers after his assassination, his belief that the war was a punishment from God for the sin of slavery: "The will of God prevails. In great contests each party claims to act in accordance with the will of God. Both *may* be, and one *must* be wrong. God cannot be *for*, and *against* the same thing at the same time. In the present civil war it is quite possible that God's purpose is something different from the purpose of either party—and yet the human instrumentalities, working just as they do, are of the best adaptation to effect His purpose. I am almost ready to say this is probably true—that God wills this contest, and wills that it shall not end yet. By his mere quiet power, on the minds of the now contestants, He could have either *saved* or *destroyed* the Union without a human contest. Yet the contest began. And having begun He could give the final victory to either side any day. Yet the contest proceeds."

Taking leave of his neighbors in Springfield, Illinois, to assume the presidency of the United States in 1861, after six states of the Union had already seceded, Lincoln had likewise expressed himself in religious terms: "My friends—No one, not in my situation, can appreciate my feeling of sadness at this parting. To this place, and the kindness of these people, I owe every thing. Here I have lived a quarter of a century, and have passed from a young to an old man. Here my children have been born, and one is buried. I now leave, not knowing when, or whether ever, I may return, with a task before me greater than that which rested upon Washington. Without the assistance of that Divine Being, who ever attended him, I cannot succeed. With that assistance, I cannot fail. Trusting in Him, who can go with me, and remain with you and be every where for good, let us confidently hope that all will yet be well. To His care commending you, as I hope in your prayers you will commend me, I bid you an affectionate farewell."[37]

Altogether, in the inaugural addresses of the thirty-six presidents who have made such addresses upon assuming office, there are more than two hundred statements about God's relationship to America, prayerful expressions of faith in God, and allusions to various concepts about God and his providence. The cynical point of view that presidents are simply politicians who tell the people what they want to hear, does not explain why the American people should want to hear an expression of religious faith from their elected chief magistrate. Nor does it explain why some presidents who are known to have been persons of deep faith—such as Woodrow Wilson—and who could be expected to use the occasion of their inaugural to express their faith at some length, made only brief religious references in their inaugural addresses. (Perhaps they felt that religious faith is too personal a matter for public expression.) Moreover, such great presidents as Jefferson, Lincoln, and Franklin Roosevelt reserved their longest commentary on religion for their final inaugural speech, when they no longer had a need to please the voters because they would never again be standing for election to the office.

Belief in God and in his protection of the United States have been consistently evidenced by the men the American people have elected to represent them in the most powerful office of their government. Although no "religious Test" is required to run for the office of president (the Constitution prohibits that), it has been generally understood that the American people would never elect to the presidency a person who was a known atheist or openly disrespectful of religion. Such a choice would be abhorrent to the importance God has in the lives of too many Americans, and contrary to the primary religious belief that is central to American culture: *God Created Nature And Human Beings*. It would also be contrary to the belief *America Is A Chosen Country*.

But (as we shall see in discussing political beliefs in a later chapter), Americans also believe that *Worship Is A Matter Of Conscience*. Because of that belief, any continual parading of religious faith by a candidate or an elected official may be viewed as unseemly political pandering to Americans' religious convictions. Along those same lines, any insistence by a candidate on a particular faith as the only true religion would end that person's political standing with the American people.

EMIGRANTS to America in the seventeenth and eighteenth centuries brought with them from Europe the beliefs *God Created Nature And Human Beings* and *God Created A Law Of Right And Wrong*, and their lives and the lives of their descendants in America strengthened and enculturated these beliefs. But it was life in America that originated and enculturated the beliefs *America Is A Chosen Country* and *God Gave Men The Same Birthrights*. These are therefore the most distinctively American religious beliefs.

Thomas Jefferson and his fellow delegates to the Second Continental Congress in 1776, in writing and ratifying the Declaration of Independence, affirmed the belief *God Gave Men The Same Birthrights* by saying that "All men are created equal" and "endowed by their Creator with certain unalienable Rights." A letter Jefferson wrote in 1826, just ten days before his death, leaves little room for doubting this meaning of those immortal phrases. In this letter, declining because of poor health an invitation to speak in Washington at the ceremony for the fiftieth anniversary of the Declaration of Independence, Jefferson writes that what he and the other delegates to the Second Continental Congress meant in declaring all men to be created equal and endowed by God with unalienable rights was that "the mass of mankind has not been born with saddles on their backs, nor a favored few booted and spurred, ready to ride them legitimately, by the grace of God."[38]

In England's aristocratic culture, that was exactly what had happened historically. There had been two categories of men: those of "noble" blood, which gave them a birthright to govern the rest of mankind, and those of "common" blood whose birthright was to let those of noble birth govern. By 1776, when the Declaration of Independence was written and proclaimed, American culture had developed the quite contrary cultural belief that *God Gave Men The Same Birthrights*. Jefferson's metaphor, comparing the relationship between the governing class in England and the rest of the English population to that of a rider on his horse, rejected the belief in a birthright to lordship. It asserted instead the revolutionary American belief that all men have the same birthrights, without distinction by class.

This belief in a God-given equality of birthrights was the cultural foundation of the American Revolution. It led to an entirely different form of government from that of aristocratic Europe in the eighteenth century. Although the belief applied only to free men, and not to free women or to the slaves in the American population, that fact does not diminish the culturally revolutionary development it represented. It made the consent of the governed the basis of government in the United States, as opposed to the right to govern of a particular class. From the beginning of their history in the wilderness, there had been among Americans no class of "noble" birth and no class with a birthright to govern. That was the meaning of the famous words in the Declaration of Independence "All men are created equal" and "endowed by their Creator with certain unalienable Rights." It was a major advance in the history of freedom in the world that such a belief—even though it was restricted to free men—was by 1776 enculturated among the American people. The same belief later formed the basis for the women's suffrage movement and for the civil rights movement of black Americans.

Jefferson and the other Founding Fathers could not have believed that all men have been created equal by God in the sense that they all have the same talents or interests. No mature person of ordinary intelligence could believe in an equality of individual endowments of that sort. Nor would any person of sound mind and some experience in the world think that all men could ever, in any sense, be made equal in their physical, mental, or moral capacities or their condition. In endorsing the statement that men are "created equal" and "endowed by their Creator" with the same rights, Jefferson and the other members of the Second Continental Congress were declaring their American belief in an equality of birthrights—the right to life, the right to liberty, the right to pursue happiness, and the right to institute the kind of government they wished to live under. The idea of an equality of birthrights had been written about in England and other countries of Europe. Generations of behavior had enculturated the belief among free men in America.

The elected representatives of the American people who produced the Declaration of Independence were culturally united in believing that by resisting the British king's violation of their birthrights, they were upholding the will of God that those rights be defended. Their belief in God was thus crucial to their assertion of independence from England. How much that belief entered into their thinking can be seen in what can be called the argument of the Declaration of Independence, which is contained in its first two paragraphs and the most substantive statements of its last paragraph. The argument rests on the belief in God as the source of equal birthrights. The Declaration both repudiated the European doctrine of the right of persons of "noble" blood to rule and asserted the non-European, democratic cultural belief in the divine right of free men to govern themselves without interference from kings:

> When in the Course of human events, it becomes necessary for one people to dissolve the political bands which have connected them with another, and to assume among the Powers of the earth, the separate and equal station to which the Laws of Nature and of Nature's God entitle them, a decent respect to

the opinions of mankind requires that they should declare the causes which impel them to the separation.

We hold these truths to be self-evident, that all men are created equal, that they are endowed by their Creator with certain unalienable Rights, that among these are Life, Liberty and the pursuit of Happiness. That to secure these rights, Governments are instituted among Men, deriving their just powers from the consent of the governed, That whenever any Form of Government becomes destructive of these ends, it is the Right of the People to alter or to abolish it, and to institute new Government, laying its foundation on such principles and organizing its powers in such form, as to them shall seem most likely to effect their Safety and Happiness. . . .

We, therefore, the Representatives of the United States of America, in General Congress, Assembled, appealing to the Supreme Judge of the world for the rectitude of our intentions, do, in the Name, and by Authority of the good People of these Colonies, solemnly publish and declare, That these United Colonies are, and of Right ought to be Free and Independent States; that they are Absolved from all Allegiance to the British crown. . . . And for the support of this Declaration, with a firm reliance on the Protection of Divine Providence, we mutually pledge to each other our Lives, our Fortunes and our sacred Honor.[39]

In sum, the argument of the Declaration is this: God has created men and has endowed them with the same birthrights; governments must respect those birthrights; the government of the king of England has not respected the God-given birthrights of his subjects in America; therefore they must remove themselves from his authority and form a new government of their own. The argument is rooted in three religious beliefs of American culture: *God Created Nature And Human Beings*, *God Created A Law Of Right And Wrong*, and *God Gave Men The Same Birthrights*.

Having the same God-given birthrights makes men politically equal. That belief alone, once it became enculturated among Americans, was enough to make their culture radically unlike any eighteenth-century European culture. (All the nations of Europe, except Switzerland, had governments headed by kings or queens or persons of lesser noble birth.) An equality of God-given birthrights is the only kind of human equality that is inherent; it is the only kind that can never be altered or taken away. Being conferred by birth, it is as unalienable as the right to rule claimed by a king's firstborn son by virtue of his birth. The principal cultural content of the Declaration of Independence, therefore, is as Jefferson said it was in 1826: the conviction that no man has been born saddled for another man, born booted and spurred, to ride.

By 1776 America had been for eight generations a society made up mainly of people who descended from self-selected immigrants who had chosen to seek, with God's help, a better and happier way of life for themselves in America. They came from the class of society known in the eighteenth century as "the lower orders"—that is, persons with little or no property at the time of their emigration to America and, of course, no "noble" blood. After eight generations of hard labor, they and their descendants had civilized by 1776 most of a vast coastal plain several times larger than the British Isles. Kings, queens, princes, princesses, earls, countesses, marquesses, marchionesses, dukes, duchesses, viscounts, viscountesses, barons, baronets, and baronesses had not settled in their midst to constitute a governing class defined by birth.

The cultural belief of Americans that *God Gave Men The Same Birthrights* has remained unchanged since the Declaration of Independence, except that it no longer applies only to free white men of age. In 1953 President Eisenhower spoke of it in terms of the "faith" Americans have that "establishes, beyond debate, those gifts of the Creator that are man's inalienable rights, and that make all men equal in His sight"; his successor in the presidency, John F. Kennedy, expressed it in 1961 by saying America was pledged to uphold "the belief that the rights of man come not from the generosity of the state, but from the hand of God." In 1925 President Calvin Coolidge spoke of "the rights of persons" having "a divine sanction." In 1841 President William Henry Harrison said an American has birthrights that derive from "no charter granted by his fellow-man" but from the fact that "he is himself a man, fashioned by the same Almighty hand as the rest of his species."[40]

Although European theologians and political philosophers in the seventeenth and eighteenth centuries and earlier wrote of the idea of human equality, no society in Europe had ever acted upon it long enough to make it a cultural belief. Rousseau and Voltaire, for example, while they proposed an enlightened philosophy, both conformed to the age-old pattern of European culture in seeking to live off the largess and patronage of noblemen and monarchs. The life of the English political philosopher John Locke, whose writings have often been thought of as a source of the American Revolution, also shows deference to a noble class. As the hired secretary of an English nobleman who was one of the lord proprietors of the Carolinas, Locke drew up an elaborate plan called "The Fundamental Constitutions of Carolina"; it authorized a landed, titled nobility in the Carolinas whose members would constitute a governing class. The model for the plan was, of course, England's aristocratic society and government. But the circumstances of life in colonial America were unsuitable to the establishment in the Carolinas, or anywhere else along the Atlantic coastal plain, of an aristocratic class. The attempt to implement "The Fundamental Constitutions of Carolina" therefore failed. When the secretary of the lord proprietors drew it up, there was already too much land in the hands of "commoners" in America, and too much additional land available to them at cheap prices, to establish a nobility of great landowners.

Professions about equality by such European philosophers as Voltaire, Rousseau, and Locke were not demonstrated in their deference to persons of noble birth and their willingness to live off the money furnished them by monarchs and lords. John Locke believed in the institution of monarchy. He believed in the differentiated, inherited political rights of lords. He believed in government dominated by highborn persons as the proper form of government. The American Revolution denied the validity of all these English cultural beliefs. Unlike the French Revolution in the eighteenth century and the Soviet revolution in the twentieth, both of which made human reason the measure of rightness and the source of freedom, equality, and brotherhood, the American Revolution was rooted in the belief that the equality of human beings and the rights of man have their origin in God. In America, it has been rightly noted, religion and politics have been "organically linked";[41] this is undoubtedly one of the chief reasons why belief in God is so important to so many Americans.

Associate Justice of the Supreme Court William O. Douglas pointed this out in writing the majority opinion of the Court in *Zorach v. Clauson* in 1951: "We are a religious people whose institutions presuppose a Supreme Being."[42] Chief Justice Earl Warren said the same thing at greater length in 1954, the year an act of Congress added the words "under God" to the phrase "one nation" in the Pledge of Allegiance:

> I believe no one can read the history of our country without realizing that the Good Book and the spirit of the Savior have from the beginning been our guiding geniuses. . . . Whether we look to the first Charter of Virginia or to the Charter of New England or the Charter of Massachusetts Bay or to the Fundamental Orders of Connecticut, the same objective is present . . . a Christian land governed by Christian principles. I believe the entire Bill of Rights came into being because of the knowledge our forefathers had of the Bible and their belief in it: freedom of belief, of expression, of assembly, of petition, the dignity of the individual, the sanctity of the home, equal justice under law, and the reservation of powers to the people. I like to believe we are living today in the spirit of the Christian religion. I also like to believe that as long as we do so, no great harm can come to our country.[43]

Eighty-six percent of Americans profess the Christian religion.[44] If that many citizens of any country professed communism, it would surely be called a Communist nation; by the same reasoning, America is a Christian nation. But it is not a nation with one, state-sanctioned religion. It is a Christian nation whose culture sanctions freedom of conscience to worship God according to one's own understanding.

CHAPTER SEVEN

Social Beliefs

Society Is A Collection Of Individuals

Every Person's Success Improves Society

Achievement Determines Social Rank

IN THESE social beliefs of American culture we again see the results of America's peculiar history: the origin of a great majority of the American population through immigration by individuals and families who chose, without governmental screening, to live in a new society; the commitment of these self-selected immigrants and their descendants to success and improvement; and the social differentiation of the population by the degree of success its members attained. This combination of social factors has caused Americans to think of their society as a collection of self-determining individuals, rather than, as in Europe, a society of birth-determined classes.

"Nowhere [in colonial America] was there anything remotely resembling a legally privileged aristocracy," the historian Jack P. Greene has observed. The thousand-year-old traditions of Britain, on the other hand, at the time of the American war for independence, were "essentially feudal and aristocratic," according to Charles M. Andrews; and "probably in no country of Europe was the law concerning land and hereditary property . . . more feudal than in the England of that period."[1]

Neither before nor after the American Revolution, however, was American society ever "classless," if by that term one means socially undifferentiated. The great difference between America and England was in how membership in the upper, middle, and lower classes was determined. Because of the fact that America had no semblance of an aristocracy buttressed by feudal laws, it was "wealth, rather than family or tradition," that was "the primary determinant of social stratification," as the historian Carl Degler has pointed out.[2] Apart from the slave class established by law in the 1660s, which existed in parts of the United States until 1865 (when slavery was forbidden throughout the nation by the Thirteenth Amendment to the Constitution, though a majority of states had abolished it decades earlier), American society has never had the kind of classes fixed by birth that one finds in European history. In America, except for the slaves, an individual's success in life determined his class. In every generation of Americans, the number of persons who rose and fell in class standing was proportionately large in comparison to European societies, where birth was the main consideration in determining class, and the movement of individuals from the middle class to the upper class was small. Class standing in America, on the other hand, was highly "mobile," and movement between classes, both up and down, was commonplace.

NO FAIRLY LARGE SOCIETY has ever remained socially undifferentiated over time, and colonial America was certainly no exception. But in comparison to colonial Spanish America, colonial Brazil, colonial Canada, and Europe before the nineteenth century, the formative period of American culture was exceptional in determining social standing through achievement. Practically speaking, this meant how much property or money an individual accumulated; and in a society where honesty and diligent work formed the best avenue to money and property, the distinction between money-making and respectable citizenship became blurred. Property was the chief outward sign in America of a presumptive honesty and the chief distinguishing mark of respectability. Success in American society required a reputation for honest dealings and being active in "doing something with your life"—that is, improving your own life and the lives of others. Those who made the greatest contribution to material improvement—a compelling requirement in a society originating in a wilderness—were respected as the most successful persons and the most deserving of higher social standing, provided their success was honestly achieved.

Cadwallader Colden, lieutenant governor of New York before the American Revolution, remarked then that "the only principle of life propagated among the young people is to get money, and men are only esteemed according to what they are worth."[3] His judgment might be applicable today, except for his use of "only." At no time in American history has money-making been the exclusive focus of the younger generation. Men and women have often been respected for reasons other than the amount of their possessions. A deserved reputation for honesty and usefulness has also been part of class membership in America. Yet, on the whole, because Americans have often regarded wealth as a sign of rectitude in one's dealings with others, as well as an indication of having done something useful in life, a person's wealth has generally been the determining feature of his social rank.

I suspect, however, that the ambition most prevalent among Americans has been to make "a decent living" rather than to attain a fortune. If this is true, success for most Americans has historically consisted of aspiring *not to be poor* rather than yearning to get rich. There is an old American joke about the farmer who, though he was always buying more land, denied that he wanted to own all the farmland in the world—he only wanted to purchase the land next to his. This is a criticism of continually piling up more and more wealth; and so is the joke about John D.

Rockefeller's reply "Just a little more," when asked how much wealth was "enough" for one man to have.

Money-making and property ownership have been seen by most Americans as a means to independence and comfort and, if possible, to leaving one's children an inheritance. Money and property have also been necessary to self-respect in a society in which the way to wealth is open to the great majority of persons. The almost universal interest of Americans in having things and making money, which foreign observers have so often noticed and so frequently condemned as unbridled and stifling materialism, reflects the need of Americans to establish themselves on their own, without reliance on their birth for social position. Many English novels concern the situation of inheriting property or the quest to marry someone who has inherited, or will inherit, an estate; but this theme is seldom found in classical American literature.

The early age at which American youths leave their families to fend for themselves and the absence of support from extended families—which have impressed observers from Europe, Asia, and other parts of the Americas as unusual—both reflect Americans' historically intense interest in making money to attain independence and self-respect. The availability of unoccupied land and other means to achieving independence in America during the formative period of its culture—opportunities comparatively lacking in Europe, Asia, and other parts of the Americas—created new norms of social behavior in America.

Nathaniel Hawthorne's novel *The House of the Seven Gables* (1851) is about the corrupting influence of the ambition to establish an aristocratic lineage based on inherited wealth. The story illustrates the cultural rightness of self-determination and independence for each generation of Americans, and the wrongness for American culture of aristocratic beliefs. Hawthorne's novel also suggests that in assessing a person's social worth, moral considerations count for as much as the amount of one's property. In this fictional study of American cultural beliefs about class, even the representative of the lowest class (the character named Uncle Venner) wants to be self-reliant and avoid dependence on public charity. *The House of the Seven Gables* stipulates in its preface the "folly" of letting loose "an avalanche of ill-gotten gold, or real estate, on the heads of an unfortunate posterity, thereby to maim and crush them"; and one notes in this statement the importance of the qualifier "ill-gotten." The villain of this novel wants more and more money and is in love with wealth for its own sake. Still, when it comes to deciding how much honestly acquired money or property is enough to assure comfort, independence, and the enjoyment of the better things of life, most Americans have a little of the John D. Rockefeller mentality in their cultural makeup. Each generation of Americans has probably acted as though it were better to have "a little more" money than too little—without, however, making the piling up of possessions and income the only goal in life.

The chief fact of American social history is that the aspiration *not to be poor* has been satisfied for most Americans. From one generation to another throughout American history, success in these terms has been attainable by most all Americans. This may be why being poor in America has come to have such a stigma attached to it—an indication that one has not tried hard enough to avoid poverty. In other words, a greater proportion of American society has historically avoided poverty and attained middle-class respectability than has been true generally in the history of other Western cultures. That, of course, is why America has received more migrants than any other nation in history, and why immigration to America has continued to be heavy despite repeated attempts in the twentieth century to control its volume. Americans expect success. It is a cultural norm in the United States.

Before the twentieth century, probably some of Europe's poor never knew of the existence of America. (I once met an old woman in a tiny village in the mountains of Lérida in the Catalan region of northeastern Spain who asked me where I was from and said, after I told her, that she had never heard of the United States of America.) But from the mid-1660s on, the poor of Europe who lived in its main seaports and the hinterlands they served certainly knew of the existence of a nation across the Atlantic called America. There, they knew, lower-class persons could hope to acquire property and middle-class status through their own efforts, and a middle-class European who had to rent land and his house from some landowner might in America own a farm, a home, or a business of his own. The attractiveness of America as a destination for self-selecting emigrants, during the centuries before quotas restricted legal migration to the United States, is sure proof that America offered real possibilities for rising in life. The convergence on America of poor people bent on rising in life has made America preeminently a middle-class society. Both before and since American independence, this great fact about American society—that historically most of its people have aspired to belong to the middle class, and most of them have been able to satisfy their aspiration—has shaped the social beliefs of American culture.

SUCCESS WAS most likely during the initial generations of settlement on the Atlantic coastal plain, when that large region of the future United States still lay open and uninhabited land was so plentiful as to be—as Americans say—"dirt cheap." Records in Maryland, the fourth of the thirteen American colonies, reveal that during its earliest period of settlement more than 90 percent of those who arrived in the colony from Europe as indentured servants (whose condition put them in the lowest class of free men because under the terms of their indentures they could not earn money for themselves) became landowners in less than a decade after they completed their years of contracted servitude and were free to work for themselves.[4] Even though this remarkable rate of success later declined—by the last decades of the 1600s in Maryland it was 70 percent—the rate of success for poor immigrants in America remained so astoundingly high by

European standards that it continued to attract more and more landless peasants and tenant farmers from Europe.

It would be fair to say that for even the poorest immigrants who arrived on American shores before the twentieth century, and who were willing to put their minds and backs to the task, the odds in favor of success were a good deal better than fifty-fifty. And in the twentieth century, success in America has not slackened appreciably. In a 1996 poll nearly two-thirds of adult Americans surveyed (61 percent) said they were financially better off than their parents had been at the same age. (Another 22 percent said they were in about the same financial condition their parents had been at their age; 75 percent said they were making more money in 1996 than they had been in 1981.)[5]

The general success of individuals in America and the enormous size of the middle class relative to the lower class have greatly weakened the European idea of "class consciousness." The Chinese minister to the United States at the turn of the century remarked about the American attitude toward class: "The dislike of distinction of classes which arises from the principle of equality is apparent wherever you go in the States. . . . It is a common thing to see [in the streetcars of Washington] a workman, dressed in shabby clothes full of dirt, sitting next to a millionaire or a fashionable lady gorgeously clothed. Cabinet officers and their wives do not think it beneath their dignity to sit beside a laborer, or a coolie, as he is called in China."[6] Certainly the American middle class has historically felt itself to be by far the most important class in American society and the ultimate repository of social respectability and political responsibility. Since early colonial times, the huge middle class has created the steadily increasing national wealth of America through its improvement-oriented behavior. Because so much of America's wealth has been held by the middle class, the European mentality of "class warfare" has not figured in American history. No majority in any state of the American Union has ever risen up against their "masters" to seize their property. Simply to state the matter in those terms indicates how different the structure and history of society in America has been in comparison to Europe's.

The self-assurance and self-confidence of the American middle class, and its feeling of being in command of the society in which it comprises the overwhelming majority of the population, are illustrated in an exchange on the subject of class which supposedly took place in the 1920s between the American writers Ernest Hemingway and Scott Fitzgerald. Fitzgerald is supposed to have observed in conversation with Hemingway: "The rich are different from you and me," to which Hemingway supposedly replied: "Yeah. They have more money." The story reflects an American attitude: that members of the upper class in America are no better as human beings than members of other classes.

Historically so many Americans have considered themselves middle class, and have earned that status through what they made on their own, that their self-respect has not suffered by comparison to members of the upper class. The wealthy have been seen by the vast majority of Americans as just like themselves, except that they have more money, comfort, and independence. In Europe, on the other hand, the class of highest respectability has been defined historically by the belief that certain persons have, because of their birth, a nobility of *being* that other human beings do not have. Although certain actions of a "nobleman" might betray his noble blood, in Europe before the twentieth century the cultural belief prevailed that a certain class of persons had a nobility of birth that could be tainted only by atrocious misbehavior.

If there has been comparatively little envy of the rich in America, it is because members of the middle class have felt they had sufficient wherewithal for comfort, enjoyment, independence, and self-respect, and because each person's degree of success, however great or little, was a contribution to the general building up of society. The imperative in American history to civilize a wilderness created a need for cooperation among Americans that greatly diminished the sharp class distinctions of

Europe. The presence of so much cheap land (the social mobility factor in American cultural history) had the same effect of blunting the kinds of class consciousness and antagonisms found in European history. The lower class in America had no general feeling that their condition was necessarily permanent and that the upper class considered them and their offspring inferior human beings.

A recent history of the founding of a town in upstate New York in the 1790s remarks about the recurring social experience in America of making new communities: "Every newly cleared and planted acre benefited not merely one family but everyone in the neighborhood. Every expansion of fields and herds increased the local supply of food while subtracting from the forest that harbored the wild predators that afflicted their livestock and crops. Settlers usually worked as distinct family groups on their own property, but because all the families labored in the same way to the same ends, they advanced a common cause."[7] Each man's gain in this society worked to the advantage of his neighbor by transforming the wilderness; the more acres someone cleared and developed, the better for everyone. Society in upstate New York in the 1790s was a collection of individuals equally focused on improving their lives, with varying results. In this kind of society, no class of persons could be seen as taking advantage of another class.

This was not a classless society, because not everyone in it had the same amount of property, the determiner of social rank; but inequality of possessions did not define a man's human worth, because every hand turned to the task of transforming the wilderness was needed and contributed to the general improvement of American society. It was a society dominated by a large, hardworking, and independent middle class whose members sought cooperation and felt no class envy over differences in success because each person acknowledged that it was up to him to get ahead and to make something of himself. The founder in the 1790s of Cooperstown, New York, William Cooper, the father of the novelist James Fenimore Cooper, started life poor. More power to him, therefore, if he succeeded in becoming wealthy from his land dealings and in the process helped other men become property owners. That attitude, which prevailed on the frontier of upstate New York, still prevails in America two hundred years later, because the behavior of generation after generation of Americans has enculturated the belief *Every Person's Success Improves Society.*

Whether every American made something of himself or not, Americans as a people have historically believed and acted on the premise that anyone may improve his condition if he is willing to make the effort. Consequently few Americans have lived their lives thinking in terms of "class consciousness," "class privilege," and "class warfare." Rather, the vocabulary of American culture has been opportunity, work, individual responsibility, and "getting ahead." The seeds of the socialist movements of the late nineteenth and early twentieth centuries—which formulated the dogma of the need for "class struggle"—found unsuitable cultural soil in America, though variants of these ideas are being kept alive even in the late twentieth century by being grafted onto American cultural beliefs. (One of the slogans of the Communist Party U.S.A. in the 1930s was "Communism Is Twentieth-Century Americanism."[8]) "Class struggle" made sense in European society because of its history of "noblemen" and "commoners," its disproportionate concentration of wealth in a tiny governing class with a monopoly on land, and its class barriers erected by birth which could be breached only rarely and with great difficulty. These characteristics of European social history, which differ so markedly from the American cultural belief *Achievement Determines Social Rank,* defined English society before the twentieth century. There one found "castes," in comparison to the so-called classless society of America. (One's birth is, after all, not something one can change; and when social rank is defined mostly by birth, classes do indeed become castes.)

Another doctrine of socialism that has made little sense in America is "equality of condition." The chief historical awareness of Americans, based on the history of their development of central North America, has been the consciousness of building something as individuals and as a collectivity of individuals. To use the laws of the land and the powers of government to take from those who have achieved something and distribute their substance to those who, for whatever reason, did not achieve as much, has seemed unjust and beyond what American law and government were intended to do. In each generation, individual Americans had to determine for themselves, through their own effort, whether they would rise to a higher class of achievers, fall in social rank, or remain in the social class into which they were born. Nothing was assured for any individual, nothing guaranteed by birth or inheritance. The "self-made man"—the man who makes something of himself through his own efforts—remains therefore the American model of success, and self-reliance and independence are still American cultural values. Successes in America, as defined by not being poor, still outnumber failures by a wide margin. The hard work, thrift, and prudent avoidance of ruinous expenses that allowed "almost any healthy man" in the Maryland of the 1640s and 1650s to "become a landowner in a short time," continue to be requirements for getting ahead in America.[9]

"The masses" in American social history have been *a propertied middle class*, not "the dispossessed" who historically formed the bulk of European society. Furthermore these American masses have determined their social rank for themselves; it has not been determined for them. In the late 1700s, on the eve of revolutions in America and France, the classes in European societies had a radically different relationship to each other than had the classes in America. The fundamental difference has been summarized by the historian Alan Taylor: "[Europe was] a relatively crowded society where resources were scarce, social mobility was uncommon, and the people lived in compact villages in which the poor and uneducated were under the supervision of their betters. But in America the relative abundance of land to population permitted most common white men to obtain substantial farms and to live remote from the oversight of magistrates and ministers."[10] In American history it has not been "every man for himself," though at times in the late nineteenth and twentieth centuries it may have seemed so to those who failed the test of self-determination. Rather, society in America has meant that every man favored success and regarded society as a collection of individuals who were generally benefited by the success of each member of the society.

Comparisons are helpful in evaluating the exceptional social history of America. The population history of Spain offers a typical case. The oldest identifiable group in Spain is the Basques; indeed, they are the oldest identifiable people in all of Europe, because their language belongs to none of the numerous languages known as Indo-European—the family of languages spoken from India through Europe. The Celts, the ancestors of the Gallegos and Asturianos who inhabit northwestern Spain today, were also an ancient, prehistoric people of Europe. The Iberians, who gave their name to the peninsula that Spain and Portugal occupy, appear to have come from North Africa. And in the south of Spain, archaeologists have dated the founding of Cádiz, Europe's oldest continuously inhabited city, to thirty-one centuries ago, when seafaring Phoenicians from the Middle East were attracted by the safe anchorage inside the Bay of Cádiz and established a trading post there. Over time, successive peoples—Romans, Suevi, Vandals, Alani, Visigoths, and Moors (a collection of various North African tribesmen, all of whom were Muslims)—invaded and settled in Spain. Each of these groups migrated as a society and imposed through conquest their rule on peoples already living in Spain. Their military leaders became a governing class over the peoples they conquered; and naturally they wished their offspring to inherit their privileges and superior social rank. Therefore, in time, the recurring pattern of invade, conquer, and rule gave rise to a belief in birth as the basis for rulership—the so-called "noble" blood of the leaders of the conquests that not just Spain but every part of Europe has experienced in its history.

Americans have no such social history. The cultural ancestors of Americans were brave, imaginative, disgruntled individuals of Christian faith from the lower and middling ranks of diverse countries of Europe. During the centuries that America was being populated by self-selected immigrants, a man who was the son of a duke in Europe was treated as an exalted and accomplished member of society and a superior human being, no matter how doltish, feckless, or incompetent he might be. In aristocratic cultures like those of Russia, England, Germany, and France, birth rank was the primary social, economic, and political fact. It determined a man's human worth, his social status, his property, and his political rights and authority. That is the meaning of the term "privileged class." A nobleman did not need to earn or prove anything. He had only to defend his birth rank and preserve the privileges that birth had conferred on him and those of his class.

The whole of the American experience was opposed to the social beliefs of Europe's aristocratic culture. In America a person's parentage was as nothing compared to his competence and character as an individual. A rich man's son still had to prove his worth by his own accomplishments. He could not rely on his parents' social standing for his self-respect or the respect of others. His birth might make more opportunities available to him, but he still had to prove his own worth through his own accomplishments. In America no more merit would have attached to the son of a nobleman than attached to the son of a man who chopped down trees—and perhaps less if he could not demonstrate some greater ability than chopping down trees, which was a much needed skill in clearing away the wilderness.

Europe's historical pattern of invasion, conquest, and lordship was classically repeated in the Spanish conquest of civilizations in the Americas. Because the Spanish commanders perfectly understood and were culturally attuned to the basic cultural beliefs of these civilizations, they were able to use the dynamics of those beliefs to overthrow the rulers of Mexico and Peru. The Spanish replaced these native lords and high priests with Spanish lords and the prelates of the state religion of Spain. In Mexico the hatred of the Aztec conqueror by other peoples was crucial to Spanish conquest, because it made available to the Spaniards tens of thousands of soldiers and porters from among those the Aztecs had subjugated. Peru at the time of its conquest had one of the most severely hierarchical civilizations known to history. When the handful of Spanish conquistadores invaded that empire and perceived its structure, they simply seized the sacred person of the Inca emperor and used his absolute authority—the cornerstone of Inca power—to forward their conquest. Steel body armor and steel weapons, war horses, ferocious dogs, and gunpowder were not nearly as important to the Spanish conquests as the Spaniards' thorough understanding of the aristocratic values of the civilizations they conquered. And during three centuries of Spanish rule in the New World, the blood of persons born in the Spanish homeland *(Peninsulares)* was always considered socially superior to the blood of persons of Spanish descent born in the Americas *(Creoles)*, whose blood might have been mixed with the Indian races the Spaniards had conquered.

Slavery was the principal fact of Brazil's historical culture, and an all-important sense of class based on birth and bloodlines pervaded its society. Even though the Portuguese had no aversion to miscegenation, the blood of the Portuguese masters of the African-descended slaves was considered superior, and the slightest bit of it elevated the class standing of even a slave. During the three and a half centuries of slavery in Brazil, persons of unmixed African blood were therefore considered inferior to persons of pure and unadulterated European descent. (When I lived in Brazil, I found it strange that none of the ministers of the government appeared to have any African ancestry, though Brazil's population is made up mostly of blacks and mulattos.) In the future United States during the formation of its culture, slavery was a minor, not the major social fact; and anyone having even the slightest bit of the blood of the slaves in the society was considered inferior to the free majority of the society—just the reverse of the situation in Brazil.

Canada's history after its conquest resembled the conquista-dor history of Spanish America, except in this case both the con-querors and the conquered were European "races." Social relations between the conquered, French-speaking "race" and the conquering, English-speaking "race" remain even today at the center of Canadian politics. In other words, the Conquest (the term is used in Canadian history books) still influences the structure of the Canadian constitution and is the foundation of its distinctive, "two-nations" culture. Immediately after the con-quest of Canada, the English conquerors delineated the rights of the French Canadians in formal political documents that be-came, and remain, part of the Canadian constitution. Thus for more than two centuries Canada has known two systems of law and political privilege: one for the descendants of the conquered French "race" and another for the descendants of the conquering English "race."

The Conquest gave French-speaking Québécois a political leverage they otherwise would not have had. And the now-enculturated division of Canada into blocs of "English speakers" and "French speakers" (classes of citizens referred to in Canadian governmental documents as Anglophones and Francophones) has worked to the advantage of French Canadians in the later twentieth century. Although the proportion of Québécois in Canada's population has declined, they have retained their con-stitutionally guaranteed group rights. As the cultural descendants of a conquered people and the inheritors of separate rights, French Canadians in some sense are, as they claim, "a distinct people."

As in Spanish America before its conquest, French Canadi-ans were accustomed to lordship at the time of their conquest. Immigration to French Canada was carefully screened in France to ensure conformity to a government-approved type of immi-grant; and feudal rights and obligations were instituted in Canada, whose government was entirely appointed by the French crown. Thus during 150 years of French lordship in

Canada, the structure of both government and society perfectly reflected Europe's history of aristocratic culture.

The English conquest of Canada did not disturb that structure. Indeed, the conservative nature of the society was reinforced a few years after the Conquest by the first large group of non-French immigrants to enter Canada. These tens of thousands of royalist refugees from the nearby, recently independent American republic, though they represented but a tiny fraction of America's population at the time (less than 2 percent), doubled Canada's small population. Loyalty to the English crown was the defining characteristic of the thinking and behavior of these immigrants who had sacrificed everything in attempting to preserve English lordship in America, and who had preferred to leave it rather than live under a republican form of government. Their presence in Canada reinforced allegiance to European culture to such a degree that Canada did not claim full independence from British rule until 1981. Even now, after full independence of the Canadian constitution from British supervision, Canada's head of state remains the reigning monarch of England.

At no time in the formative period of American culture did a conquered people form the major part of its population. Nor has a sense of aristocratic bloodlines and its associated class distinctions ever existed in America. Going to colonial America did not make an immigrant automatically—as it did in Spanish America and Brazil—a member of a small class of persons of one European "race" who, because of their "race," shared a sense of lordship over conquered races. America was, as the American poet Walt Whitman said in 1855, "a race of races," because the ancestors of most Americans had come from various "races" of Europe by their own choice and had frequently intermarried in America.[11] They arrived in America with no special privilege because of their "race" and no special status as socially, economically, or politically superior to the majority of the colonial society they were joining. Rather, the descendants of free immigrants made up the overwhelming majority of American society. Each member of this society had to establish his social rank through individual achievements and contributions to society, aided by whatever help might be received from relatives, friends, or other immigrants. Except for the consequences of mischance and certain kinds of mental incapacity, poverty and lower-class status in America are still, for most persons, the result of poor decisions, lack of imagination in seeing opportunities, or indifference to improving their lives.

CHAPTER EIGHT

Political Beliefs

The People Are Sovereign

The Least Government Possible Is Best

A Written Constitution Is Essential
To Government

A Majority Decides

Worship Is A Matter Of Conscience

IN AMERICA during the 1600s and early
1700s, the sovereignty of "We the People" replaced the European belief in the sovereignty of persons of "noble" birth. Thus
in 1776, when elected representatives of the thirteen American
states declared the independence of the United States, they did
so "in the Name, and by Authority of the good People of these
Colonies."[1] Twelve years later, other assemblies of elected representatives of the American people wrote and ratified a constitution for the government of the United States, a document that
required the approval of a majority of the people in three-fourths
of the states to take effect. These numerous elected assemblies
that produced the Constitution and gave it authority acted as
representatives of the sovereign people in each state in the

165

Union and in the nation as a whole. No other people in history had ever used this method of establishing a national government.

Through their elected representatives, the American people created a national government limited to certain specific powers, enumerated in a written constitution, all other powers being reserved to the people, in their respective states and as a whole population. Only the people, acting through their elected representatives, could amend the Constitution. Then they placed themselves under the government they had established.

In the Constitution the powers of the national government—legislative, executive, judicial—were kept separate to prevent governmental power from becoming concentrated in any branch of government and thus being a potential source of oppression. The Constitution also declared the people's rights as the sovereign power, which the government was forbidden to infringe. As the servant and instrument of the people, the national government was limited in power; the people as the originating source of governmental power were not limited, except as they agreed to be, under law. Americans consented to live under the Constitution, and under other laws they empowered their representatives to make, in order to secure, as the Preamble to the Constitution states, "the Blessings of Liberty" to themselves and their descendants. "There were two levels of law," the historian R. R. Palmer wrote, "a higher law or constitution that only the people could make or amend through constitutional conventions or bodies similarly empowered; and a statutory law, to be made and unmade, within the assigned limits, by legislators to whom the constitution gave this function."[2]

ENGLAND in its history has never known such a sovereign power or a constitution like this. English government had been established not by an elected assembly of representatives, but by a thirteenth-century arrangement between a king and a body of lords. In the fifteenth century an elected "commons," representing important taxpayers, was added to the unwritten English constitution through the mutual agreement of the lords and the king. In the seventeenth century the lords and "commons" took away most of the crown's powers. In the twentieth century the "commons" did the same thing to the lords and became the dominant power in government. Never during this long history did England have a written constitution approved by the people and limiting the authority of those in power; nor does it have such a constitution today. In eighteenth-century America, on the other hand, a written constitution was already regarded as essential and as representing the sovereign authority of the people. In England and the rest of Europe at that time, the state held that authority. Only in the twentieth century has most of Europe, influenced by the American example, come to have governments based on written constitutions approved by the people.

The constitution of England was unwritten—in the sense that it was an accumulation of documents, laws, and treaties produced by those in power who not only comprised the state but could, at any moment at their discretion, change the constitution as they saw fit. (In contrast to this power, which still pertains today under England's unwritten constitution, thousands of amendments to the U.S. Constitution have been proposed in Congress, but only twenty-seven have been ratified and become part of the Constitution.) England has no supreme court to interpret its constitution. That function is performed by those in power, the same persons who on their own authority can alter the constitution as they wish. Nor is there under this arrangement of government any separation of the power to make laws and to execute them. The chief executive of the government of England (the prime minister) is a member of the legislature, as are all the other executive officers of the government who make up the chief executive's cabinet of advisers. These ministers function simultaneously as legislators who propose and vote on laws and as administrators who execute the laws they vote on. Under the unwritten English constitution, the government has no limits on its power apart from those its members approve; and the people have no specified, guaranteed constitutional rights. The state is the sovereign authority.

To put the matter most simply: on the matter of sovereignty, Englishmen have a different cultural history from Americans. The United States constitutionally abolished monarchy more than two centuries ago. England has yet to do that because the sovereignty vested in those with power to govern is still associated with the institution of monarchy that has been central to the cultural history of England. Americans have the government they have because of their culture, which is appropriate to them as a people. Englishmen have a government that is appropriate to their own cultural history.

WHEN IN 1787–1788 elected representatives of the people wrote and ratified the Constitution of the United States, and gave that constitution the authority of a supreme law, it was the second time in history that a national government had been so established. The first time was during the American Revolution, when the Second Continental Congress wrote and the thirteen state legislatures ratified the Articles of Confederation and Perpetual Union, which went into effect in 1781, two years before the war's end. (Most of the American Revolution was fought without a national constitution and, amazingly, without a chief executive.) At an even earlier date, in 1754, long before the American Revolution, Americans had tried a somewhat similar process of writing a constitution, when delegates representing a majority of the colonies met and wrote a plan for an intercolonial government having only enumerated powers. This first American attempt to produce a united government was intended to strengthen and coordinate the military capacity of the colonies, but this so-called Albany Plan (named for the city where it was proposed) failed to be ratified by either the crown or the colonial assemblies.

The revolution in America was the enculturation during the 1600s and early 1700s of a belief in the sovereignty of the people, as manifested in a written constitution. The first statement in the Constitution articulates the source of its authority: "We the people . . . ordain and establish this Constitution for the United States of America."[3] Charles Pinckney, one of the most influential leaders in the convention that wrote the Constitution—a twenty-nine–year-old South Carolinian who had served in the Continental Army and was to be a four-term governor of South Carolina, a U.S. representative, U.S. senator, and minister to Spain—said of the sovereignty of the American people:

> We [Americans] have been taught here to believe that all power of right belongs to the people; that it flows immediately from them, and is delegated to their officers for the public good; that our rulers are the servants of the people, amenable to their will, and created for their use. How different are the governments of Europe! There, the people are the servants and subjects of their rulers; there, merit and talents have little or no influence; but all the honors and offices of government are swallowed up by birth, by fortune, or by rank. From the European world are no precedents to be drawn for a people who think they are capable of governing themselves.[4]

The principal leader in America's war for independence and revolution in government agreed with that sentiment. When George Washington retired from his long career of service to his country, he wrote a farewell address to the American people in which he stated: "The basis of our political systems is the right of the people to make and to alter their constitutions of government." Washington's belief in the right of the people of America to constitute their national and state governments echoes that of the fifty-six signers of the Declaration of Independence who asserted in that document "the Right of the People to alter or to abolish [an insufferable government], and to institute new Government."[5] That belief has been manifest in the Albany Plan (failed of ratification in 1754), the Articles of Confederation (ratified 1781), the Constitution of the United States (ratified 1788), constitutions of every state of the Union, and in every amendment to those constitutions over the past two centuries. The authority for American nationhood and American government at both the state and national levels has been the belief of the American people in their sovereignty.

The people of America developed a nation from a wilderness, declared its independence, and organized its governments. Operating through their elected representatives, they decided what powers their governments should have. Tocqueville recognized the effects of the American belief *The People Are Sovereign* during his tour of the United States in 1831–1832, and from the perspective of his European culture wrote a book called *Democracy in America.* "The people reign in the American political world as the Deity does in the Universe," he observed. "They are the cause and aim of all things; everything comes from them, and everything is absorbed in them." Abraham Lincoln called this sovereignty "government of the people, by the people, for the people."[6]

The Constitution has been the greatest political achievement of American culture. Only six nations in the world today (Great Britain being one of them) have not imitated it by writing a supreme national law ratified by a vote of the people who agree to live under its authority.[7]

THE THREE THOUSAND MILES of ocean separating America from England had much to do with the formation of the belief in their sovereignty among Americans during their colonial history. But colonial Brazilians, colonial Spanish Americans, and colonial French Canadians lived at even greater distances from their European rulers, and during their colonial histories developed no belief in their sovereignty. The peculiar character of the American colonial population, as much as geography, accounts for Americans' belief in their sovereignty. Being descended primarily from free immigrants who chose to live in America, the colonial population of the future United States had more reason for believing in their sovereignty than the slaves who made up roughly four-fifths of the colonial population of Brazil, or the conquered peoples who made up an even higher proportion of the colonial population of Spanish America, or the inhabitants of French Canada who lived under a government appointed and paid for by the king of France. The colonial populations of Brazil, Spanish America, and Canada were excluded in these various ways from the exercise of political authority. But even these fundamental demographic differences do not entirely explain the unique development in colonial America of a cultural belief in the sovereignty of the people.

The development among Americans of a belief in their sovereignty can be traced in large part to the fiscal policy of the English crown toward the inhabitants of its American colonies: the crown gave them responsibility for defending their land frontiers and paying the costs of their governments.

In French Canada the kings of France assumed responsibility for the administrative costs of government and maintained garrisons of troops sent over from France to defend the colony. After the conquest of Canada by England, the English crown paid the salaries of the governors it appointed to Canada and sent regiments of troops to garrison the fortresses of its newly conquered territories, lest France retake them. These garrisons were maintained until the 1870s. But in the colonies that were to become the United States of America, the English crown made the colonists themselves responsible for providing the manpower and money to defend their frontiers and for paying the salaries of the governors whom the crown appointed over them. From the beginning of settlement in 1607, until 1768, only minor posts of English troops were maintained on American soil. Regiments of the British army did participate in seaborne assaults against fortifications of Spain and France in the New World, but no British soldiers engaged in warfare on the inland frontiers of North America before General Edward Braddock's ill-fated expedition to the headwaters of the Ohio in 1755 in western Pennsylvania.[8] Royal troops were garrisoned in America only in 1768, a century and a half after the first permanent English settlement on the North American mainland.

The intention of the crown's fiscal policy toward the American colonies was, of course, to shift the expense of colonization to others. In the 1600s English kings authorized colonization of the Atlantic coastal plain of North America because it claimed that territory by right of exploration. Vast grants of wild land were given to individual "proprietors" and private corporations through written charters that authorized not only the occupation of territories but the organization of government in them—with the stipulation that no colonial government was ever to make a law contradictory to English law.

The motives of the colonial proprietors and corporations varied. Some sought nothing but commercial profit; others— Massachusetts, Pennsylvania, Maryland, and Georgia—had a religious or utopian motivation. But no proprietor or corporation, regardless of the nature of its interest, could indefinitely pay the cost of maintaining a colony. These founders expected the colony they financed to become either profitable or self-sustaining. Thus sooner or later the colonists themselves would have to bear the cost of transforming a wilderness into settlements and of defending and administering the colony in which they lived. The king's charters therefore authorized the proprietor or the corporation to allow the inhabitants of the colony to elect an assembly of representatives in order to set taxes to pay the salaries of the appointed governors. The charters also allowed the colonists to organize militias for the purpose of defense, which were likewise to be supported by the taxes collected in the colony.

No other colonies in the Americas had such basic fiscal responsibilities or the delegated political and military authority that went with them. Nor did the people of England at the same time. To protect itself from expense, the English crown granted its American colonies the power to tax; in doing so, it unwittingly started these colonies on the road to independence. The consequences of the policy became apparent in the 1760s.

Virginia's House of Burgesses, the first elected assembly in America, convened in 1619. Over the next 150 years, as generations of Americans in each of the colonies exercised through their assemblies the authority to tax themselves, and as they experienced the efficacy of their own resources of men and money, the importance of the English king's distant authority diminished in their thinking.

By the latter half of the 1600s, the English crown decided it needed more direct control over the American colonies. Therefore it began to eliminate the corporate and proprietary governments, placing as many colonies as possible under royal government. By 1752 only Maryland and Pennsylvania still had a proprietor, and no colony remained in the hands of a private corporation. In making these changes the crown did not, however, have the wisdom and foresight to assume the costs of government and defense of the eleven colonies it brought under royal supervision. It continued the old fiscal policy of making the colonists pay these costs. Consequently—as far as the thinking of the colonists was concerned—the switch to royal government made little difference. All that changed after New Hampshire, Massachusetts, Rhode Island, Connecticut, New York, New Jersey, Delaware, Virginia, North Carolina, South Carolina, and Georgia became "royal colonies" was that a governor appointed by the king, rather than a governor appointed by a proprietor or a corporation, now received the salary the colonists paid. Either way, the colonists continued to tax themselves through their elected representatives. The practice made them feel they had at least as much power over their affairs as the king had, and the feeling was justified. A governor who depends on elected representatives of the people for his pay becomes, in effect, the paid servant of that people, regardless of how he received his appointment.

The election by Americans of the officers who commanded their local militias also contributed to the development among them of a belief in their own sovereignty. The armed forces of these colonies were colonial, not royal, forces. Even under proprietary and corporate government, the same taxpayers who elected the assemblies (which decided the taxes that would pay the costs of military campaigns) also filled the ranks of the militias and provided their officers, whom the colonial assemblies commissioned. The money, the manpower, and the martial skills of the colonists themselves constituted their military power. And although the king's navy had responsibility for defending America's coasts, even those royal forces were augmented in time of war by numerous ships built, owned, manned, armed, provisioned, and commanded by Americans. Like the colonial militias, the ships of these colonial naval forces, called "privateers," carried the commission of a colony's elected assembly, not a commission from the king.

Besides the chronic warfare with Indians on every frontier and recurring conflicts with Spanish forces on the southern frontier of colonial America, England's four wars with France in the seventeenth and eighteenth centuries for imperial dominance in North America also developed the martial skills of Americans. They attacked French bases in Canada both independently and alongside troops from Britain. The capture of French strongholds in Canada by all-American forces in 1654, 1697, 1710, 1745, and 1755 (particularly the successful assault on Louisbourg, second only to the fortress at Quebec as the principal French bastion in the New World) were remarkable feats of valor and military tactics, as was the performance in 1741 of American troops (though few survived the assault) who took the heights above Cartagena, the principal Spanish strong point in South America, during England's unsuccessful expedition to capture that strategic fortification.[9] By the time the American Revolution began in 1775, the civilian soldiers of America had a long military tradition and reason to think of themselves as at least the equals of British troops in conceiving and carrying out military campaigns on American soil.

The self-confidence that American colonists derived from their experiences in self-government and self-defense greatly strengthened the sense of independence they had developed in creating a civilization out of wilderness. These colonists became during the 1600s and early 1700s a self-determining society unlike any other in the New World. Through their behavior they steadily enculturated a belief in their own sovereignty. In declaring their independence from England in 1776, Americans were acknowledging a reality that had developed during the previous century and a half.

ONLY ONE PART of England's government had ever been elected; and the House of Commons of the English Parliament differed markedly from the colonial assemblies in America. Members of Commons were often related by blood or marriage to members of the House of Lords. Before the twentieth century one could find in the Commons brothers, brothers-in-law, uncles-in-law, sons, sons-in-law, nephews, and grandsons of members of the House of Lords, some of whom were themselves titled noblemen.[10] Judged by American standards, the House of Commons in the 1600s and 1700s scarcely deserved the name.

In America, as one historian has commented, "the right to vote had nowhere been very narrowly restricted." Although America's national wealth in the 1600s and 1700s was nowhere near as great as England's, the wealth it did have was much more evenly distributed, and the wide availability of land allowed most of the male freemen in the population to meet the property qualification for voting in elections. Consequently the portion of the American population that could qualify to elect representatives to the colonial assemblies was far greater than the proportion of England's population that elected the House of Commons. In early Virginia and Massachusetts, for instance, almost every adult white male who was not an indentured servant could vote. When the American Revolution began in 1775, probably three-fourths of the free males of age in America were eligible to participate in elections.[11] And during the next half-century that proportion increased.

Just the opposite was true in England. In 1775 few Englishmen had the vote, and half a century later even fewer had it. Property during the fifty years from 1775 to 1825 became more and more concentrated in fewer hands, with the result that in England in 1825 only about one person in thirty met the property qualification for voting. England did not become a "full democracy" until 1928.[12]

Another important difference between representative government in the colonies and in England was how that representation was assigned. In the colonies it was distributed by population. In England some places had many more representatives in proportion to their population than others; and some had none at all. Towns that had once flourished but had lost nearly all their inhabitants nonetheless continued to elect the same number of persons to Parliament as they had elected before their decline in population, while burgeoning new towns with large populations sent no representatives to parliament. (Before the passage of the Reform Bill of 1832, 150 persons might elect 3 representatives to the House of Commons. Voting districts where such disproportionate representation was possible were rightly referred to as "rotten boroughs.") Great landlords who owned hundreds of square miles could sometimes personally decide, through their influence over the votes of their tenants, the election of as many as half a dozen members to the House of Commons.

Representation in the House of Commons was also accorded to the once-powerful craft guilds, which were holdovers from the Middle Ages, and to the two universities of England that educated the sons of the governing class. In terms of disproportionate representation of special interests, however, the greatest irregularity in the legislature of England was the fact that the number of Lords Spiritual (bishops of the state church of England) and Lords Temporal (titled noblemen) in the House of Lords was just about equal to the number of representatives elected to the House of Commons—even though the number of titled noblemen and bishops was minuscule in comparison to the total population. Before 1911 these unelected, lifetime members of Parliament who held their seats by birth and royal appointment could prevent any bill from becoming law, because their assent was constitutionally required. Thus before the twentieth century, representation in the British Parliament was heavily weighted in favor of a few hundred aristocratic families, who truly constituted a "ruling class."

Yet in the 1700s, despite the historical weakness of elected representation in England's government, English constitutional theory claimed that Parliament represented all the people of the realm. This doctrine—known as "virtual representation"—held that even though the vast majority of English males of age had no voice in electing the House of Commons, their interests were nonetheless represented in both the Lords and the Commons because members of Parliament, however they got their seats, could be depended on to put the interests of society as a whole above their own personal and class interests. Therefore there was no need to make representation proportional to population or to increase the numbers of voters.

This theory of virtual representation was also a holdover from the Middle Ages: a variation of the doctrine of noblesse oblige by which every gentleman, from the king down to the lowliest knight, was obliged by personal honor to care for his inferiors in social rank and political privilege and see that they received fair treatment. It was a lovely theory, but it was not congenial to American beliefs. By the 1760s Americans had been living for generations under circumstances that demanded they take care of themselves. Their experience had made them self-determining, even though as colonials they were supposed to be subordinate to the authority of the king.

The first American political essay to circulate widely in the colonies in the years preceding the American Revolution addressed this theory of virtual representation. Its author was Daniel Dulany, a Marylander. Published in a Maryland newspaper in 1765 and republished in other colonial newspapers, Dulany's essay, "Considerations on the Propriety of Imposing Taxes in the British Colonies for the Purpose of Raising a Revenue by Act of Parliament," denounced the doctrine of virtual representation by name as "a mere cob-web, spread to catch the unwary, and entangle the weak." That Americans had a theoretical representation in the English parliament and should therefore be content with their virtual representation seemed to Dulany wholly unwarranted. The taxation of Americans had always been decided by their elected representatives in each colony, not by any theoretical, "virtual" representation on the other side of the Atlantic.[13]

Belief in virtual representation was consistent with England's aristocratic history and culture, but not with America's history and culture. Government by lords was centuries old in England. No such domination ever formed part of the historical experience of Americans, since no class of Lords Temporal and Spiritual had ever existed in America. Thus Americans were not culturally disposed to accept what the mass of Englishmen had long accepted: that they were "virtually" represented by their social betters. In terms of the culture of colonial America, virtual representation could not be taken seriously. By the 1760s Americans had been taxing themselves through their elected colonial assemblies for seven generations. They wanted to continue to exercise that power of government.

To Americans—who had never bowed low before bishops of a state church and ermined lords of "noble birth"—it seemed too much to ask of a self-respecting man of common sense to believe that he should open his purse and allow faraway lords and other men of exalted rank to help themselves. Americans had never done so before the 1760s, and they were not culturally disposed to begin doing so. The only tradition of nobility that existed in America's history was the nobility of usefulness and the self-respect that comes from it. The English cultural traditions of noblesse oblige and virtual representation had, as Daniel Dulany said metaphorically in his essay, about as much meaning to an American as a spider's cobweb spun across some woodland path.

ENGLISHMEN, as Christians, believed that one God had created human beings as well as a moral law by which human beings should live. In these beliefs they were like Americans. But they did not share with Americans the belief that God had endowed all men with the same birthrights. For in the eyes of an Englishman there was an immense difference between the political rights of a tinker's brat and those of a duke's oldest son. That should be self-evident to any man of sense, Englishmen thought. And it was self-evident in terms of English history and culture, which by the middle 1700s was not the culture of Americans.

The argument in the 1760s between those in power in England and the American people, over who should decide what taxes Americans ought to pay, brought home to Americans that something besides three thousand miles of ocean separated them from England. An enormous difference in their beliefs about sovereignty also lay between them.

Unlike most Englishmen, the great majority of men in America owned property, usually in the form of land; and some of them possessed considerable fortunes. No American in the 1700s, however, commanded anywhere near the immense wealth of some English lords. Americans as a people aspired to a freer and more prosperous way of life than their immigrant ancestors had known, wherever in Europe they had come from. America represented a new ethos of social, economic, and political behaviors because it was a society chiefly descended from self-selected immigrants seeking improvement. The way to wealth there was through diligent personal effort; in England the way to wealth lay in patronage and inheritance.

The bulk of America's real estate was owned by persons who in England were known as commoners. And in America commoners were constantly creating more and more property from raw wilderness. Commoners also elected the legislatures of the thirteen colonies, which decided how much of the wealth they had created from the wilderness would be given over to meet the expenses of government and defense. Naturally they expected their elected representatives, and the governors who were appointed by the king of England and whose salaries they paid, to be frugal public servants, spend the hard-earned tax money entrusted to them to the best effect, and avoid costly ceremony and expensive pomp. Colonial American society had little tolerance for salaried place-servers.

In England, with its dukes and earls and princes and archbishops, costly shows of pomp and parades of authority were norms of behavior. Many men found through their ties of blood or marriage "a place in government" or "a living in the Church of England" or a commission in the British army or navy. Who got what was decided by those who were highborn or married well. In England, power originated at the top and flowed downward. On the western side of the Atlantic, where property was still in the process of being created from a primeval forest, it was comparatively easy for a man to acquire the minimal amount of property required to become a voter (forty shillings, or two pounds sterling) and to participate in government when he came of age. On the expanding frontiers of America, where property had yet to be created from the wilderness, participation in government had an even simpler basis: any freeborn male able to bear arms in the defense of his community, regardless of his age, had a say in who was elected to leadership in the military and civil affairs of the community.[14]

At the beginning of English settlement in America, it was believed in London that the kings of England could keep these colonies subject to their authority by mandating that no law passed in a colonial assembly could take effect until it had been reviewed and approved by the crown. But in the 1620s, a few years after the first two English colonies had been planted in America, a struggle began in England to change the constitution of England's government, a struggle that was not to be resolved until the late 1680s. This six-decades-long conflict over political power in England included recurring war, the trial and execution of a reigning king, seven years of military dictatorship, the restoration of the son of the executed king, the bloodless overthrow of another king, and finally, in 1688, the offer of the crown of England to a new royal line, the Dutch prince William of Orange and his English wife Mary, on the condition that they and their heirs would accept Parliament's supremacy.

It was during these sixty years of political turmoil in England that almost all the English colonies on the Atlantic coastal plain of North America were established. The timing is important, because had the English crown not been distracted by its life-and-death struggle with Parliament during the seventeenth century, England's colonies might not have developed the degree of independence they did in comparison with other European colonies in the Americas. (Both France and Spain had particularly powerful monarchies when they established their colonies on the American continents.)

By the late 1750s the spirit of independence among Americans had reached such a level of development that a king's veto over the laws of colonial assemblies appeared no longer sufficient to keep the Americans as subjects. A drastic step was therefore adopted in London: the king would simply announce through his minister for colonial affairs that the crown would henceforth be the legislative power for the colonies. Under England's unwritten constitution, which allowed those in power to make constitutional changes, this was a legitimate act, since the crown had always been constitutionally in charge of colonial affairs. The king's decision to become the lawmaker for colonies was revealed to Americans in the summer of 1757 in a conference between George II's minister for American affairs, Lord Granville, and the principal lobbyist in London for American interests, Benjamin Franklin, whom Granville summoned to his mansion for the purpose. In his autobiography Franklin described the meeting from notes he took at the time:

> . . . Mr. Hansbury called for me and took me in his Carriage to [Lord Granville's residence], who receiv'd me with great Civility; and after some Questions respecting the present State of Affairs in America, & Discourse thereupon, he said to me, "You Americans have wrong Ideas of the Nature of your Constitution; you contend that the King's Instructions to his Governors are not Laws, and think yourselves at Liberty to regard or disregard them at your own Discretion. But those Instructions are not like the Pocket Instructions given to a Minister going abroad, for regulating his Conduct on some trifling

Point of Ceremony. They are first drawn up by Judges learned in the Laws; they are then considered, debated & perhaps amended in Council, after which they are signed by the King. They are then so far as relates to you, the *Law of the Land*; for THE KING IS THE LEGISLATOR OF THE COLONIES." I told his Lordship this was new Doctrine to me. I had always understood from our Charters, that our Laws were to be made by our Assemblies, to be presented indeed to the King for his Royal Assent, but that being once given the King could not repeal or alter them. And as the Assemblies could not make permanent Laws without his Assent, so neither could he make a Law for them without theirs. He assur'd me I was totally mistaken. I did not think so however. And his Lordship's Conversation having a little alarm'd me as to what might be the Sentiments of the Court concerning us, I wrote it down as soon as I return'd to my Lodgings.—[15]

Franklin was not the only American who found the king's claim alarming. When he communicated the news to the four colonial assemblies whose interests he represented in London, there was an outcry of protest in America.

By the mid-1750s self-government had reached so advanced a state in America that a written plan for organizing "one General Government" for the thirteen colonies had been approved by a group of colonial delegates meeting in Albany, New York. (In order to take effect, the Albany Plan of 1754 stipulated that it must be ratified by the colonial assemblies and the king.) It provided for a central legislature, whose members were to be elected by the assemblies in each colony, and a "President General" whom the king would appoint and pay. Under the provisions of this plan, which Benjamin Franklin drafted and presented to his fellow delegates in Albany, the proposed intercolonial legislature would have "power to make laws, and lay and levy such general duties, imposts, or taxes, as to them shall appear most equal and just." Tax money could be spent, however, only on matters specifically authorized by a majority of the legislature and with the approval of the king's representative, the President General.[16] The Albany Plan was the first clear indication of the developing American sense of nationhood.

The colonial assemblies did not ratify this 1754 proposal because they thought it gave the king too much power, specifically the power to nominate the officers to command the colonial militias. The king also refused his assent, but for the opposite reason: because he thought it contained "too much of the *democratic*."[17] Indeed, his attempt in 1757 to become the lawmaker for the colonies may have been a reaction to indications in the Albany Plan that his subjects in America were on a path to nationhood.

American protests against the king's claim to be their legislator were so strong and widespread that the crown withdrew the claim. A few years later, however, after England's conquest of Canada, another attempt was made to bring the American colonials into proper subordination to the English government. This time Parliament took the lead. Since 1688 it had been acknowledged as the supreme power in England's unwritten constitution of government. Beginning in 1764, a year after the peace treaty with France gave England possession of Canada, Parliament initiated a series of laws taxing Americans. Again American protests were immediate and vigorous. For 140 years Americans had been taxing themselves through their own elected assemblies and paying their own costs of government and military defense. It therefore seemed intolerable to them to be taxed by any other legislative body.

In 1766 the constitutional conflict between Parliament and the American colonies was clearly focused by Parliament's passage of "An act for the better securing the dependency of his Majesty's dominions in America upon the crown and the parliament of Great Britain." It declared:

> . . . the said colonies and plantations in *America* have been, are, and of right ought to be, subordinate unto, and dependent upon the imperial crown and parliament of *Great Britain*; and

the King's majesty, by and with the advice and consent of the lords spiritual and temporal, and commons of *Great Britain*, in parliament assembled, had, hath, and of right ought to have, full power and authority to make laws and statutes of sufficient force and validity to bind the colonies and people of *America*, subjects of the crown of *Great Britain*, in all cases whatsoever.[18]

As far as the king and Parliament were concerned, this resolution had the weight of a formal clarification of a matter of great constitutional importance (the supremacy of Parliament) and was indeed an amendment to England's unwritten constitution. For Parliament, allowing any exception to its supremacy would have disturbed the foundation of the English constitution.

This constitutional struggle between England and America was much different from the struggle in the 1600s between the crown and Parliament, which had ended in establishing Parliament's supremacy. Again, the crisis concerned sovereignty: Who was the supreme authority for America? Were laws for Americans to be made by the king and the colonists reaching agreement with each other, as the colonial charters stipulated; the king acting alone (as he had tried to claim in 1757); or Parliament acting alone? And if the unwritten constitution of England were to be changed with regard to the power to make laws for Americans, by whom would it have to be changed? Would Americans have to agree to the change? Those in power in London believed they alone should decide such matters; the elected representatives of the American people sitting in the thirteen colonial capitals of America believed they had an equal voice in the decision. These opposite views were framed by a difference in culture: England's ancient aristocratic culture, where power flowed from the top, versus America's newly formed democratic culture, where power had always effectively rested with the majority of freemen.

AMERICANS mounted a variety of coordinated protests against the taxes laid on them by Parliament. They resisted through resolutions passed in the colonial assemblies, through the election of an extraordinary body of representatives from nine of the thirteen colonies to deal with the matter (the Stamp Act Congress), and through the organization of intercolonial boycotts against the English goods on which Parliament had laid a tax for Americans. Those were the peaceful ways. There were also orchestrated mob attacks in American seaports against tax collectors.

These various protests, in which all classes of American society participated, and the loss of trade they occasioned British merchants, forced Parliament to repeal the taxes. But Parliament could not allow Americans to force a retreat from the vital principle of parliamentary supremacy, Parliament's *right* to legislate for the colonies "in all cases whatsoever," as set forth in the 1766 resolution. To exemplify and uphold that right, the House of Lords and the House of Commons refused to rescind the tax on tea. And in 1768 four regiments of British regulars were sent to Massachusetts to make certain that the symbolic tax on tea was collected—the first time a large contingent of British troops was stationed in America.

But American resistance to the English concept of sovereignty continued nonetheless. In 1770 a squad of the king's troops fired on a Boston mob that was taunting them, killing seven Americans; three years later, in 1773, three shiploads of tea from England were destroyed by Americans in Boston harbor in an incident that became affectionately known among Americans as the Boston Tea Party. (So many chests of tea had to be brought on deck from the holds of these ships, broken open, and dumped in the harbor that the job took almost all night; the next morning Boston harbor was covered with floating gobs of tea and smashed remnants of the tea chests.[19]) Finally, on April 19, 1775—seven years after the first regiments of British regulars were garrisoned in America—an all-day battle was fought between American militia and a contingent of the king's troops in the villages of Lexington and Concord in eastern Massachusetts and along the road leading from those villages to Boston. About 100 Americans and some 250 British were killed and wounded in the daylong fight. When the other twelve colonies received word of the events in Lexington and Concord, they began immediately to raise troops and gather military stores to send to Massachusetts and elected a Second Continental Congress to organize a "Continental Army."

The war between Britain and America that followed—after more than two decades of political resistance by Americans, going back to 1757 and the king's claim to be able to legislate for Americans—was the longest ever fought by Americans. It manifested the belief of the American people in their sovereignty. Seen in this way, the American Revolution, unlike the French Revolution, was not an attempt to create a new culture but to defend an existing culture, one that had begun to be formed when the first land became available to commoners and the first colonial assembly was elected in America.

THE AMERICAN BELIEF *The People Are Sovereign* has also been manifested in the process of forming new states of the United States, something which began soon after the American Revolution. Vermont, the first of thirty-seven new states that followed the original thirteen, was admitted to the Union in 1791; Kentucky, the first state to be organized west of the Appalachians, followed the next year. Tennessee was admitted in 1796; Ohio in 1803; Louisiana in 1812; Indiana in 1816; Mississippi in 1817; Illinois in 1818; Alabama in 1819; Maine in 1820; and Missouri, the first state located entirely west of the Mississippi River, in 1821. In these eleven states and the twenty-six others that were admitted to the Union between 1836 and 1959, elected representatives in the territory that was to become the new state initiated the process for an elected government, wrote and ratified a constitution, and petitioned Congress for admission to the Union on an equal political footing with the existing states of the United States, as provided for in the Constitution. This way of settling territory and organizing new governments is distinctively American. In giving each new state a "Republican Form of Government," as required by the Constitution, the settlers of the territory, not the federal government, took the initiative. The process expresses the American belief in the sovereign power of the people to create government and to limit its power in a written instrument of their devising.

Because *The People Are Sovereign* is an American cultural belief, it is difficult for Americans to conceive how the transition from colonial dependence to national independence could have been achieved and a national government established except through elected bodies representing the people. The Second Continental Congress declared America's independence from England and commissioned George Washington to command the military forces that Congress authorized to fight the war against England. Washington and other officers commissioned by Congress obeyed this elected legislature as the supreme authority of the land because it represented the people. At the end of the war for independence, the peace treaty with England was negotiated by agents commissioned by Congress. During most of the war, there was no national authority other than the Continental Congress. Not even a written constitution existed until two years before the end of the war, when the state legislatures ratified the Articles of Confederation. The entire war was fought under the authority of the Congress elected by the people, without an elected president.

That was not how independence for Brazil, Canada, or Spanish America was achieved.

Canada gained independence gradually during the two centuries following England's conquest of French Canada, and at every stage of the process the British government had the final say. Parliament gave Canada its first, embryonic semblance of nationhood in 1867 (the British North America Act); another act of Parliament in 1981, signed into law by the queen of England in 1982, finally gave Canadians complete control over their constitution. (Before 1982, if Canadians wanted to change their government, they had to submit the proposal to the British government for approval.) The act of the Canadian legislature in 1981 asking Britain to give Canada complete control over its unwritten constitution begins in these terms: "To the Queen's Most

Excellent Majesty: Most Gracious Sovereign: We, Your Majesty's loyal subjects, the House of Commons of Canada in Parliament assembled, respectfully approach Your Majesty, requesting that you may graciously be pleased to cause to be laid before the Parliament of the United Kingdom a measure . . . ," etc. etc.[20] Granted that these words are an ancient formula with little real meaning today; they nonetheless reflect a nondemocratic culture. Even under the present sovereignty of Canada, the reigning English monarch remains, in Canada's unwritten constitution, the head of state of Canada. It is culturally inconceivable that any American would permit the head of state of another nation to be also the head of state of the United States.

Independence for Brazil was established in 1822 through a solemn pronouncement made by Portugal's crown prince to a small gathering of Brazilian notables, as he stood in the open air on the banks of a Brazilian river. On the authority of this European crown prince's words, Brazil became a sovereign nation; by the authority and approval of this same man of royal blood, a constitutional monarchy was created in Brazil which designated him emperor of Brazil. (Dom Pedro I rejected the first draft of the constitution submitted to him for his approval by the committee he had appointed to write it because, in his judgment, it gave him too little power.) A European prince of royal blood was thus the constituting authority of Brazilian nationhood and government. And the government he instituted lasted until 1889, when a junta of Brazilian military officers overthrew his son, Dom Pedro II, the second emperor of Brazil, in a bloodless coup. Two years later Brazil adopted a constitution for a republican form of government. Since 1891, however, high-ranking general officers of the Brazilian armed forces have been repeatedly involved in the exercise of what is called in Brazilian constitutional theory "the moderating power"—that is, the authority the emperor once exercised in the name of the people of Brazil to change the government according to what the "moderating power" thinks is in the best interest of the people. This "moderating power" was most recently asserted in the 1960s, '70s, and

'80s by Brazilian generals. Thus the people of Brazil have yet to achieve a fully enculturated sovereignty that has been in place more than three generations.

Spanish-American independence was established in still another way, in a series of armed rebellions against Spanish rule. They began in Mexico in 1808, spread to South America, and escalated into full-blown warfare throughout the mainland of Spanish America until all of this largest cultural region of the Americas was in arms against the imperial authority of Spain. These armed conflicts continued until the last Spanish garrison, occupying the castle of Callao, Peru, surrendered in 1826. Since the wars in Spanish America took place over such immense distances and in such difficult terrain, and because they lasted for such a long time, they naturally lacked the unity of command and coordinated direction that characterized the American Revolution, where land communications were a matter of hundreds, not thousands, of miles.

More important from a cultural point of view, the wars for independence in Spanish America were conducted on the authority of self-commissioned generals, who did in the 1810s and 1820s what the Spanish conquistadores had done three centuries earlier: they made themselves lords of the lands they conquered. This is not to say that the *idea* of popular sovereignty did not exist in Spanish America at the time of its independence from Spain. It surely did. But it was not an enculturated belief. Those who initiated and waged the wars of independence in Spanish America spoke often and passionately of instituting the sovereignty of the people; and they proclaimed more than once, on their own authority, not only that they embodied that sovereignty but had instituted it. Yet they acted like dictators. The history of Spanish America since its independence is replete with such expressions of "the sovereignty of the people," as one military strong man has replaced another.

Because of its elongated, high-mountain geography, Spanish America had little real chance for political unity. But even the regional political unities that were established in some places—

such as in the immense nation known as Gran Colombia in northwestern South America—broke apart into separate nations soon after independence from Spain was won. And within the resulting sixteen nations of mainland Spanish America, there have been numerous local *caudillos* or strong men who have governed by armed force. Even the most famous and revered leader of Spanish America's wars of independence, "the George Washington of South America," Simon Bolívar, once he took up the sword to liberate the people of his native continent, found it difficult to put the sword down. After his military exploits had given him political power, he continued to regard himself as the benevolent protector of the people, ruling in their best interest. He not only proclaimed on his own personal authority the independence of large areas of South America, he also wrote constitutions himself and proclaimed them. Of course, none of Bolívar's republican constitutions lasted because none of them had the indispensable support of an enculturated belief in the sovereignty of the people.

The idea of popular sovereignty did not die in Spanish America. Despite repeated, sometimes bloody suppressions of the idea by military dictators—all of whom professed to be acting in the name of the people—the idea has persisted in Spanish America. (Cuba's Fidel Castro in 1994 set the record for the longest rule by a *caudillo*, surpassing in that year the previous record of thirty-five continuous years of dictatorial rule by Paraguay's dictator Alfredo Stroessner.) It is now, however, the ninth generation since the overthrow of the sovereignty of Spanish kings in Spanish America, and the persistence of Spanish Americans in trying to act on the idea that the people are sovereign may at last have caused it to become enculturated.

BECAUSE they could be self-determining, the American people enculturated a belief in their sovereignty. And like any sovereign power, they preferred the least possible governmental limits. In America the people have granted limited powers to those they elect to office but are not limited in their own power except by their consent. They remain the ultimate *human* authority over the government they have created. (The matter must be stated in this way because of Americans' cultural belief in the higher authority of God's moral law.) From the belief *The People Are Sovereign*, which is the fundamental political belief of American culture, comes the corollary belief *The Least Government Possible Is Best*. Nowhere is it more evident than in the sequence of the three national constitutions that were proposed by the elected representatives of the people for ratification. During the thirty-three years between 1754 and 1787 when these three constitutions were put forward, a workable balance was being achieved between the sovereignty of the people and the government they needed in order to remain united and prosperous.

After the rejection of the Albany Plan of 1754, because it would have surrendered a cherished power to the king of England, a second constitution, the Articles of Confederation and Perpetual Union, was drafted in 1777, during the American Revolution. This was truly a proposal for a national government and was ratified in 1781 by the legislatures of all thirteen states. The powers the Articles granted the national government were so limited, however, that real uncertainty arose about whether the Union organized under the Articles might disintegrate, allowing England to pick up the pieces and make Americans once more the subjects of the English king. When the Articles proved unworkable because they limited the power of the national government too greatly, a third constitution was written by representatives elected by the people in twelve of the thirteen states and ratified in 1790 by specially elected constitutional conventions in every state. This constitution has now been in effect for more than two centuries.

But the Constitution of the United States—the third American plan for a national government—like its two predecessors, granted only limited powers to the national government. And it was ratified only after the state ratifying conventions agreed to append to it a specific list of the people's rights. This Bill of Rights (the first ten amendments to the Constitution, ratified two years after the Constitution went into effect) specified certain rights that the national government might not infringe or diminish. The tenth of these rights addresses the matter of the people's sovereignty and the limited power they grant to their government: "The powers not delegated to the United States by the Constitution, nor prohibited by it to the States, are reserved to the States respectively, or to the people." All unenumerated powers remain with the people as a whole and the people in each state; only the enumerated powers specified in the Constitution are delegated by the people to their national government. This is the most fundamental concept in the Constitution and is the main purpose of having a written constitution, as opposed to England's unwritten document. As part of the American belief *The Least Government Possible Is Best*, the limited powers allotted the legislative, executive, and judicial branches of the federal government are kept separate and are balanced against one another so that each branch will keep an eye on the other two branches and restrain their actions, thus ensuring that no part of the national government becomes too powerful.

Another distinctly American belief is *A Written Constitution Is Essential To Government*. England has never had such a single, written warrant and plan for national government produced by the elected representatives of the people and specifically limiting the government's powers. The unwritten constitution of England exists in laws and pronouncements that have accumulated during the eight centuries since the most powerful lords of England in 1215 forced the king of England at sword's point to recognize their rights. That Magna Carta set the pattern that those in power would decide the constitution of England. In America, however, an amendment to the Constitution is not approved by the same body of representatives that writes it, because patently what is written and passed by any body has its approval. Rather, the two functions are kept separate. If the people are to retain their sovereign right to create new provisions of their nation's constitution, and not to have it altered by those "in power," they themselves must retain the ultimate authority to create constitutional law.

The American people apparently developed the belief *A Written Constitution Is Essential To Government* in imitation of the royal charters that established England's colonies on the Atlantic coastal plain of North America. Specifying how and by whom those colonies were to be governed, and how the expenses of their governments were to be met, the crown thus delegated some of its sovereign power in written warrants for government. In the quarrel between England and her thirteen American colonies during the mid-1700s, the colonial charters were a constant reference of Americans as they explained their views of their constitutional rights. Their principal argument was that the crown had given their ancestors certain rights of government *in writing*—most important, the right to elect assemblies to determine their taxes—and could not amend those written agreements without the consent of the people whose lives would be affected by the change.

By the eighteenth century, the belief in a constitution as a written agreement for government was encultured in the political thought and behavior of an overwhelming majority of Americans. This is evidenced by the willingness of Americans to take on the king's military forces if he, or Parliament, claimed a right to change the terms of the colonial charters. To wage the American Revolution required great dedication to and a readiness to make sacrifices for the cause that Americans went to war to defend, part of which was the proposition that a written charter for government could not be amended without the consent of the people who had agreed to live under its authority. While it is true that the colonists had had no say in writing or agreeing to the provisions of these colonial charters, Americans had nonetheless consented to live under them. The charters allowed them real power over their affairs, acting through the elected assemblies authorized in the charters.

AMERICAN DEMOCRACY is founded on the belief in the constituting power, or sovereignty, of the people. But what has made that sovereignty practicable is the belief in majority rule. The cultural belief *A Majority Decides* is therefore every bit as important in American culture as the beliefs *The People Are Sovereign, The Least Government Possible Is Best,* and *A Written Constitution Is Essential To Government.*

The kings of England in the 1600s, in requiring their American subjects to pay for their governments, allowed them to elect assemblies to raise necessary taxes. But apart from that, the election of representatives by majority vote was also a practical solution to the problem of how to organize communities in the wilds of America, given the absence of a class of persons whose right to govern was culturally recognized in their birth and education, as was true in English culture. Circumstances in America were not suitable for a governing class based on "noble" bloodlines and a near monopoly of land; the exercise of governmental authority therefore had to be established on some other basis.

In the earliest settlements, one man sometimes had to step forward when survival was at stake, and make decisions in order to avert disaster—as Captain John Smith notably did in Virginia. But one-man rule, even in the short term, was not a dependable way to organize the government of frontier communities. Men whose combination of good judgment, moral integrity, strength of will, and bravery could command obedience in a rough-and-tumble wilderness community were too rare. More important, the circumstances of daily life in such communities—where even gentlemen had to work—tended to reduce every man to the same footing and made one-man rule, or even rule by a small group of men, more or less obnoxious. Leaders therefore were those who could persuade a majority of the community that their judgment on a certain course of action was in the majority's best interest, because it took the willing cooperation of the community to carry out solutions to problems. In communities established under harsh conditions by volunteers, it is difficult to command the inhabitants to do anything without their consent, and majority rule is an eminently practical way to decide consent.

Majority rule recognizes that no man is infallible and that men are seldom, if ever, entirely selfless in making decisions. These basic truths were especially evident in communities struggling with the unfamiliar challenges that civilized Europeans faced in a Stone Age wilderness. When the consequences of a decision might affect the very survival of the community, the most practical way of deciding what ought to be done and who ought to carry out the decision was by consulting opinions in the community and abiding by the opinion of the majority. Since no two men will have exactly the same interests or knowledge, it is next to impossible even in small communities that everyone should have the same opinion on a matter. Thus the will of the majority, or something close to a majority, as expressed in a poll of voters, is an orderly way of reaching a decision which men and women of good sense will abide by as fair.[21]

Allowing the voice of a majority to decide political matters does not, of course, make their decision any wiser than the judgment of one well-informed person. But neither is the will of a majority more likely to be in error. There is no evidence in the history of government that one man governs better than a majority. A monarchy is not an inherently better form of government than a democracy, and perpetuity in office can easily create a delusion of infallibility. In a government controlled by one man or one party, one man or a majority of the leaders of the one party decide what is best for everyone else; in a republic the people ultimately determine what is in their best interests. In a wilderness society made up mostly of self-determining individuals, republican government and majority rule were the most natural forms for government to take.

Every human being has his own beliefs, based on personal interests and his own experiences. The spirit of majority rule in American political history respects that natural diversity of people's interests and was clearly evident in the creation of the Constitution. The year-long process of writing and ratifying the Constitution, in the national constitutional convention in Philadelphia and in the subsequent conventions in the thirteen states, was throughout a process of reconciling opposing ideas and interests and reaching compromises based on the will of a majority. That process would not have been possible if the delegates elected to represent the people of the United States in these conventions had not recognized their fallibility of judgment, and if they had not had the cumulative example in their history, going back to 1619, of deciding issues by majority vote in their colonial assemblies.

At the close of the convention that wrote the Constitution—when the final vote was about to be taken to decide whether it would be sent to the Confederation Congress for transmission to state conventions for debate and approval—the oldest delegate, Benjamin Franklin, spoke to his fellow delegates. He intended to sign the document, he said, not because he agreed with every one of its provisions, which he did not, but because "when you assemble a number of men, to have the advantage of their joint wisdom, you inevitably assemble with those men all their prejudices, their passions, their errors of opinion, their local interests, and their selfish views." He had learned during the course of a long life (he was then eighty-two) that, like every other man, he was liable to be influenced by his prejudices. Therefore he hoped that every delegate who disagreed, as he did, with some part of the constitution they had written together, would "doubt a little of his own infallibility" and sign it.[22]

In the event, only three of the delegates who had regularly attended the sessions of the convention withheld their signatures. The other thirty-six signed the Constitution, though most of them, like Franklin, probably had some reservation about a particular article or clause or the absence of a provision they favored.

This same willingness on the part of Americans to abide by the decision of a majority has manifested itself generation after generation. In innumerable votes taken in operating city, county, and state governments, as well as the federal government, and in countless meetings of shareholders, service clubs, professional organizations, and other groups, decisions are reached by majority rule. The transition in 1787–1788 from the authority of the Articles of Confederation to the more workable and stronger authority of the Constitution without violence or bloodshed among Americans of different, strongly held political views would have been impossible without a fully enculturated belief in majority rule. Perhaps nothing is culturally more natural to an American than to take a vote to decide a question.

Only once in the political history of the nation has a national election been overturned by armed force by a minority that refused to abide by the decision of a majority. Before the election of Abraham Lincoln to the presidency in 1860, political leaders in some Southern states vowed that if he were voted into office they would lead their states out of the Union. When Lincoln won the election, they kept their vow. (He received 180 votes in the Electoral College; the other three candidates for president in 1860 received a total of 123.) The war over secession that followed shows just how firmly and how seriously most Americans took their belief in majority rule and in government under a written constitution.

James Madison, a leader in the Philadelphia convention that wrote the Constitution, said in one of his essays favoring its ratification:

> As long as the reason of man continues fallible, and he is at liberty to exercise it, different opinions will be formed. As long as the connection subsists between his reason and his self-love, his opinions and his passions will have a reciprocal influence on each other; and the former will be objects to which the latter will attach themselves. The diversity in the faculties of men . . . [is] an insuperable obstacle to a uniformity of interests.[23]

Diversities of interest and opinion among human beings are unavoidable. As long as men are free to express and act on the various interests that develop from their individuality, the continuance of freedom and popular sovereignty depends on abiding by decisions reached by majority vote. These same diversities among human beings naturally prevent the *same* majority from deciding all issues by acting in agreement on all occasions. It is a misconception of human nature to suppose that any consistent and permanent uniformity of judgment, opinion, and interest exists among any sociologically defined group. In other words, the same majority does not exist on every question.

WORSHIP IN ENGLAND has historically been a matter of government, not conscience, because for hundreds of years the government supported a state church and used the powers of government to enforce conformity to the principle of one state, one church.

The Church of England, in turn, exerted its religious authority in support of the English state and was part of the government. Englishmen who refused to conform to this state-sanctioned and state-supported church were disqualified from voting and holding government office. The reigning monarch was simultaneously the head of state and the head of the state church. The bishops of the state church received their office from the king and, with some exceptions, became voting members for life of the House of Lords in Parliament. Even in the twentieth century, this state church has yet to be "disestablished," that is, separated from the government of England. The monarch remains, under England's unwritten constitution, the head of the Church of England; its bishops continue to have seats in the legislature; and final authority for the form of worship in the Church of England still rests with Parliament, not with the church's bishops acting alone. These features of the principle of one state, one church in English history must be clearly understood if one is to appreciate what a "religious establishment" is and what is truly meant by "separation of church and state."

The Constitution of the United States ensures separation of church and state simply by prohibiting any religious test for holding any office or position of trust in the national government at any level, and by prohibiting Congress from establishing a church as part of the government of the United States. The First Amendment denies to Congress the power to make any law respecting any establishment of religion. It also denies to Congress power to make any law prohibiting the free exercise of religion. The complete text of this part of the Constitution reads: "Congress shall make no law respecting an establishment of religion, or prohibiting the free exercise thereof; or abridging the freedom of speech, or of the press, or the right of the people peaceably to assemble, and to petition the Government for a redress of grievances." Article VI, paragraph 3, reads in its entirety: "The Senators and Representatives before mentioned, and the Members of the several State Legislatures, and all executive and judicial Officers, both of the United States and of the several States, shall be bound by Oath or Affirmation, to support this Constitution; but no religious Test shall ever be required as a Qualification to any Office or public Trust under the United States." Together the First Amendment and Article VI of the Constitution articulate the American cultural belief that *Worship Is A Matter Of Conscience* rather than a matter of government.

In prohibiting Congress from establishing a church as part of the government or making laws that would interfere with the "free exercise" of religion, the Constitution does not grant to federal judges the authority to interfere through judicial decisions with the "free exercise" of religion. It would be inconsistent to suppose that the Constitution would allow either the judicial or the executive branch of the federal government to interfere with religious freedom when that power is explicitly prohibited to the legislative branch. Only when a conflict can be shown to exist between a religious practice and some overriding interest of society, such as the protection of life—as would arise, for instance, from the attempt to practice a form of worship requiring the sacrifice of human life—could government have grounds for interfering with the free exercise of religion guaranteed by the First Amendment. The responsibility of the Supreme Court and lesser federal courts under the Constitution is to see that the "free exercise" of religion is protected.

Such free exercise of religion as the prayers offered at the beginning of each session of Congress and at presidential inaugurations, or the custom of displaying symbols of faith on public properties during certain religious holidays, might be thought of as forms of free speech. But freedom of religion—which includes public manifestations and expressions of faith in God—is protected and provided for in its own right in the first two clauses of the First Amendment, apart from freedom of speech. The free exercise of religion is therefore not considered in the First Amendment to be a subspecies of free speech.

Thomas Jefferson's view of the federal government's powers in respect to the practice of religion, which he expressed in his second inaugural address, is the correct one: it has none. "In matters of religion," Jefferson said, "I have considered that its free exercise is placed by the Constitution independent of the powers of the General Government."[24] This is the fundamental separation of church and state that the Constitution recognizes and upholds. In a letter written on January 1, 1802, to an association of Baptists, Jefferson expressed his view that "a wall of separation between Church and State" *already existed* in the United States and should never be breached: "Believing with you that religion is a matter which lies solely between man and his God, that he owes account to none other for his faith or his worship, that the legislative powers of government reach actions only, and not opinions, I contemplate with sovereign reverence that act of the whole American people [the Constitution] which declared that their legislature should 'make no law respecting an establishment of religion, or prohibiting the free exercise thereof,' thus building a wall of separation between Church and State."[25] Jefferson wrote this letter in reply to a request he had received from the Baptists to declare a national day of fasting. He refused to do it for the reason quoted above: that the federal government has no constitutional authorization to involve itself in religious matters.

So null is the power of the federal government with respect to religion that the people of a state might have an established church if they desired one. The Establishment Clause in the First Amendment, in denying Congress the power to make any law that would establish a national state church, or to interfere with any established churches, clearly leaves the matter of religious practices to the people living in each state.

It should also be noted that any appeal to the federal judiciary by a citizen or group of citizens to prevent or interfere with the exercise of freedom of religion by others is contrary to the First Amendment's "free exercise" clause. *No provision of the Constitution protects any citizen from being offended by the religious practices of another citizen.* Americans who have no religious beliefs, or who oppose all or some religious beliefs as (in their opinion) false, repugnant, or pernicious, may not invoke their abhorrence of religion in general or any particular religious tenant or practice as a reason for asking a federal court to suppress it. It has been well stated in a study of the Constitution's religious content: "The Constitution, the nation's fundamental law, cannot legitimately be construed to afford redress to every citizen who takes offense at public expressions, whether religious or secular in content."[26]

On the other hand, the federal judiciary *is* bound by the First Amendment to protect the free exercise of religion. To hold otherwise would void the protection afforded freedom of religion in *two* clauses of the First Amendment to the Constitution. To suppose that people have a right to freedom from annoyance over the public expression of a religious belief, and to insist that federal powers be used to protect that supposed right, would create a right not specified in the Constitution to the detriment of a right that is specified. It would make the federal judiciary responsible for supervising religious expression in public places, and permit the censorship of public expressions of faith in God. As with freedom of speech, the First Amendment in regard to freedom of religion makes no distinction between public and private religious expressions. Both are protected. The First Amendment imposes no obligation on federal courts to suppress the free exercise of religion in public places, any more than the free-speech clause in the First Amendment obliges federal courts to purge public places of speech that might offend a person, or even a large number of persons.

When Englishmen settled the Atlantic coastal plain of North America in the early 1600s, they brought with them the English political principle of one state, one church, though they obviously disagreed on which religion should be established by law. Virginia established the Church of England while Massachusetts established a Puritan form of worship; other colonies established other religious forms. The English crown did not insist on the establishment of the same church in every colony. To have done so would have impeded emigration from England of troublesome religious nonconformists, such as Quakers and Puritans, whom the kings of England were pleased to be rid of. In some colonies, most notably Pennsylvania and Rhode Island, freedom of religion was proclaimed from the start. No state church was ever established in them, or any religious qualification ever required for election to office. So it was always possible for an immigrant to find in one or another of the colonies the religious climate he preferred. Because the crown allowed each colony to decide whether to have an established church, and which church to establish, a proliferation of religious practices arose in England's colonies. (One European visitor to colonial Pennsylvania reported so many "doctrines and sects" that it was "impossible to name them all."[27]) And no one church gained a preeminent importance. Thus the English principle of one state, one church was doomed to extinction in America.

Other factors in the life of these colonies also affected the English cultural belief that worship was a matter of government. For one thing, the ability of a person to help civilize the wilderness was a more important consideration than how he worshiped God. For another, the rapid growth, extraordinary mobility, and general self-determination that characterized life in America often resulted in marriages between persons of different faiths, which fostered religious tolerance and undermined the principle of one state, one church.

In the two decades before the beginning of the American Revolution (1755–1775), nine of the thirteen American colonies had either a weak religious establishment (Georgia, South Carolina, North Carolina, Maryland, the southern counties of New York) or no religious establishment at all (Delaware, New Jersey, Pennsylvania, Rhode Island). The other four had either a fairly strong religious establishment (Virginia) or a very strong one (Massachusetts, Connecticut, New Hampshire). The religion established by law in 1775 in the southern counties of New York and in Virginia, Maryland, North Carolina, and South Carolina was the Church of England. That establishment vanished in 1776 when America declared its independence from England, because American patriotism would not tolerate the continued establishment—that is, state support—of a church headed by the king of England when America was at war with England. Thus at the beginning of American nationhood only four states had an established religion (New Hampshire, Massachusetts, Connecticut, and Georgia); and because of the several factors mentioned above, the belief *Worship Is A Matter Of Conscience* had already been enculturated.

The state constitutions written during and immediately after the Revolution are remarkably consistent in their provisions regarding religious freedom. This is so even in the states that continued to have an established church. *Virginia, June 12, 1776:* ". . . all men are equally entitled to the free exercise of religion, according to the dictates of conscience. . . ." *Massachusetts, October 25, 1780:* ". . . [no one who is subject to the jurisdiction of Massachusetts law] shall be hurt, molested, or restrained, in his person, liberty, or estate, for worshiping God in the manner and season most agreeable to the dictates of his own conscience." *New York, April 20, 1777:* ". . . the free exercise and enjoyment of religious profession and worship, without discrimination or preference, shall forever hereafter be allowed within this State, to all mankind: *Provided* That the liberty of conscience, hereby granted, shall not be so construed as to excuse acts of licentious-ness, or justify practices inconsistent with the peace or safety of this State." *New Hampshire, June 2, 1784:* ". . . no [one] shall be hurt, molested, or restrained in his person, liberty or estate for worshiping God, in the manner and season most agreeable to the dictates of his own conscience, or for his religious profession, sentiments or persuasion; provided he doth not disturb the pub-lic peace, or disturb others in their religious worship."

New Jersey, July 3, 1776: ". . . no person shall ever, within this Colony, be deprived of the inestimable privilege of worship-ping Almighty God in a manner agreeable to the dictates of his own conscience; nor, under any pretense whatever, be compelled to attend any place of worship, contrary to his faith and judg-ment; nor shall any person, within this Colony, ever be obliged to pay tithes, taxes, or any other rates, for the purpose of build-ing or repairing any other church or churches, place or places of worship, or for the maintenance of any minister or ministry, con-trary to what he believes to be right, or has deliberately or volun-tarily engaged himself to perform." *Delaware, September 11, 1776:* ". . . all men have a natural and unalienable right to wor-ship Almighty God according to the dictates of their own con-sciences and understandings; and . . . no man ought or of right can be compelled to attend any religious worship or maintain any ministry contrary to or against his own free will and consent, and . . . no authority can or ought to be vested in, or assumed by any power whatever that shall in any case interfere with, or in any manner controul [sic] the right of conscience in the free ex-ercise of religious worship." *Maryland, November 11, 1776:* ". . . no person ought by any law to be molested in his person or estate on account of his religious persuasion or profession, or for his religious practice; unless, under the colour of religion, any man shall disturb the good order, peace or safety of the State, or shall infringe the laws of morality, or injure others, in their nat-ural, civil, or religious rights; . . ." *North Carolina, December 18, 1776:* ". . . all men have a natural and unalienable right to wor-ship almighty God according to the dictates of their own con-sciences." *Georgia, February 5, 1777:* "All persons whatever shall have the free exercise of their religion; provided it be not repugnant to the peace and safety of the State; . . ."[28] Well before the end of the eighteenth century, then, the belief of English culture that worship is a matter of government had been supplanted in America by the belief *Worship Is A Matter Of Conscience.*

This does not mean that American history has been free of persecution for differences in religious belief. For instance, in colonial times Jews were deprived of some civil rights because of their religion; and in the 1600s in Massachusetts Quakers were physically punished, and in a few instances executed, because of their repeated disruptions to the church services of the established religion of that colony. (Seventeenth-century Quakers, in the name of religious freedom, harassed Puritans—who, in the name of the one church, one state they believed in, retaliated with far greater harshness.) And in the nineteenth century, prejudice against Roman Catholics and Mormons also erupted in occasional acts of violence, including murder. But overall, Americans in their history have tolerated rather than persecuted religious differences. The extraordinary number of religions historically practiced in America has prevented any one church from being dominant and has made systematic persecution for religious differences difficult to contemplate. Undoubtedly the presence of so many religions and churches in America from the beginning accounts for the absence of religious warfare in America. Europe, on the other hand, has repeatedly suffered such wars.

CHAPTER NINE

Beliefs on Human Nature

Almost All Human Beings Want To Do
What Is Right

Human Beings Will Abuse Power When
They Have It

THE RANGE OF diversity among human beings—in bodily appearance, vigor, interests, habits, strength, intellect, abilities, knowledge, language, judgment, character, and attainments—is impressive. So are the many differences in morality, politics, religion, and opinions of all kinds; and, in regard to the subject of this book, the many cultural differences among peoples. Most of these differences are superficial; they do not affect what we consider to be a person's humanity. (The human status of a short person is not altered by his shortness.) Other differences are less superficial—intellect, for example, because below a certain level of reason a human being begins to lose some, though certainly not all, of his humanity. As for the raving lunatic who must be physically restrained to keep him from injuring himself or others: we may still recognize him as a fellow human being, but we usually regard him as having an impaired humanity.

However, despite their diversity, human beings have a certain basis of sameness. To notice the cultural differences among peoples, for instance, is to accept the fact that all human beings belong to some culture. Likewise, all human beings have an intellect; all have a need for some sort of food and shelter; all have a moral sense (even moral relativists declare their relativism to be more righteous than any moral code). It is also characteristic of human beings to ponder the meaning of their lives. And no human being in his right mind has ever lived into adulthood without becoming conscious—through a rather mysterious process—of his mortality. Traits do exist, therefore, that pertain to every human being, and others exist among so many persons that for all practical purposes they may be considered universal traits of "human nature."

From their experience on the Atlantic coastal plain of North America in the seventeenth and eighteenth centuries, the cultural ancestors of Americans derived certain fundamental beliefs regarding "human nature," a phrase that occurs frequently in the writings of the Founding Fathers. Perhaps the unique "racial" diversity of these European immigrants, as compared with other post-1492 European populations in the Americas; their isolation in a wilderness apart from the rest of civilization, which forced them to cooperate with one another; and their common goal of improving their lives in America, brought home to them a particularly vivid sense of the ways people resemble one another. Certainly from the experience of rapidly civilizing a continental space the size of Europe, Americans acquired a strong awareness of a basic interest that cut across individual differences. American history has been a new beginning, a starting over once more of mankind's continual history of civilizing nature. That experience unified an unusually diverse collection of human beings by giving them a common focus on one monumental task, and in the process enculturated certain beliefs about human nature.

FOR THREE CENTURIES, beginning in the early 1600s, men and women from throughout Europe came to America speaking many languages and practicing various religions. They worked together. They intermarried. And if they arrived in America not knowing how to speak English, their common purpose in coming to America to improve their lives and make a new home for themselves motivated them in most cases to want to learn the language being commonly spoken in America. For unless they could communicate, they were handicapped in their effort to accomplish the imagined improvement that had compelled their emigration. As they worked alongside people from the many "races" of Europe in America, they discovered they were not so different from one another as they had thought while living in multilingual Europe.

One of the deepest and most ancient convictions about the differences among human beings is the idea of "race." Like the distinction between "noble" and "common" blood, this idea underwent a basic alteration in America. The discovery among immigrants from Europe's multitude of "races" and their descendants born in America, that they had similar interests and shared needs in facing the dangers of a Stone Age wilderness and in striving to "get ahead," began a slow but steady breakdown in thinking of an English, a German, or an Irish race. Life in America made individual talent a vastly more important consideration than racial classifications. Americans began to think less in terms of belonging to the English race or the French race or the German race—distinctions that were normal in Europe—and to think more in terms of being an Irish American or a Norwegian American, insofar as such distinctions continued to be made at all in a society where most people had ancestors from several of the "races" of Europe. Because free cooperation and association were basic to the pursuit of a better life, the sense of racial differences among the free immigrants to America were usually lost by the third generation of the immigrants' American-born descendants.

As the European sense of race diminished in America, it was replaced by beliefs about "human nature." But that happened only among descendants of the free immigrants to America, who have historically made up roughly 85 percent of the American population. The other portion of the population during the formative period of American culture—the descendants of forced immigrants, mostly from the many "races" of West Africa—did not benefit from this shift in judging persons according to their individuality rather than for presumed racial differences.

As slaves, those Americans who descended from the forced immigrants from Africa continued to be judged according to traits of generic classification. They were regarded as fundamentally different from the overwhelming majority of the population which they, or their ancestors, had been forced to join. And the condition of their lives *was* fundamentally different from the lives of the 85 percent of the population who were free. This was no fault of theirs but the result of the many debasements of their humanity inherent in their enforced, lifelong enslavement—a debasement they were forced to pass on to their descendants. The superficial characteristic of color—white for the freemen, whose ancestors had chosen to come to America out of Europe's many "races," and black for the slaves, whose ancestors had been brought out of Africa to America by force—became a mark of distinction that even the achievements of highly talented individuals of African descent could not entirely overcome. Thus age-old convictions about racial differences and how the "nature" of races was inherent—which in the main were cultural constructs—was reduced in America to a much simpler, bipolar concept of race: the dark-skinned race (the color of slaves) and the fair-skinned race (the color of free men and women). All that was left in America in the way of racial classification was the sense of being either "black" or "white"—though these classifications often bore little relation to any real purity of color. Part of this bipolarization of race was the loss among the slave portion of the American population of belonging to one or another of the many "races" of Africa, as they too, like the European-descended immigrants, intermingled and inter-bred.

The abbreviation in America of the "races" of man to two represented a great cultural advance in reducing the potential causes of conflict among human beings. But the sense of racial differences, though greatly reduced, was not eliminated. Indeed, by being reduced to just two "races," it may in fact have been intensified, especially since whiteness was associated with free-dom—something American culture prized highly—and black-ness with freedom's opposite: inherited servitude. Nevertheless this radical reduction of racial consciousness made it possible to dream of eventually eliminating the concept of racial differ-ences and replacing it with the egalitarian concept of human na-ture.

COMPARED TO EUROPE, there was too much moving around, too much need for productive workers, too many opportunities to be imagined in America—especially in the choice of marriage partners—for any group of immigrants to remain permanently apart from the mainstream of American society (unless, like the Amish, they deliberately chose to remain "different"). Because of the diminished sense of racial and class differences among Amer-icans, their manners became simpler and less formal than the manners of Europeans. Even in colonial times, it appears, Amer-icans had that inquisitive friendliness that still causes them to ini-tiate conversations with strangers, and to ask rather personal questions on short acquaintance—a behavior that is uncommon in European culture.

In America there are no strangers for very long. Even in the twentieth century this propensity of Americans for affable rela-tions with everyone nearby and for instant friendships continues to impress foreign observers as a distinctly American trait. A 1993 anthology of views by fourteen anthropologists and schol-ars from Africa, Asia, and Europe, who had studied America as a foreign culture, repeatedly makes that observation. Perhaps the most telling of their remarks is that from a Zairian who earned a doctorate at the University of Chicago and became a professor on its faculty:

> The Bantu custom is in sharp contrast with the American custom of using first names or nicknames between close friends and with most in-laws. In the beginning [of my stay in the United States in 1974], I found it bizarre to see ascending and descending in-laws (fathers- and mothers-in-law and sons- and daughters-in-law, respectively) address each other by their first names and to see them interact casually with each other. (In my background, ascending and descending in-laws maintain avoidance relationships.) The new custom gave me the impression that Americans did not care much about these special, affined ties and that all social relations were of the same kind. I also assumed then that Americans did not distinguish between acquaintances and friends. In addition, I thought that Americans became personal with people they had just met rather quickly.[1]

Various explanations of this American trait are offered by these foreign observers. One of the European anthropologists thought the tendency among Americans to speak to, or at least smile at, strangers with whom they made eye contact on the street or in stores might be an "effort at establishing an amicable truce with potential enemies." My own understanding of this American characteristic, as I have noted, is that in a society historically constituted by strangers, Americans have had an acute historical need to get along. This has meant forming effective work relationships among groups of individuals thrown together by chance and common goals and needs. From this kind of experience, and the behaviors it involved, a cultural conviction of a common humanity gradually developed among Americans. Manners became like those described by the Zairian commentator quoted above: "all social relations were of the same kind."

The loneliness of life on the frontier and in rural, post-frontier America, before the use of automobiles became widespread in the early 1900s, also led Americans to value friendliness. In the newly built suburbs of America after World War II, this developed into a phenomenon known as the "welcome wagon": a system for greeting recent arrivals in a neighborhood and making them feel at home. This was an extension of earlier behaviors on the frontier. (Perhaps only in America would it occur to persons to try to *organize* friendship.) I tend to doubt—though I do not know for certain—that any country of Europe, including England, has ever seen the equivalent of an American "welcome wagon."

Probably by the mid-1700s, American experience had validated the cultural belief that "human nature" can generally be trusted to want to do what is right. Generations of Americans have found that a person's individual interests are best served in cooperation with others. In American society, doing the right thing reflected the desire to be treated fairly and forthrightly by others. To observers from places where social relations were historically based on the inherited authority of an upper class constituted by birth, the American belief that most people want to do what is right seemed the height of innocence and nonsense. But during the formative period of American culture (apart from the great exception of the enslaved minority), birth seldom entered into the evaluation of a person's social worth and respectability. In determining one's status in society, personal qualities and individual achievement were far more important than sociological categories such as class origin.

From my own observations and experiences in America and abroad, it seems to me that one of the reasons Americans are more often friendly toward strangers than other people are, is because they look upon everyone they encounter as having the same basic nature as themselves. Instead of smiling at a stranger to disarm a potential enemy, as the European anthropologist thought, more likely such behavior reflects a view of strangers as potential friends, having the same interests. In American society, respectability has been founded on good behavior rather than proper manners—a distinction often pointed out by Henry James, the American expatriate, in his many novels and stories comparing European and American culture (most famously in his short story "Daisy Miller," about a young American woman traveling in Switzerland and Italy).

American beliefs about human nature are based on historical experiences that convinced the great majority of Americans in every generation that human beings have certain wholesome interests in common. Their experience as a people also convinced them that the satisfaction of those interests required trusting other human beings and treating them as equals. The cultural belief *Almost All Human Beings Want To Do What Is Right* differs markedly from the belief that only certain men—those of superior birth and breeding—can be trusted to act honorably and responsibly in their relations with others. That aristocratic belief, which associates virtue with a certain social class constituted by birth and superior education, did not square with the historical experience of Americans.

ANOTHER BELIEF about human nature that developed among Americans was negative rather than positive.

Europe's aristocratic culture concentrated governing power in the hands of a few persons who were considered to have superior bloodlines. The corollary to this outlook is that persons who do not belong to the superior class cannot be trusted with responsibility because of their inferior nature and lack of "breeding." American culture is democratic because Americans came to have a different view: that those in positions of power could not be trusted and had to be watched constantly to prevent their abuse of power.

This skeptical view of persons in power did not apply to a category of human beings. *All* human beings when they acquired power—not just some—were viewed as susceptible to the temptation to abuse it. No distinction was made regarding the *nature* of persons with power and persons without power. In American thought, powerful persons have the same human nature as powerless persons; and people who are poor and those who are rich are believed to have the same human nature. Thus, in American political thought, a majority may be just as tyrannical as a minority. The belief that almost everyone can be trusted to want to do right by their fellow human beings made the institutions of democracy in America possible. The belief in the inevitable abuse of power by those who have it has enabled American democracy to endure.

The belief *Human Beings Will Abuse Power When They Have It* holds that all men and women (not just those who are aristocrats) are capable of evil as well as good; that the freedom which is part of human nature consists of the ability to do wrong as well as good. Intrinsically, freedom itself is neither a virtue nor a vice. Whether it is a virtue depends entirely on how it is used. In trusting human nature, American culture has not attributed evil to one class of human beings, whose elimination would remove the basis of evil from human affairs. Rather, America's democratic culture has recognized a potential for the abuse of power in all human beings. In believing that *Human Beings Will Abuse Power When They Have It*, Americans attribute evil to a potential in themselves and other human beings that is not created by the conditions of their upbringing or the experiences of their social relations or a particular genetic inheritance.

In American culture neither nurture nor nature is ultimately responsible for what human beings do. American culture requires each individual to accept his human nature and be responsible for whether he does good or evil. It is a culture in which every person uses freedom to determine what his life will be. The desire to do the right thing is inherent to our natures, according to the beliefs of American culture, but so is our potential to succumb to the temptation to abuse others when we are in a position to do so.

Undoubtedly the conviction that the potential for wrongdoing lies in us as human beings (rather than as members of a particular category of human beings) became a part of American culture because Americans of lowly origin were constantly rising to positions of wealth and authority, and were sometimes seen to abuse their power as much as persons born of powerful parents.

In America it was not possible to attribute wrongdoing to the corruption or unrestrained excesses of the highborn.

Beliefs about human nature in American culture include the ancient wisdom that man's freedom of choice (as in the story of the Garden of Eden) will sooner or later lead him to disregard his innate desire to do what is right and to fall into wrongdoing. As one of the Founding Fathers, James Madison, said, referring to the checks and balances he and his fellow leaders had structured into the federal government:

> It may be a reflection on human nature, that such devices [as the balance of powers in government] should be necessary to control the abuses of government. But what is government itself but the greatest of all reflections on human nature? If men were angels, no government would be necessary. If angels were to govern men, neither external nor internal controls on government would be necessary. In framing a government which is to be administered by men over men, the great difficulty lies in this: you must first enable the government to control the governed; and in the next place oblige it to control itself. A dependence on the people is, no doubt, the primary control on the government; but experience has taught mankind the necessity of auxiliary precautions.[2]

No more succinct statement regarding the essential points of the American outlook on government, and the connection between the structure of American government and the negative belief of American culture about human nature, has ever come to my attention.

The belief that human beings, as human beings, have the potential to abuse whatever power they may have over others, prevents excusing abuses of power by attributing them to some outside influence. It places responsibility for wrongdoing squarely on the abuser, as a human being. Doctrinaire socialists, on the other hand, such as Marxists, attribute evil to the private ownership of property; and therefore conclude that in order to improve human affairs all power must be concentrated in a political party dedicated to the elimination of private property—and, if they resist expropriation, the elimination of the former owners of property.

To attribute wrongdoing to the special nature of a category of persons—defined by class, occupation, gender, or race—opens the door to the persecution of those persons. But when wrongdoing is regarded as part of the nature of all human beings, and responsibility for it is centered squarely in each individual and in his freedom to choose between right and wrong—regardless of the influences on him or his social status—persecution of categories of persons becomes much less likely. Only when wrongdoers are stripped of their humanity and placed in a special category, whose alleged wrongdoing is said to be specific to their class, is the fury of unrestrained persecution let loose. Categorizing human beings can also exonerate whole classes of persons from the possibility of individual wrongdoing.

Identifying categories of evildoers discourages the judgment of a person's individual behavior. A person who falls into such a category is liable to persecution, no matter how admirably he may behave as an individual. Justice is complicated enough, but when the alleged behavior of a category of persons becomes part of the context for passing judgment on a person, the concept of justice itself is muddled. It becomes a kind of Alice-in-Wonderland construct where saying something makes it so, and words take on whatever whimsical or arbitrary meaning is assigned to them. For an individual, the consequences of such arbitrariness can be dire. American culture contains a belief in the unavoidable potential for wrongdoing among human beings; but it rejects the idea that anyone's descendants inherit, or can be held accountable for, the sins of their parents.

If we believe in something called human nature, the consequences are momentous. So are the consequences of the particular beliefs we may hold about human nature. If we believe that human beings are by nature ungovernable except through coercion, we will construct authoritarian regimes that take into account that view of human nature. If we believe that only certain categories of human beings are capable of wrongdoing, we will try to suppress those categories. If we believe that most human beings are born to be governed by a few human beings capable of disinterested virtue and compassion, we will support rule by such a class of persons. As Joseph Wood Krutch, a wise American writing in the mid-twentieth century, has said: "Among the most important of [man's] ideas, convictions, and beliefs are those which concern his own nature. . . ."[3]

Another wise American made this comment in the 1700s about human nature:

> It is the Opinion of some People, that Man is a Creature altogether selfish, and that all our Actions have at Bottom a View to private Interest; If we do good to others, it is, say they, because there is a certain Pleasure attending virtuous Actions. But how Pleasure comes to attend a virtuous Action, these Philosophers are puzzled to shew, without contradicting their first Principles, and acknowledging that Men are *naturally* benevolent as well as selfish. For whence can arise the Pleasure you feel after having done a good-natured Thing, if not hence, that you had *before* strong humane and kind Inclinations in your Nature, which are by such Actions in some Measure gratified?

The author of this statement, Benjamin Franklin, continued: ". . . the Fact is certain, that we do approve and disapprove of Actions which cannot in the least influence our present Affairs. How could this happen, if we did not in contemplating such Actions, find something agreeable or disagreeable to our natural Inclinations as Men, that is, to our benevolent Inclinations?"[4]

Franklin in his autobiography tells of a project he attempted in his early twenties, just after his return from his first residence in Europe: "the bold and arduous Project of arriving at moral Perfection" through the systematic cultivation of a series of thirteen virtues arranged in an order that would make each of them progressively easier to attain. (The ultimate virtue in the list was

"Humility."[5]) This youthful project failed, Franklin confesses with considerable amusement, though it did help him rid himself of a few bad habits. Mostly what he learned from his attempt to be morally perfect was that the ambition was "a kind of Foppery," or ridiculous vanity.

Young Franklin's impulse to be a better person, and his belief that he could do so if he had a method and applied himself, reflect the interest of American culture in self-improvement and self-determination. His tolerance of imperfection in himself and others during his more mature years, when he wrote his autobiography, reflects his American belief in the mixed character of human nature (starting with himself). Franklin came to recognize the impossibility of ever excluding immoral and unjust behavior from human affairs, though we should try to be better persons. Knowing the mixture of good and bad in our own nature should make us more willing to forgive others their shortcomings and wrongdoing. Men are, as Franklin said, by nature both benevolent and self-centered. They are interested at the same time in doing good and in putting their own interests ahead of the interests of others.

In America, recognizing this fact has led to a certain tolerance of differences of opinion. And it has led to an understanding that the attempt to cure social, political, and economic problems may produce more ills than the problems themselves.

"Liberty is to faction what air is to fire, an [element] without which it instantly expires," James Madison wrote during the debate over whether to ratify the Constitution. "But it could not be less folly to abolish liberty, which is essential to political life, because it nourishes faction than it would be to wish the annihilation of air, which is essential to animal life, because it imparts to fire its destructive agency."[6] Because human beings have the freedom to pursue selfish ends, they will inevitably be selfish and come into conflict with the interests of others. To eliminate these possibilities of conflict and wrongdoing, one would have only to eliminate the freedom to pursue one's interests. But such a society—at least in America, with its extraordinary history of freedom of self-determination—would not be worth living in, even supposing it were possible to prevent individuals from pursuing their own interests.

A conclusive overview of the positive and negative American beliefs about human nature, and how they have influenced the institutions of American government, is expressed in this passage from one of the essays in *The Federalist*, favoring ratification of the Constitution:

> As there is a degree of depravity in mankind which requires a certain degree of circumspection and distrust, so there are other qualities in human nature which justify a certain portion of esteem and confidence. Republican government presupposes the existence of these qualities in a higher degree than any other form. Were the pictures which have been drawn by the political jealousy of some among us faithful likenesses of the human character, the inference would be, that there is not sufficient virtue among men for self-government; and that nothing less than the chains of despotism can restrain them from destroying and devouring one another.[7]

A people's cultural beliefs both derive from and sustain their historical behavior. They are what make them a people. For Americans, two of those beliefs are *Almost All Human Beings Want To Do What Is Right* and *Human Beings Will Abuse Power When They Have It.*

CHAPTER TEN

American Culture Today, and Tomorrow

EXAMINED AS A SET, American beliefs reveal certain themes or principles. Improvement. Practicality. Freedom. Responsibility. Equality. Individuality. During the four centuries of their history, Americans in their behavior have generally manifested these principles. And the principles themselves have considerable unity. Responsibility complements freedom; equality restrains individuality; and practicality balances improvement. This is to say that freedom, individuality, and improvement are impulses to action; responsibility, equality, and practicality limit the destruction that unrestrained freedom, individuality, and improvement could cause. Historically the dynamics of American beliefs has been responsible individuals having equal freedom making practical improvements.

The distinctive achievements of the American people illustrate the distinctive dynamics of their historical beliefs. Beginning in 1607, self-selected immigrants and their descendants created in central North America a new kind of society by consent. Today it has assimilated some 55 million people from almost every country, race, religion, and language on earth—without producing a babel of languages or a loss of American identity. This society has grown nearly seventyfold from the 3.9 million who inhabited the United States in 1790 when the first census was taken. In the second century of their history, the American people invented a new form of governmental authority: a constitution written and approved by specially elected constitutional conventions. During the past two centuries, thirty-seven new states have been organized under the Constitution of the United States and added to the original thirteen states of the nation. The government of each of these fifty states was created by the people living in them. Most wonderful of all, perhaps, the American people civilized a Stone Age wilderness as big as the continent of Europe (3.8 million square miles) in just four centuries, a fraction of the sixty centuries it took Europeans to bring Europe from a Stone Age condition to a comparable state of civilization. And the continental nation Americans made is now the world's most productive, wealthy, and powerful country.

In achieving these prodigies of creativity, growth, and unity, the access of Americans to Europe's technologies and the untapped resources of a continent-size wilderness was of great importance. But that access to resources and technology does not in itself explain what has happened in American history. Even with access to the technology of Europe and control over a much vaster extent of land, with greater untapped resources, the Russian people from the seventeenth to the nineteenth centuries did not match American achievements during that time. As Lawrence E. Harrison in *Who Prospers? How Cultural Values Shape Economic and Political Success* (1992) and David S. Landes in *The Wealth and Poverty of Nations* (1998) have recently explained, cultural values play a crucial role in determining a people's wealth or poverty.

Practical improvement is a kind of "super belief" of American beliefs. For the self-selected immigrants who initiated America's creation, the whole point in going to America was to improve their lives; thus beliefs that could produce benefits were acted on and became part of American culture. English immigrants in the 1600s no less than Chinese immigrants in the 1800s had to learn from practical experience in America how to better their lives. Improvement may be called the psyche of American culture, but the culture's imperative has been practicality.

Equal freedom—the conviction that each citizen has a right only to the liberty enjoyed by every other citizen—has been another "super belief" of American culture. Whether everyone will, or can, accomplish what all are equally free to do is, of course, another matter. (Anyone born in America who is at least thirty-five and has resided in America for fourteen years has a right to become president of the United States; yet only a few Americans have actually attained the office.) Equal freedom in American culture is equal opportunity, not equal result. It is a freedom to do something, not a freedom from something—particularly not from the responsibility of making choices beneficial to oneself and one's society.

Conditions in America from the beginning of its history made possible exceptional degrees of freedom to imagine opportunities, form associations, make independent judgments, and move about in a big space and upward in society. With this extraordinary freedom came extraordinary responsibilities for every individual. And the combination of freedom and responsibility generated a "super belief" in the responsible individual.

Responsible individuals are constructive agents, not people who wait for something to be done for them or to have someone direct their lives. As heirs of a culture formed through self-selected immigration, responsible individuals believe human beings make their world; the world does not make them. The responsible individual is dedicated to "getting the job done" and doing it right. He regards others as having the same basic nature and the same birthrights from God that he has. In his view, society is a collection of individuals, not a collection of groups classified by characteristics peculiar to each. Persons like this, who accepted responsibility for their own well-being and the institutions of their society, have built America.

AMERICANS believe in improvement, not decline. But should the formative and unifying set of beliefs that has been crucial to America's astonishingly rapid rise to prominence ever become deformed, the United States would surely decline. The past four decades (1960–2000) have seen troubling signs of such cultural deformation.

In no period of American history before the last forty years have families in every class of American society been so disrupted by marital infidelity and divorce (half of all American marriages now end in divorce), out-of-wedlock pregnancies (in 1963, 6.5 percent of Americans were born out of wedlock; in 1993, 30 percent[1]), abortions (now averaging over one million a year) and new venereal diseases such as AIDS and herpes—the cumulative results of the "revolution" against "middle-class morality" on American campuses in the 1960s called the "counterculture," and the 1973 Supreme Court decision on abortion (*Roe v. Wade*). During these same forty years, federal courts across the land have been busy suppressing prayer in public schools and prohibiting the display of the Ten Commandments in public buildings. There has also been an unprecedented surge of drug abuse, the effects of which are now felt in every city, town, and rural community in America and in every class and age group. Criminal acts of many kinds have also risen to record levels and include such disturbing new features of life in America as killers under the age of twelve, recreational murder, and on-the-job and in-school multiple killings—all of which have necessitated record expenditures of public and private resources on personal security, uniformed police forces, and prison facilities.

The same period has likewise seen a growing disrespect for community standards of decency, reflected in speech patterns, obscenity in film and print media, violent song lyrics, and the burning of the American flag—all justified as nothing more than freedom of expression. And never before have so many Americans in all classes of society depended so heavily on government. (Taxes to support government spending now consume 40 percent of a typical American family's earnings. Put another way, the average American family works about three hours a day for tax collectors.[2]) Still another basic change has occurred in public schooling in America: a shift of emphasis from teaching knowledge and skills to teaching "self-esteem"—making it possible for some students to spend twelve years in the system and emerge functionally illiterate. A rewriting of American history as an uninterrupted tale of oppression and victimization has also occurred during these same forty years; and the idea of "multiculturalism" has entirely displaced America's national culture in the thinking of some Americans.

Since the mid-1960s, the growing reluctance of America's schools and universities to flunk students who are not measuring up to minimum standards of performance is part of a larger trend in American society: an unwillingness to pronounce any conduct as wrong. Americans have been made to feel in the past forty years that being "nonjudgmental" is a kind of higher morality. Tolerance and choice—*no matter what is tolerated or chosen*—have been presented as values that override every other. Sophistication, in the minds of too many Americans, has become a more important consideration than shame.

As alarming as these symptoms of cultural decline may seem—and they are certainly alarming—they do not lead to the conclusion that American culture has yet been deformed. For one thing, most of the behavioral trends just cited are coming under increasingly heavy criticism, or have leveled off, or have been reversed. And some American beliefs, such as *Helping Others Helps Yourself* and *God Gave Men The Same Birthrights*, have actually been extended and strengthened since the 1960s. Most important, an overwhelming portion of the adult and young adult population of America still consists of responsible individuals.

For example, the Roper Center of Public Opinion Research in 1994 found that Americans across four generations (persons in their late teens to their late sixties and older) agreed that hard work is the key to getting ahead in America; that broadening opportunities is more important than ensuring equality of income; that big government is the greatest threat to America's future; and that they were generally satisfied with their personal lives.[3] Another national poll, taken in 1997, revealed that regardless of region, race, class, or age, most Americans still believe that "people have the power to shape their own lives, no matter what their circumstances, and that the best solutions are reached when people work together, cooperatively." Specifically in this poll, 83 percent agreed that "the USA is the greatest nation on Earth"; 95 percent that "freedom must be tempered by personal responsibility"; 89 percent that people have a "responsibility to help those less fortunate"; 79 percent that "people who work hard in this nation are likely to succeed"; and 81 percent that "a spiritual or religious belief is essential to a fulfilling life."[4]

Predictions of American decline have been made before and have proven false. And it is encouraging to remember that in the forty years from 1840 to 1880, which included a civil war, American beliefs survived. Cultures are tough. After all, cultural beliefs persist because they are durable.

Americans must nonetheless recognize that many of their beliefs as a people have been weakened in the last four decades, particularly the belief *America Is A Chosen Country*, which now seems to embarrass some Americans. (Had the 1997 poll that found an 83 percent agreement that "the USA is the greatest nation on Earth" been taken in 1957, I suspect the percentage of agreement would have been somewhere above 90.) Other American beliefs which—though still strong—have been somewhat diminished are the religious and moral beliefs *God Created Nature And Human Beings*, *God Created A Law Of Right And Wrong*, and *Doing What Is Right Is Necessary For Happiness*; the social and economic beliefs *Everyone Must Work*, *Society Is A Collection Of Individuals*, *Each Person Is Responsible For His Own Well-Being*, and *Opportunities Must Be Imagined* (as opposed to being provided by the government); the political beliefs *A Majority Decides* and *The Least Government Possible Is Best*; and the belief about human nature *Human Beings Will Abuse Power When They Have It* (whose weakening is suggested by judicial decisions nullifying state laws to limit the number of terms of elected representatives).

The end result of the simultaneous weakening of so many American beliefs has been to alter the dynamics of American culture. To account for how and why these beliefs have been weakened is beyond the scope of this book, but it is certain that since World War II some principles of American culture have been emphasized to the detriment of others. The principle of freedom, for instance, has been promoted without regard to responsibility; calls for improvement have been made without regard to practicality; and equality has sometimes been demanded with a zeal that ignores differences among individuals. Too often in the last forty years of the twentieth century, it seems, America's cultural history has been set aside in favor of uncompromising ideologies.

As always, America's future depends on the unity of the American people, just as George Washington said it did in his Farewell Address in 1796, three years before his death. And that unity is, as always, mostly a matter of the beliefs that Americans share and act on as a people.

Appendix

LIST OF AMERICAN CULTURAL BELIEFS

PRIMARY BELIEFS
Everyone Must Work
Persons Must Benefit From Their Work
Manual Work Is Respectable

IMMIGRANT BELIEFS
Improvement Is Possible
Opportunities Must Be Imagined
Freedom Of Movement Is Needed For Success

FRONTIER BELIEFS
What Has To Be Done Will Teach You How To Do It
Each Person Is Responsible For His Own Well-Being
Helping Others Helps Yourself
Progress Requires Organization

RELIGIOUS AND MORAL BELIEFS
God Created Nature And Human Beings
God Created A Law Of Right And Wrong
Doing What Is Right Is Necessary For Happiness
God Gave Men The Same Birthrights
America Is A Chosen Country

SOCIAL BELIEFS
Society Is A Collection Of Individuals
Every Person's Success Improves Society
Achievement Determines Social Rank

POLITICAL BELIEFS
The People Are Sovereign
The Least Government Possible Is Best
A Written Constitution Is Essential To Government
A Majority Decides
Worship Is A Matter Of Conscience

BELIEFS ON HUMAN NATURE
Almost All Human Beings Want To Do What Is Right
Human Beings Will Abuse Power When They Have It

Notes

Preface

1. Thomas Jefferson to James Monroe, June 17, 1785, in Thomas Jefferson, *Writings*, ed. Merrill D. Peterson (New York: Library of America, 1984), p. 808.

1. What Do We Mean By "Culture"?

1. I am indebted to the late Russell Kirk for making me aware of "the moral imagination" as a distinguishing characteristic of human beings.

2. T. S. Eliot, in his *Notes Towards the Definition of Culture*, rightly says: "If we include as education all the influences of family and environment, we are going far beyond what professional educators can control—though their sway can extend very far indeed; but if we mean that culture is what is passed on by our elementary and secondary schools, or by our preparatory and public schools, then we are asserting that an organ is an organism. For the schools can transmit only a part, and they can only transmit this part effectively, if the outside influences, not only of family and environment, but of work and play, of newsprint and spectacles and entertainment and sport, are in harmony with them. . . . So the instructive point is this, that the more education arrogates to itself the responsibility [of the reformation and direction of culture instead of keeping to its place as one of the activities through which a culture realises itself] the more systematically will it betray culture" (London: Faber and Faber, 1962, pp. 106–107). The failure of the Communist party of the Soviet Union to create a Communist culture in the Soviet Union, despite its total control over the educational system (a failure admitted in the preface to the 1977 constitution of the Soviet Union), certainly corroborates Eliot's point.

2. How American Culture Formed

1. *Documents of American History*, 9th ed., ed. Henry Steele Commager (Englewood Cliffs: Prentice-Hall, 1973), I, 15–16.

2. William Donovan summarized in *The Native Population of the Americas* (Madison: University of Wisconsin Press, 1976) the widely varying estimates of native populations in the Americas before European settlement, and the difficulties in making such estimates. My reasoning on this problem is given in *Finding Freedom: America's Distinctive Cultural Formation* (Carbondale: Southern Illinois University Press, 1989), pp. 23–24. *The Americas Before and After 1492: Current Geographical Research* in *Annals of the Association of American Geographers*, 82, No. 3, (September 1992), 343–398, contains a great deal of information on the issue. David Henige, *Numbers from Nowhere: The American Indian Contact Population Debate* (Norman: University of Oklahoma Press, 1998) is the most thorough and recent investigation of the subject.

3. In the year American independence was declared, there were in the United States approximately 450,000 slaves, descended from forced immigrants from Africa—18 percent of a population estimated at 2,530,000 (Thomas Fleming, "America 1776," *Reader's Digest*, July 1976, p. 224, and *The World Almanac and Book of Facts 1997*, p. 378). In the most recent U.S. Census (1990), six generations after the abolition of slavery in the United States, Americans who claim African descent make up 12 percent of the population (*World Almanac 1997*, p. 379).

4. *The Barbarian Invasions*, ed. Katherine Fischer Drew (Huntington: Robert E. Krieger Publishing, 1977), provides an overview of this subject. See also J. M. Wallace-Hadrill, *The Barbarian West, 400–1000* (London: Hutchinson, 1952).

5. Florentino Diaz Loza, *Doctrina política del ejército* (Buenos Aires: A. Peña Lillo, 1975), p. 39.

3. Primary Beliefs of American Culture

1. Charles M. Andrews, *The Colonial Period of American History*, 4 vols. (New Haven: Yale University Press, 1934), I, 110.

2. John Smith, *Travels and Works*, 2 vols., ed. Edward Arber (New York: Burt Franklin, 1967), II, 390.

3. Smith, *Travels*, II, 390, 407, 442–445, 516, and John Smith, *Advertisements for the Unexperienced Planters of New England, or Anywhere: or, The Pathway to Erect a Plantation* (Boston: William Veazie, 1865), pp. 15–16, 40. Smith had concluded early on, from his frequent encounters with the natives of the Chesapeake, that there was no gold to be had in Virginia because the ornaments worn by the natives showed no sign of it.

4. Quoted in Smith, *Travels*, II, 516.

5. Smith, *Travels*, II, 516, and *Advertisements*, pp. 40–41.

6. William Bradford, *History of Plymouth Plantation, 1620–1647*, 2 vols. (New York: Russell and Russell, 1968; reissue of 1912 ed.), I, 156.

7. Probaby a form of typhus introduced by a European ship whose infected crew came ashore in New England. Bradford, *Plymouth*, I, 221, n1.

8. Bradford, *Plymouth*, I., 288–291.

9. Bradford, *Plymouth*, I, 300–302.

10. Edward Winslow, *Good Newes from New-England: or A true relation of things very remarkable at the plantation of Plimouth in New-England* (London: Printed by I. D[awson] for W. Bladen and I. Bellamie, 1624), p. 48.

11. Bradford, *Plymouth*, II, 152.

12. Bradford, *Plymouth*, II, 152–153.

13. W. Stitt Robinson, Jr., *Mother Earth: Land Grants in Virginia, 1607–1699* (Williamsburg: Virginia 350th Anniversary Celebration Corp., 1957), p. 74. Carl N. Degler, *Out of Our Past: The Forces That Shaped Modern America*, revised ed. (New York: Harper and Row, 1970), p. 43. Jack P. Greene, *Pursuits of Happiness: The Social Development of Early Modern British Colonies and the Formation of American Culture* (Chapel Hill: University of North Carolina Press, 1988), p. 195.

14. Benjamin Franklin, "Information to Those Who Would Remove to America," *Writings* (New York: Library of America, 1987), p. 978.

15. Michel-Guillaume-Saint-Jean de Crèvecoeur, *Letters from an American Farmer*, ed. Albert E. Stone (New York: Penguin, 1986), p. 67. According to James T. Lemon, the phrase "the best poor man's country" was often used by western Europeans in the 1700s in reference to Pennsylvania (*The Best Poor Man's Country: A Geographical Study of Early Southeastern Pennsylvania* [New York: W. W. Norton, 1976], p. 229, n1).

16. Fleming, "America 1776," p. 55. Also Greene, *Pursuits*, p. 182.

17. Thomas Jefferson to John Adams, October 28, 1813. Jefferson, *Writings*, p. 1309. Fleming, "America 1776," p. 55. Clyde C. Griffen, "Upward Bound," *Wilson Quarterly* (Winter 1987), p. 102.

18. Commager, *Documents*, I, 123–124.

19. Commager, *Documents*, I, 412–413.

20. Franklin, *Writings*, p. 978. T. H. Hollingsworth, *Historical Demography* (Ithaca: Cornell University Press, 1969), p. 179.

21. Barbara Kaye Greenleaf, *America Fever: The Story of American Immigration* (New York: New American Library, 1970), p. 13.

22. Degler, *Past*, p. 27.

23. "The twenty Africans who were put ashore at Jamestown in 1619 by the captain of a Dutch frigate were not slaves in a legal sense. And at the time the Virginians seemed not to appreciate the far-reaching significance of the introduction of Africans into the fledgling colony. These newcomers, who happened to be black, were simply more indentured servants." John Hope Franklin, *From Freedom to Slavery: A History of Negro Americans*, 5th ed. (New York: Alfred A. Knopf, 1980), pp. 54–55. On the connection between indentured servitude and the development of chattel slavery in America, see also Winthrop D. Jordan, *White Over Black: American Attitudes Toward the Negro, 1550–1812* (Baltimore: Penguin, 1969), pp. 52–53, 71–80, and Herbert S. Klein, *Slavery in the Americas: A Comparative Study of Virginia and Cuba* (Chicago: Ivan R. Dee, 1989), pp. 40–47.

4. Immigrant Beliefs

1. Joel Dorfman, Gerard Casale, and Charles Pappa, "The Immigration Crisis: An Inside View," *Christian Science Monitor*, September 16, 1981, p. 22; Charles B. Keely, "Illegal Migration," *Scientific American*, 246, No. 3, (March 1982), p. 41.

2. Gary B. Nash, *Red, White, and Black: The Peoples of Early America*, 2nd ed. (Englewood Cliffs: Prentice-Hall, 1982), p. 200; also, American Historical Association, *Annual Report*, I, 1931, 124–125, 310.

3. Crèvecoeur, *Letters*, pp. 74, 68–70.

4. Kay Haugaard, "More Than Ever, a Melting Pot," *Wall Street Journal*, December 30, 1993, p. A8.

5. Theodore Roosevelt, *The Winning of the West*, 4 vols. (New York: G. P. Putnam's Sons, 1903), I, 20. This history of the settlement of the trans-Appalachian territories of the United States after the American Revolution was first published in 1889–1896.

6. Crèvecoeur, *Letters*, p. 70.

7. Herman Melville, "Supplement," *John Marr and Other Poems* (Princeton: Princeton University Press, 1922), p. 121.

8. "Immigrant War Heroes," *Wall Street Journal*, November 11, 1996, p. A16.

9. Henry Steele Commager, *The American Mind: An Interpretation of American Thought and Character Since the 1880's* (New Haven: Yale University Press, 1950), p. 4; and John Keegan, *Fields of Battle: The Wars for North America* (New York: Alfred A. Knopf, 1996), pp. 24–25. Keegan, an Englishman, was drawing on his memory of England during World War II; Commager was an American serviceman stationed in England.

10. James Truslow Adams, *A Searchlight on America* (London: George Routledge and Sons, 1930), p. 180.

11. *Washington Post*, May 16, 1991, pp. D1, D4.

12. Quoted in Degler, *Past*, p. 47.

13. Ralph Waldo Emerson, *English Traits* (Boston: Fields, Osgood, 1869), p. 305.

14. Samuel L. Clemens, *Innocents Abroad: or, The New Pilgrims' Progress* (New York: Heritage Press, 1962), p. 194.

15. O. E. Rölvaag, *Giants in the Earth: A Saga of the Prairie*, trans. Lincoln Colcord and the author (New York: Harper & Brothers, 1929), pp. 111–112.

16. Rölvaag, *Giants*, p. 358.

17. Rölvaag, *Giants*, p. 385.

18. Rölvaag, *Giants*, p. 425.

19. James Fenimore Cooper, *The Pioneers, or The Sources of the Susquehanna: A Descriptive Tale* (Albany: State University of New York, 1980), p. 321.

20. Cooper, *Pioneers*, p. 183.

21. Stephen Vincent Benét, *America* (New York: Farrar and Rinehart, 1944), p. 60.

22. Timothy Dwight, *Travels in New England and New York*, 4 vols., eds. Barbara Miller Solomon with Patricia M. King (Cambridge: Belknap Press of Harvard University Press, 1969), II, 212.

23. Dwight, *Travels*, IV, 18.

24. Concluding page of the preface. Webster's italics. A facsimile of this great work of Noah Webster, originally published in 1828, was issued by the Foundation for American Christian Education in 1989.

25. *World Almanac and Book of Facts 1997*, p. 387.

26. Griffen, "Upward Bound," p. 99.

5. Frontier Beliefs

1. Roosevelt, *West*, I, 116.

2. "A Volunteer Spirit Asks, Where's the Fire?" by Edward Koren describes a contemporary small-town, volunteer fire department (*New York Times*, December 9, 1997, p. G19).

3. Commager, *Documents*, II, 532–534.

4. Andrew Greeley, "The Other Civic America: Religion and Social Capital," *American Prospect*, May–June 1997, pp. 68–69, 72–73.

5. *World Almanac and Book of Facts 1997*, p. 713. Susan Jacoby, "Why Do We Donate? It's Personal," *New York Times*, December 9, 1997, p. G1.

6. Franklin, *Writings*, pp. 1422–1424.

7. James Truslow Adams, *Provincial Society, 1690–1763* (New York: Macmillan, 1928), pp. 260–264.

8. Alexis de Tocqueville, *Democracy in America*, trans. Henry Reeve, rev. by Francis Bowen, ed. with further corrections by Phillips Bradley, 2 vols. (New York: Alfred A. Knopf, 1945), II, 106.

9. Robert H. Bremner, *American Philanthropy* (Chicago: University of Chicago Press, 1960), pp. 89–90.

10. *World Almanac and Book of Facts 1997*, pp. 620–631.

11. R. R. Palmer, *The Age of Democratic Revolution: A Political History of Europe and America, 1760–1800*, 2 vols. (Princeton: Princeton University Press, 1959), I, 214–215.

6. Religious and Moral Beliefs

1. *Index to International Public Opinion Survey, 1993–1994*, eds. Elizabeth Hann Hastings and Philip K. Hastings (Westport: Greenwood Press, 1995), p. 441.

2. Floris W. Wood, *An American Profile—Opinions and Behavior, 1972–1989* (Detroit: Gale Research, 1990), p. 361.

3. *Index to International Public Opinion Survey, 1995*, p. 440.

4. UNESCO survey summarized in *Wilson Quarterly* (Winter 1996), p. 128. Patrick Glynn, *God, the Evidence: The Reconciliation of Faith and Reason in a*

Postsecular World (Rocklin: Prima Publishing, 1997), p. 10. Mark A. Noll, *A History of Christianity in the United States and Canada* (Grand Rapids: William B. Eerdmans, 1992), p. 475, states that "well over 95 percent of the [U.S.] population has persistently affirmed belief in God" in twentieth-century polls.

5. Tocqueville, *Democracy*, I, 319.

6. Rand McNally *Almanac of World Facts, 1995*, p. 44.

7. In 1990 more than eleven hundred of these storms were reported in North America. Rand McNally *Almanac of World Facts, 1995*, p. 37.

8. Rebecca and Edward Burlend, *A True Picture of Emigration*, ed. Milo Milton Quaife (Secaucus: Citadel, 1968), pp. 10–14ff.

9. Gottlieb Mittelberger, *Journey to Pennsylvania in the Year 1750 and Return to Germany in the Year 1754*, ed. & trans. Oscar Handlin and John Clive (Cambridge: Belknap Press of Harvard University Press, 1960), p. 14.

10. Franklin, *Writings*, p. 983.

11. Mittelberger, *Journey*, p. 48–50. Francisco de Miranda, *The New Democracy in America: Travels of Francisco de Miranda in the United States, 1783–84*, trans. Judson P. Wood, ed. John S. Ezell (Norman: University of Oklahoma Press, 1963), p. 182.

12. Chapter XXII in James Fenimore Cooper's novel *The Pioneers* (1823) describes the shooting of migrating passenger pigeons. The kill in such slaughters was measured by the wagonload.

13. Greene, *Pursuits*, p. 188.

14. Franklin, *Writings*, p. 978.

15. Franklin, *Writings*, pp. 1307–1308.

16. Henry David Thoreau, *The Illustrated Walden*, ed. J. Lyndon Shanley (Princeton: Princeton University Press, 1973), p. 218.

17. Commager, *Documents*, I, 100.

18. *Tracts of the American Revolution, 1763–1776*, ed. Merrill Jensen (Indianapolis: Bobbs-Merrill, 1977), pp. 423, 427.

19. *Tracts*, pp. 275, 276.

20. Commager, *Documents*, I, 173.

21. Franklin, *Writings*, pp. 1358–1360.

22. Franklin, *Writings*, p. 1396.

23. Franklin, *Writings*, p. 168.

24. *Faulkner in the University*, eds. Frederick L. Gwynn and Joseph L. Blotner (Charlottesville: University of Virginia Press, 1959), pp. 133–134.

25. William Faulkner, "Speech on Acceptance of the Nobel Prize, 1950," in *An American Primer*, ed. Daniel J. Boorstin (Chicago: University of Chicago Press, 1966), pp. 924–925.

26. Jerome R. Reich, *Colonial America*, 2nd ed. (Englewood Cliffs: Prentice-Hall, 1984), p. 200.

27. Roger Finke and Rodney Stark, *The Churching of America, 1776–1990* (New Brunswick: Rutgers University Press, 1992), p. 15, state that "By 1970 church adherence was about 62 percent"; Noll, in *A History of Christianity in the*

United States and Canada, p. 475, reported church membership in 1990 at 69 percent. Finke and Stark, pp. 274–275, found growth in church membership has historically been fastest among churches making the greatest demands on their members.

28. Franklin, *Writings*, pp. 475–476.

29. Denis Brogan, *U.S.A.: An Outline of the Country, Its People and Institutions* (London: Oxford University Press, 1941), p. 70.

30. *Inaugural Addresses of the Presidents of the United States . . . [to] 1973* (Washington, D.C.: U.S. Government Printing Office, 1974), p. 257.

31. *New York Times*, January 21, 1989, p. A10.

32. *New York Times*, January 21, 1977, p. B1.

33. *Inaugural Addresses*, pp. 1–4.

34. *Inaugural Addresses*, pp. 16, 15, 21.

35. *Inaugural Addresses*, pp. 239, 249.

36. Abraham Lincoln, *Selected Speeches and Writings* (New York: Library of America, 1992), p. 450. The verses Lincoln quoted and paraphrased are, in the King James version of the Bible that Lincoln customarily read: "And unto Adam he said, Because thou hast hearkened unto the voice of thy wife, and hast eaten of the tree, of which I commanded thee, saying, Thou shalt not eat of it: cursed is the ground for thy sake; in sorrow shalt thou eat of it all the days of thy life; Thorns also and thistles shall it bring forth to thee; and thou shalt eat the herb of the field; In the sweat of thy face shalt thou eat bread, till thou return unto the ground; for out of it wast thou taken: for dust thou art, and unto dust shalt thou return" (Genesis 3:17–19). "Judge not, that ye be not judged" (Matthew 7:1). "Judge not, and ye shall not be judged: condemn not, and ye shall not be condemned: forgive, and ye shall be forgiven" (Luke 6:37). "Woe unto the world because of offences! for it must needs be that offences come; but woe to that man by whom the offence cometh!" (Matthew 18:7). "The fear of the Lord is clean, enduring for ever: the judgments of the Lord are true and righteous altogether" (Psalms 19:9).

37. *Selected Speeches and Writings*, pp. 344, 277.

38. Thomas Jefferson to Roger C. Weightman, June 24, 1826, in Jefferson, *Writings*, p. 1517.

39. Commager, *Documents*, I, 100–102.

40. *Inaugural Addresses*, pp. 259, 267, 221, 73.

41. Paul Johnson, "The Almost-Chosen People," *Wilson Quarterly* (Winter 1985), p. 89.

42. Quoted in Russell Kirk, *The Roots of American Order* (LaSalle: Open Court, 1974), p. 438.

43. Quoted in Richard John Neuhaus, "A Strange New Regime: The Naked Public Square and the Passing of the American Constitutional Order," Salvatori Lecture, October 8, 1996, No. 572, Heritage Foundation, Washington, D.C., 1996, p. 2.

44. *New York Times*, April 10, 1991, p. A1.

7. Social Beliefs

1. Greene, *Pursuits*, p. 186. Charles M. Andrews, *The Colonial Background of the American Revolution* (New Haven: Yale University Press, 1924), p. 185.

2. Degler, *Past*, p. 5.

3. Colden was writing in 1748. Quoted in Reich, *Colonial*, p. 163.

4. Russell R. Menard, "From Servant to Freeholder: Status Mobility and Property Accumulation in Seventeenth-Century Maryland," in *Colonial America: Essays in Politics and Social Development*, 3rd ed., eds. Stanley N. Katz and John M. Murrin (New York: Alfred A. Knopf, 1983), p. 74.

5. Rachel Wildavsky, "Are You Getting Ahead?" *Reader's Digest* (December 1996), p. 55.

6. Wu Tingfang, *America Through the Spectacles of an Oriental Diplomat* (Taipei: Ch'Eng-Wen Publishing Co., 1968), pp. 84–85.

7. Alan Taylor, *William Cooper's Town: Power and Persuasion on the Frontier of the Early American Republic* (New York: Vintage Books, 1996), pp. 97–98.

8. Robert Bendiner, *Just Around the Corner: A Highly Selective History of the Thirties* (New York: E. P. Dutton, 1968), pp. 94, 98–99.

9. Menard, "From Servant to Freeholder," p. 86. For the seven characteristics shared by contemporary American millionaires, see Thomas J. Stanley and William D. Danko, *The Millionaire Next Door: The Surprising Secrets of America's Wealthy* (Atlanta: Longstreet Press, 1996), pp. 3–4.

10. Taylor, *Cooper's Town*, p. 42.

11. During the time that most immigrants to America were coming from Europe, there were four separate "races" in Britain: the Irish, the English, the Welsh, and the Scots, whom the English had unified into a single kingdom, chiefly through conquest.

8. Political Beliefs

1. Commager, *Documents*, I, 102.

2. Palmer, *Democratic*, I, 214–215.

3. Commager, *Documents*, I, 139.

4. Quoted in W. Cleon Skousen, *The Making of America: The Substance and Meaning of the Constitution* (Washington, D.C.: National Center for Constitutional Studies, 1985), pp. 168–169. See also the entry on Pinckney in Robert G. Ferris and James H. Charleton, *The Signers of the Constitution* (Flagstaff: Interpretive Publications, 1986), pp. 202–204.

5. Commager, *Documents*, I, 172, 100.

6. Tocqueville, *Democracy*, I, 60. Lincoln, "The Gettysburg Address, " *Selected Speeches and Writings*, p. 405.

7. A. E. Dick Howard, "Exporting the Constitution," *Wilson Quarterly* (Spring 1987), p. 126. Besides Britain, Israel and New Zealand are also committed to an unwritten constitution that can be altered by a simple majority vote of their parliaments. Saudi Arabia, Oman, and Libya accept the Koran as their supreme written law.

8. *American Military History*, Army Historical Series, general ed. Maurice Matloff (Washington, D.C.: Center of Military History, U.S. Army, 1985), p. 33.

9. A half-brother of George Washington was among the American officers in this expedition to South America, and named his estate in Virginia "Mount Vernon" in honor of Edward Vernon, the English commander of the naval forces that besieged Cartagena for three months in 1741 without taking it.

10. James Fenimore Cooper, *Gleanings in Europe: England* (Albany: State University of New York Press, 1982), pp. 137–138.

11. J. Franklin Jameson, *The American Revolution Considered as a Social Movement* (Princeton: Princeton University Press, 1926), p. 39. Robert E. Brown and B. Katherine Brown, *Virginia 1705–1786: Democracy or Aristocracy?* (East Lansing: Michigan State University Press, 1964), pp. 125–134, and Robert E. Brown, *Middle-Class Democracy and the Revolution in Massachusetts, 1691–1780* (Ithaca: American Historical Association and Cornell University Press, 1955), pp. 401–404. Alfred H. Kelly, Winfred A. Harbison, and Herman Belz, *The American Constitution: Its Origins and Development*, 6th ed. (New York: W. W. Norton, 1983), p. 36.

12. Emerson, *Traits*, pp. 183–184, 299. Robert Rhodes James, *The British Revolution: British Politics, 1880–1939* (London: Methuen, 1978), p. 613.

13. Dulaney's essay can be found in *Tracts of the American Revolution, 1763–1776*, pp. 94–107.

14. Dale Van Every, *A Company of Heroes: The American Frontier, 1775–1783* (New York: Morrow, 1962), pp. 14–15.

15. Franklin, *Writings*, pp. 1465–1466.

16. Commager, *Documents*, I, 44. Franklin, *Writings*, pp. 378–401.

17. Franklin, *Writings*, pp. 1430–1431.

18. Commager, *Documents*, I, 60–61. Americans in 1776 obviously had the wording of this parliamentary resolution of 1766 in mind in saying in their Declaration of Independence: "these United Colonies are, and of Right ought to be Free and Independent States." Commager, *Documents*, I, 102.

19. George Hewes, one of the participants in the Boston Tea Party, wrote an account of the event which can be found in *The Spirit of Seventy-Six*, eds. Richard B. Morris and Henry Steele Commager (New York: Harper and Row, 1967).

20. *The Canadian Constitution 1981: A Resolution Adopted by the Parliament of Canada, December, 1981* (Ottawa: Minister of Supply and Services Canada, 1981), p. 1.

21. In elections in the Soviet Union before its collapse, candidates for office were routinely elected by 98 percent of the eligible voters. The Communist party, which set up and supervised all elections, saw to it that only one candidate was put forward for each office, and all eligible voters were required to cast a vote. This sham reinforced in the public a sense of the party's power, for men and women were forced to perform a ritual they knew in advance could have no

meaning as an expression of the will of a majority. The party perpetually in power had already decided who would be "elected."

22. Franklin, *Writings*, pp. 1139-1141.

23. Alexander Hamilton, James Madison, and John Jay, *The Federalist Papers* (New York: New American Library, 1961), Madison, No. 10, p. 78.

24. *Inaugural Addresses*, p. 18.

25. Thomas Jefferson to the Danbury Baptist Association, January 1, 1802. Quoted in Edwin S. Gaustad, *Sworn on the Altar of God: A Religious Biography of Thomas Jefferson* (Grand Rapids: William B. Eerdmans, 1996), p. 99.

26. Arlin M. Adams and Charles J. Emmerich, *A Nation Dedicated to Religious Liberty: The Constitutional Heritage of the Religious Clauses* (Philadelphia: University of Pennsylvania Press, 1990), p. 85.

27. Mittelberger, *Journey*, p. 21.

28. Adams and Emmerich, *Liberty*, pp. 116-120.

9. Beliefs on Human Nature

1. *Distant Mirrors: America as a Foreign Culture*, eds. Philip DeVita and James D. Armstrong (Belmont: Wadsworth, 1993), p. 64; also pp. 23, 90, 94, 114.

2. Madison, *Federalist Papers*, No. 51. p. 322.

3. Joseph Wood Krutch, *Human Nature and the Human Condition* (New York: Random House, 1959), p. 97.

4. Franklin, "Men Are Naturally Benevolent as Well as Selfish," *Writings*, pp. 200-201.

5. Franklin, *Writings*, pp. 1383-1385.

6. Madison, *The Federalist Papers*, No. 10, p. 78.

7. Madison, *The Federalist Papers*, No. 55, p. 346.

10. American Culture Today, and Tomorrow

1. Dorothy Rabinowitz, "A New Eye on American Culture at CBS," *Wall Street Journal*, February 23, 1994, p. A18.

2. "The Outlook" column, *Wall Street Journal*, January 31, 1994, p. 1; *Arizona Daily Star*, January 23, 1994, p. E1. It must also be noted that we are now not only tolerating higher taxation than in any previous period of American history but also record levels of federal borrowing to fund "entitlement" programs, the biggest share of which—43 percent according to Peter G. Peterson in *Facing Up* (New York: Simon and Schuster, 1993), p. 30—goes to persons with annual incomes ranging from $30,000 to $200,000. *Hamilton's Blessing* (New York: Walker, 1997), John Steele Gordon's study of the funding of federal spending through borrowing, as well as the creative bookkeeping of the federal government, provides a needed historical perspective on this serious problem and proposes concrete actions to correct it.

3. *Reader's Digest*, January 1995, pp. 49-54.

4. Poll results summarized by Stephen Covey in "The Beliefs We Share," *USA Weekend*, July 4-8, 1997, pp. 4-6.

Bibliography

WORKS BY foreign visitors to America comprise the largest category among the books consulted because observers from outside a culture are often more able to perceive its distinctive features than persons within the culture. In reading many accounts of America by foreign observers in different centuries, one begins to acquire a sense of the historical belief-behaviors of Americans. The works in this selected bibliography that I found most useful are marked with an asterisk (*).

COMPARATIVE STUDIES

Clark, J. C. D., *The Language of Liberty, 1660–1832: Political Discourse and Social Dynamics in the Anglo-American World* (Cambridge: Cambridge University Press, 1994).

*Eliot, T. S., *Notes towards the Definition of Culture* (London: Faber and Faber, 1948).

Greene, Jack P., *The Intellectual Construction of America: Exceptionalism and Identity from 1492 to 1800* (Chapel Hill: University of North Carolina Press, 1993).

*Harrison, Lawrence E., *Underdevelopment Is a State of Mind: The Latin American Case* (Lanham: Center for International Affairs, Harvard University, and University Press of America, 1985).

Harrison, Lawrence E., *Who Prospers? How Cultural Values Shape Economic and Political Success* (New York: Basic Books, 1992).

Hartz, Louis, *The Founding of New Societies: Studies in the History of the United States, Latin America, South Africa, Canada, and Australia* (New York: Harcourt, Brace & World, 1964).

Keegan, John, *Fields of Battle: The Wars for North America* (New York: Alfred A. Knopf, 1996).

*Kirk, Russell, *The Roots of American Order* (LaSalle: Open Court, 1974).

Landes, David S., *The Wealth and Poverty of Nations: Why Some Are So Rich and Some So Poor* (New York: W. W. Norton, 1998).

Lippy, Charles H., Robert Choquette, and Stafford Poole, *Christianity Comes to the Americas, 1492–1776* (New York: Paragon House, 1992).

Lipset, Seymour Martin, *Continental Divide: The Values and Institutions of the United States and Canada* (Washington, D.C.: Canadian-American Committee, 1989).

Mayer, Arno J., *The Persistence of the Old Regime: Europe to the Great War* (New York: Pantheon Books, 1981).

*Palmer, R. R., *The Age of Democratic Revolution: A Political History of Europe and America, 1760–1800*, 2 vols. (Princeton: Princeton University Press, 1959).

Sowell, Thomas, *Race and Culture: A World View* (New York: Basic Books, 1994).

Webber, Carolyn, and Aaron Wildavsky, *A History of Taxation and Expenditure in the Western World* (New York: Simon and Schuster, 1986).

ENGLAND

*Cannadine, David, *The Decline and Fall of the British Aristocracy* (New Haven: Yale University Press, 1990).

Dunn, John, *The Political Thought of John Locke* (London: Cambridge University Press, 1969).

Hibbert, Christopher, *Cavaliers and Roundheads: The English Civil War, 1642–1649* (London: HarperCollins, 1993).

*James, Robert Rhodes, *The British Revolution: British Politics, 1880–1939* (London: Methuen, 1978).

Lilburne, John, William Walwyn, and Richard Overton, *The Levellers in the English Revolution*, ed. G. E. Aylmer (Ithaca: Cornell University Press, 1975).

THE AMERICAN "CHARACTER," "GENIUS," "MIND," "SPIRIT"

Boorstin, Daniel, *The Genius of American Politics* (Chicago: University of Chicago Press, 1973).

*Brogan, Denis W., *The American Character* (New York: Alfred A. Knopf, 1956).

Commager, Henry Steele, *The American Mind: An Interpretation of American Thought and Character Since the 1880's* (New Haven: Yale University Press, 1950).

Johnson, Frederick Ernest, *Wellsprings of the American Spirit* (New York: Institute for Religious and Social Studies, 1948).

Savelle, Max, *Seeds of Liberty: The Genesis of the American Mind* (Seattle: University of Washington Press, 1965).

Wright, Louis B., *The American Tradition: National Characteristics, Past and Present* (New York: F. S. Crofts, 1941).

AMERICAN COLONIAL HISTORY

Andrews, Charles M., *The Colonial Background of the American Revolution* (New Haven: Yale University Press, 1924).

*Andrews, Charles M., *The Colonial Period of American History*, 4 vols. (New Haven: Yale University Press, 1934).

Degler, Carl N., *Out of Our Past: The Forces That Shaped Modern America*, rev. ed. (New York: Harper and Row, 1970).

Furnas, J. C., *The Americans: A Social History of the United States, 1587–1914* (New York: G. P. Putnam's Sons, 1969).

Galenson, David, *White Servitude in Colonial America: An Economic Analysis* (New York: Cambridge University Press, 1981).

*Greene, Jack P., *Pursuits of Happiness: The Social Development of Early Modern British Colonies and the Formation of American Culture* (Chapel Hill: University of North Carolina Press, 1988).

Jameson, J. Franklin, *The American Revolution Considered as a Social Movement* (Princeton: Princeton University Press, 1926).

Jordan, Winthrop D., *White Over Black: American Attitudes Toward the Negro, 1550–1812* (Chapel Hill: University of North Carolina Press, 1968).

Reich, Jerome R., *Colonial America* (Englewood Cliffs: Prentice-Hall, 1984).

Ver Steeg, Clarence L., *The Formative Years, 1607–1763* (New York: Hill and Wang, 1964).

BRAZIL, CANADA, AND SPANISH AMERICA

Bothwell, Robert, *Canada and Quebec: One Country, Two Histories* (Vancouver: University of British Columbia Press, 1995).

Brundage, Burr Cartwright, *Lords of Cuzco: A History and Description of the Inca People in Their Final Days* (Norman: University of Oklahoma Press, 1967).

Burns, Bradford E., *A History of Brazil*, 2nd ed. (New York: Columbia University Press, 1980).

Crow, John A., *The Epic of Latin America*, 3rd ed. (Berkeley: University of California Press, 1980).

Eccles, W. J., *The Canadian Frontier, 1534–1760*, rev. ed. (Albuquerque: University of New Mexico Press, 1983).

*Fuentes, P. D., ed., *The Conquistadors: First-Person Accounts of the Conquest of Mexico* (New York: Orion Press, 1963).

*Gibson, Charles, *Spain in America* (New York: Harper and Row, 1966).

McAlister, Lyle N., *Spain and Portugal in the New World, 1492–1700* (Minneapolis: University of Minnesota Press, 1984).

*Morton, W. L., *The Canadian Identity* (Madison: University of Wisconsin Press, 1961).

Munro, William Bennett, *The Seigneurs of Old Canada: A Chronicle of New-World Feudalism* (Toronto and Glasgow: Brook and Co., 1935).

Padden, R. C., *The Hummingbird and the Hawk: Conquest and Sovereignty in the Valley of Mexico, 1503–1541* (Columbus: Ohio State University Press, 1967).

Parry, J. H., *The Spanish Seaborne Empire* (New York: Alfred A. Knopf, 1966).

Roett, Riordan, *Brazil: Politics in a Patrimonial Society*, 3rd ed. (New York: Praeger, 1984).

*Vega, Garcilaso de la, *The Incas: The Royal Commentaries of the Inca* (New York: Orion Press, 1961).

THE AMERICAN REVOLUTION

Bailyn, Bernard, *The Ideological Origins of the American Revolution*, enlarged ed. (Cambridge: Belknap Press of Harvard University Press, 1992).

Conklin, Paul K., *Self-Evident Truths: Being a Discourse on the Origins & Development of the First Principles of American Government—Popular Sovereignty, Natural Rights, and Balance & Separation of Powers* (Bloomington: Indiana University Press, 1974).

Corwin, Edward S., *The "Higher Law" Background of American Constitutional Law* (Ithaca: Cornell University Press, 1965).

The Federalist Papers: A Collection of Essays Written in Support of the Constitution of the United States from the Original Text of Alexander Hamilton, James Madison, and John Jay (Baltimore: Johns Hopkins University Press, 1981).

Hyneman, Charles S., and Donald S. Lutz, eds., *American Political Writing During the Founding Era, 1760–1805*, 2 vols. (Indianapolis: Liberty Press, 1983).

*Jensen, Merrill, ed., *Tracts of the American Revolution, 1763–1776* (Indianapolis: Bobbs-Merrill, 1977).

Levinson, Sanford, *Constitutional Faith* (Princeton: Princeton University Press, 1988).

Levy, Leonard W., *The Establishment Clause: Religion and the First Amendment* (New York: Macmillan, 1986).

*Skousen, W. Cleon, *The Making of America: The Substance and Meaning of the Constitution* (Washington, D.C.: National Center for Constitutional Studies, 1985).

*Tocqueville, Alexis de, *Democracy in America*, 2 vols., trans. Henry Reeve, rev. by Francis Bowen, ed. with further corrections by Phillips Bradley (New York: Alfred A. Knopf, 1945).

Wood, Gordon S., *The Creation of the American Republic, 1776–1787* (Chapel Hill: University of North Carolina Press, 1969).

*Wood, Gordon S., *The Radicalism of the American Revolution* (New York: Alfred A. Knopf, 1992).

IMMIGRANTS AND IMMIGRATION

Blegen, Theodore C., ed., *Land of Their Choice: The Immigrants Write Home* (Minneapolis: University of Minnesota Press, 1955).

Budd, Thomas, *Good Order Established in Pennsilvania & New-Jersey* (n.p.: Readex Microprint Corporation, 1966).

*Burlend, Rebecca, and Edward Burlend, *A True Picture of Emigration*, ed. Milo Milton Quaife (Secaucus: Citadel Press, 1968).

Coleman, Terry, *Going to America* (New York, Pantheon Books, 1972).

*Crèvecoeur, Michel-Guillaume-Saint-Jean de, *Letters from an American Farmer*, eds. Henri L. Bourdin, Ralph H. Gabriel, and Stanley T. Williams (New Haven: Yale University Press, 1925).

Dinnerstein, Leonard, and David M. Reimers, *Ethnic Americans: A History of Immigration*, 3rd ed. (New York: Harper and Row, 1988).

Jones, Maldwyn Allen, *American Immigration*, 2nd ed. (Chicago: University of Chicago Press, 1992).

*Morrison, Joan, and Charlotte Fox Zabusky, eds., *American Mosaic: The Immigrant Experience in the Words of Those Who Lived It* (New York: E. P. Dutton, 1980).

Namias, June, ed., *First Generation: In the Words of Twentieth-Century American Immigrants*, rev. ed. (Urbana: University of Illinois Press, 1992).

Reimers, David M., *Still the Golden Door: The Third World Comes to America*, 2nd ed. (New York: Columbia University Press, 1992).

Wheeler, Thomas C., ed., *The Immigrant Experience: The Anguish of Becoming American* (New York: Dial Press, 1971).

THE ENCOUNTER WITH WILDERNESS

Bakeless, John, *The Eyes of Discovery: The Pageant of North America as Seen by the First Explorers* (Philadelphia: J. B. Lippincott, 1961).

*Bartram, William, *Travels Through North & South Carolina, Georgia, East & West Florida* (Salt Lake City: Peregrine Smith, 1980; first published in 1791).

*Bradford, William, *History of Plymouth Plantation, 1620–1647*, 2 vols. (New York: Russell and Russell, 1968).

*Burrage, Henry S., ed., *Early English and French Voyages, Chiefly from Hakluyt, 1534–1608* (New York: Charles Scribner's Sons, 1932).

Byrd, William, *The Writings of Colonel William Byrd*, ed. John Spencer Bassett (New York: Doubleday, Page, 1901).

Every, Dale Van, *A Company of Heroes: The American Frontier, 1775–1783* (New York: William Morrow, 1962).

Every, Dale Van, *Ark of Empire: The American Frontier, 1784–1803* (New York: Arno Press, 1976).

Every, Dale Van, *The Final Challenge: The American Frontier, 1804–1845* (New York: William Morrow, 1964).

Hall, Clayton C., ed., *Narratives of Early Maryland, 1633–1684* (New York: Scribner's, 1910).

Lawrence, Bill, *The Early American Wilderness as the Explorers Saw It* (New York: Paragon House, 1991).

Meinig, D. W., *The Shaping of America: A Geographical Perspective on 500 years of History*, 4 vols. (New Haven: Yale University Press, 1986–1993).

Morgan, Ted, *Wilderness at Dawn: The Settling of the North American Continent* (New York: Simon and Schuster, 1993).

Nash, Roderick, *Wilderness and the American Mind*, 3rd ed. (New Haven: Yale University Press, 1982).

Norman, Charles, *Discoverers of America* (New York: Thomas Y. Crowell, 1968).

*Núñez Cabeza de Vaca, Àlvar, *Adventures in the Unknown Interior of America* (New York: Collier Books, 1961; first published in 1542).

*Roosevelt, Theodore, *The Winning of the West*, 4 vols. (New York: G. P. Putnam's Sons, 1903).

Sauer, Carl O., *Seventeenth-Century North America* (Berkeley: Turtle Island, 1980).

Sauer, Carl O., *Sixteenth-Century North America: The Land and The People as Seen by the Europeans* (Berkeley: University of California Press, 1971).

*Smith, John, *Travels and Works*, 2 vols., ed. Edward Arber (New York: Burt Franklin, 1967).

Taylor, Alan, *William Cooper's Town: Power and Persuasion on the Frontier of the Early American Republic* (New York: Alfred A. Knopf, 1995).

RELIGION IN AMERICAN NATIONAL LIFE

*Adams, Arlin M., and Charles J. Emmerich, *A Nation Dedicated to Religious Liberty: The Constitutional Heritage of the Religious Clauses* (Philadelphia: University of Pennsylvania Press, 1990).

Cord, Robert, *Separation of Church and State: Historical Fact and Current Fiction* (New York: Lambeth Press, 1982).

*Cousins, Norman, ed., *"In God We Trust": The Religious Beliefs and Ideas of the American Founding Fathers* (New York: Harper and Brothers, 1958).

*Evans, M. Stanton, *The Theme Is Freedom: Religion, Politics, and the American Tradition* (Washington, D.C.: Regnery, 1994).

Griffin, Keith L., *Revolution and Religion: American Revolutionary War and the Reformed Clergy* (New York: Paragon House, 1994).

Sandoz, Ellis, ed., *Political Sermons of the American Founding Era, 1730–1805* (Indianapolis: Liberty Press, 1990).

FOREIGN VIEWS OF AMERICA

Anburey, Thomas, *Travels Through the Interior Parts of America*, 2 vols. (London: W. Lane, 1789).

Ashe, Thomas, *Travels in America*, 3 vols. (London: R. Phillips, 1808).

Baxter, William Edward, *America and the Americans* (London and New York: G. Routledge, 1855).

Bradbury, John, *Travels in the Interior of America in the Years 1809, 1810, and 1811* (n.p.: Readex Microprint Corporation, 1966; first published in 1817).

*Brissot de Warville, Jacques-Pierre, *New Travels in the United States of America, 1788* (Cambridge: Belknap Press of Harvard University Press, 1964; first published in 1792).

Brothers, Thomas, *The United States of North Americas as They Are; Not as They Are Generally Described* (London: Longman, Orme, 1840).

Burnaby, Andrew, *Burnaby's Travels Through North America* (New York: A. Wessels, 1904; first published in 1775).

*Carver, Jonathan, *Travels Through the Interior Parts of North America in the Years 1766, 1767, and 1768* (London: J. Walter, 1778).

Castiglioni, Luigi, *Travels in the United States of North America, 1785–87*, trans. and ed. Antonio Pace (Syracuse: Syracuse University Press, 1983; first published in 1790).

Chastellux, François Jean, *Travels in North-America in the Years 1780–81–82*, trans. G. Grieve (London: G. G. J. and J. Robinson, 1787).

Cobbett, William, *A Year's Residence in America* (London: Chapman and Dodd, 1922; first published in 1818).

Coke, Thomas, *Extracts of the Journals of the Rev. Dr. Coke's Five Visits to America* (London: G. Whitfield, 1793).

*Commager, Henry Steele, ed., *America in Perspective: The United States Through Foreign Eyes* (New York: Random House, 1947).

*Danckaerts, Jasper, and Peter Sluyter, *Journal of a Voyage to New York & a Tour in Several of the American Colonies in 1679–1680*, trans. and ed. H. C. Murphy (Brooklyn: Long Island Historical Society, 1867).

Davis, John, *Travels of Four Years and a Half in the United States of America* (London: Ostell and Caritat, 1803).

*DeVita, Philip, and James D. Armstrong, eds., *Distant Mirrors: America as a Foreign Culture* (Belmont: Wadsworth, 1997).

Duden, Gottfried, *Report on a Journey to the Western States of North America and a Stay of Several Years Along the Missouri (During the Years 1824, '25, '26, and 1827)*, trans. and eds. George H. Kellner, Elsa Nagel, Adolf E. Schroeder, W. M. Senner (Columbia: State Historical Society of Missouri, 1980).

Evans, J. Martin, *America: The View from Europe* (San Francisco: San Francisco Book Co., 1976).

Fearon, Henry B., *Sketches of America: A Narrative of a Journey of Five Thousand Miles* (London: Longman, Hurst, Rees, Orme, and Brown, 1818).

Finch, Marianne, *An English Woman's Experience in America* (London: R. Bentley, 1853).

Grund, Francis J., *The Americans in Their Moral, Social, and Political Relations*, 2 vols. (London: Longman, 1837).

Hall, Basil, *Travels in North America*, 3 vols. (Edinburgh and London: Simpkin and Marshall, 1829).

Haliburton, Thomas Chandler, *The Americans at Home*, 3 vols. (London: Hurst and Blackett, 1854).

Handlin, Oscar, ed., *This Was America: True Accounts of People and Places, Manners and Customs, as Recorded by European Travelers to the Western Shore in the Eighteenth, Nineteenth, and Twentieth Centuries* (Cambridge: Harvard University Press, 1949).

Handlin, Oscar, and Lilian Handlin, eds., *From the Outer World: Perspectives on People and Places, Manners and Customs in the United States, as Reported by Travelers from Asia, Africa, Australia, and Latin America* (Cambridge: Harvard University Press, 1997).

Hasty, Olga Peters, and Susanne Fusso, trans. and eds., *America Through Russian Eyes, 1874–1926* (New Haven: Yale University Press, 1988).

Hesse-Wartegg, Ernst von, *Travels on the Lower Mississippi, 1879–1880: A Memoir*, trans. and ed. Frederic Trautmann (Columbia: University of Missouri Press, 1990).

*Joseph, Franz M., and Raymond Aron, *As Others See Us: The United States Through Foreign Eyes* (Princeton: Princeton University Press, 1959).

Josselyn, John, *An Account of Two Voyages to New-England* (London: G. Widdows, 1674).

*Kalm, Peter, *The America of 1750: Peter Kalm's Travels in North America, The English Version of 1770*, 2 vols., revised from the original Swedish and ed. by Adolph B. Benson (New York: Dover Publications, 1966).

Kohl, Johann Georg, *Travels in Canada and Through the States of New York and Pennsylvania* (London: G. Manwaring, 1861).

Lambert, John, *Travels Through Canada and the United States of North America, in the Year 1806, 1807, & 1808*, 2nd ed. (London: C. Cradock and W. Joy, 1813).

Macrae, David, *The Americans at Home*, 2 vols. (Edinburgh: Edmonston and Douglas, 1870).

*Mariás, Julián, *America in the Fifties and Sixties*, ed. Michael Aaron Rockland (University Park: Pennsylvania State University Press, 1972) [title refers to the 1950s and 1960s].

*Miranda, Francisco de, *The New Democracy in America: Travels of Francisco de Miranda in the United States, 1783–84*, trans. Judson P. Wood, ed. John S. Ezell (Norman: University of Oklahoma Press, 1963).

*Mittelberger, Gottlieb, *Journey to Pennsylvania*, trans. and eds. Oscar Handlin and John Clive (Cambridge: Belknap Press of Harvard University Press, 1960).

Münsterberg, Hugo, *American Traits from the Point of View of a German* (Boston: Houghton, Mifflin, 1901).

Niemcewicz, Julian Ursyn, *Under Their Vine and Fig Tree: Travels Through America in 1797–1799, 1805, with Some Further Account of Life in New Jersey*, trans. Metchie Budka (Elizabeth: Grassman Publishing Co., 1965).

Rapson, Richard L., *Britons View America: Travel Commentary, 1860–1935* (Seattle: University of Washington Press, 1971).

Raumer, Friedrich von, *America and the American People*, trans. William W. Turner (New York: J. and H. G. Langley, 1846).

Rochefoucault-Liancourt, François Alexandre Frederick, duc de la, *Travels Through the United States of North America, the Country of the Iroquois, and Upper Canada, in the Years 1795, 1796, and 1797*, 2 vols. (London: R. Phillips, 1799).

Ros, John Frederick Fitzgerald de, *Personal Narrative of Travels in the United States and Canada in 1826* (London: W. H. Ainsworth, 1827).

*St. Méry, Moreau de, *Moreau de St. Méry's American Journey [1793–1798]*, trans. and eds. Kenneth Roberts and Anna M. Roberts (Garden City: Doubleday, 1947).

Sarmiento, Domingo Faustino, *Travels in the United States in 1847*, trans. Michael Aaron Rockland (Princeton: Princeton University Press, 1970).

Schöpf, Johann David, *Travels in the Confederation, 1783–1784*, trans. Alfred J. Morrison, 2 vols. (New York: Bergman, 1968; first published in 1911).

Schultz, Christian, *Travels on an Inland Voyage Through the States of New-York, Pennsylvania, Virginia, Ohio, and Tennessee . . . Performed in the Years 1807 and 1808*, 2 vols. (New York: Isaac Riley, 1810).

Sealsfield, Charles, *America: Glorious and Chaotic Land*, trans. E. L. Jordan (Englewood Cliffs: Prentice-Hall, 1969).

Tallack, William, *Friendly Sketches in America* (London: A. W. Bennett, 1861).

Weld, Isaac, Jr., *Travels Through the States of North America and the Provinces of Upper & Lower Canada During the Years 1795, 1796, & 1797*, 4th ed., 2 vols. (New York: Augustus Kelley, 1970; first published in 1799).

Wright, Frances, *Views of Society and Manners in America* (London: Longman, Hurst, 1821).

*Wu, Tingfang, *America Through the Spectacles of an Oriental Diplomat* (Taipei: Ch' Eng-Wen Publishing Company, 1968).

AMERICAN VIEWS

Adams, James Truslow, *A Searchlight on America* (London: George Routledge and Sons, 1930).

*Barlow, Joel, *Advice to the Privileged Orders in the Several States of Europe* (Ithaca: Great Seal Books, 1956; first published in 1792).

Becker, Carl L., *Freedom and Responsibility in the American Way of Life* (New York: Alfred A. Knopf, 1945).

*Cooper, James Fenimore, *The American Democrat* (New York: Alfred A. Knopf, 1931; first published in 1838).

Cooper, James Fenimore, *Gleanings in Europe: England* (Albany: State University of New York Press, 1982; first published in 1837).

*Dwight, Timothy, *Travels in New England and New York*, ed. Barbara Miller Solomon with Patricia M. King, 4 vols. (Cambridge: Belknap Press of Harvard University Press, 1969; first published in 1821–22).

*Franklin, Benjamin, *Writings*, ed. J. A. Leo Lemay (New York: Library of America, 1987).

Hamilton, Alexander, *Gentleman's Progress; The Itinerarium of Dr. Alexander Hamilton, 1744*, ed. Carl Bridenbaugh (Chapel Hill: University of North Carolina Press, 1948).

Inaugural Addresses of the Presidents of the United States: From George Washington 1789 to Richard Milhous Nixon 1973 (Washington, D.C.: U.S. Government Printing Office, 1974).

*Jefferson, Thomas, *Writings*, ed. Merrill D. Peterson (New York: Library of America, 1984).

Knight, Sarah Kemble, *The Journal of Madame Knight [1704]*, ed. George Parker Winship (New York: Peter Smith, 1935).

Krutch, Joseph Wood, *Human Nature and the Human Condition* (New York: Random House, 1959).

*Lincoln, Abraham, *Selected Speeches and Writings*, ed. Don E. Fehrenbacher (New York: Library of America, 1992).

Stewart, George R., *American Ways of Life* (Garden City: Doubleday, 1954).

Wilder, Thornton, *American Characteristics and Other Essays*, ed. Donald Gallup (New York: Harper and Row, 1979).

PARTICULAR BEHAVIORS

Bremner, Robert H., *American Philanthropy* (Chicago: University of Chicago Press, 1988).

Cochran, Thomas C., *200 Years of American Business* (New York: Basic Books, 1977).

Ebeling, Walter, *The Fruited Plain: The Story of American Agriculture* (Berkeley: University of California Press, 1979).

Gutman, Herbert G., *The Black Family in Slavery and Freedom, 1750–1925* (New York: Pantheon, 1976).

*Johnson, Daniel M., and Rex R. Campbell, *Black Migration in America: A Social Demographic History* (Durham: Duke University Press, 1981).

Nevins, Allan, *The State Universities and Democracy* (Urbana: University of Illinois Press, 1962).

THE TWO MOST RECENT GENERATIONS (1960–2000)

Carter, Stephen L., *The Culture of Disbelief: How American Law and Politics Trivialize Religious Devotion* (New York: Basic Books, 1993).

Bernstein, Richard, *Dictatorship of Virtue: Multiculturalism and the Battle for America's Future* (New York: Alfred A. Knopf, 1994).

Eberly, Don E., ed., *The Content of America's Character: Recovering Civic Virtue* (Lanham: Madison Books, 1995).

Farber, Daniel A., and Suzanna Sherry, *Beyond All Reason: The Radical Assault on Truth in American Law* (New York: Oxford University Press, 1997).

*Geyer, Georgie Anne, *Americans No More* (New York: Atlantic Monthly Press, 1996).

*Gordon, John Steele, *Hamilton's Blessing: The Extraordinary Life and Times of Our National Debt* (New York: Walker, 1997).

Handlin, Oscar, *The Distortion of America* (Boston: Little, Brown, 1981).

*Himmelfarb, Gertrude, *The De-moralization of Society: From Victorian Virtues to Modern Values* (New York: Alfred A. Knopf, 1995).

Hollander, Paul, *Anti-Americanism: Critiques at Home and Abroad, 1965–1990* (New York: Oxford University Press, 1992).

*Howard, Philip K., *The Death of Common Sense: How Law Is Suffocating America* (New York: Random House, 1994).

Kazin, Michael, *The Populist Persuasion: An American History* (New York: Basic Books, 1995).

Kosmin, Barry A., and Seymour Lachman, *One Nation Under God: Religion in Contemporary American Society* (New York: Harmony Books, 1993).

*Moskos, Charles C., and John Sibley Butler, *All That We Can Be: Black Leadership and Racial Integration the Army Way* (New York: Basic Books, 1996).

Lasch, Christopher, *The Revolt of the Elites and the Betrayal of Democracy* (New York: W. W. Norton, 1994).

Naylor, Larry L., *American Culture: Myth and Reality of a Culture of Diversity* (Westport: Greenwood Publishing Group, 1998).

Neuhaus, Richard John, *The Naked Public Square: Religion and Democracy in America*, 2nd ed. (Grand Rapids: W. B. Eerdmans, 1986).

Novak, Michael, *Unmeltable Ethnics: Politics and Culture in American Life*, 2nd ed. (New Brunswick: Transaction, 1996).

Olasky, Marvin, *The Tragedy of American Compassion* (Washington, D.C.: Regnery Gateway, 1992).

*Richburg, Keith B., *Out of America: A Black Man Confronts Africa* (New York: Basic Books, 1997)

Rothwax, Harold J., *Guilty: The Collapse of Criminal Justice* (New York: Warner Books, 1996).

*Schlesinger, Arthur M., Jr., *The Disuniting of America: Reflections on a Multicultural Society* (New York: W. W. Norton, 1992).

Smith, Tony, *America's Mission: The United States and the Worldwide Struggle for Democracy in the Twentieth Century* (Princeton: Princeton University Press, 1994).

Stanley, Thomas J., and William D. Danko, *The Millionaire Next Door: The Surprising Secrets of America's Wealth* (Atlanta: Longstreet Press, 1996).

*Steele, Shelby, *The Content of Our Character: A New Vision of Race in America* (New York: St. Martin's Press, 1990).

Thernstrom, Stephen, and Abigail Thernstrom, *America in Black and White: One Nation, Indivisible* (New York: Simon and Schuster, 1997).

FROM THE above sources I especially recommend T. S. Eliot's *Notes towards the Definition of Culture*, a highly intelligent, concise statement about the nature of culture by someone who was thoroughly informed on the subject. For a vivid sense of the cultural and physical contrasts in the Americas before the permanent settlement of the future. United States, you could do no better than to read Garcilaso de la Vega Inca's account of the South American civilization of his mother's people (*The Royal Commentaries of the Inca*), followed by a reading of Àlvar Núñez Cabeza de Vaca's account of his ten years on foot in the Stone Age wilderness of central North America, which took him from Florida to the deserts of the Southwest. Michel-Guillaume-Saint-Jean de Crèvecoeur's *Letters from an American Farmer*, Rebecca Burlend's *A True Picture of Emigration* and *American Mosaic* (a collection of twentieth-century statements by immigrants) represent a three-century chronicle of the immigrant mentality which has played so large a part in shaping American beliefs. For understanding the fundamental historical experience of the American people—their civilization of a Stone Age wilderness of continental dimensions in just three centuries—the writings of Captain John Smith about the Chesapeake Bay region in the early seventeenth century and Timothy Dwight's writings about New England and New York in the late eighteenth century are indispensable. Many of the beliefs of American culture, which was fully formed before the American Revolution and which impelled the American determination to be independent of England, are expressed in Joel Barlow's *Advice to the Privileged Orders in the Several States of Europe* and in the selection from Benjamin Franklin's writings made by J. A. Leo Lemay for the Library of America. Barlow was a diplomat, international businessman, poet, and political writer; Franklin's practical genius, wide-ranging civic and scientific accomplishments, and rise to fortune from humble beginnings remain the quintessence of the American idea of success. John Dos Passos, in *Prospects of a Golden Age,* has given us the most readable overview of the revolutionary generations that Barlow and Franklin were part of.

Acknowledgments

THANKS ARE OWED first to members of my family—Giselle, Helen, Laurie, Lisa, John, Kevin, and Ony—for their help during the writing and production of this book. I am also more than a little grateful to Darren Bruce, Yontaek Choi, Brian Molina, Michael Moore, Greg Neidhart, and John Segesta, who took my seminar on American culture and helped me refine my list of American beliefs.

Colleagues in the Department of English of the University of Arizona and friends who have been supportive through their recommendations, information, and interest include Peter Wild, the late Jim Tuttleton, Rudy Troike, Jim Smith, Paul Rosenblatt, Caroline Rehder, Jan Lipartito, Gene Koppel, the late Russell Kirk, Annette Kirk, Bob Houston, Reka Hoff, John Fortier, Larry Evers, and Bernard Bergesen.

For reading parts of the manuscript I am grateful to Bob Burns, Jack Cox, Joseph Crapa, Emory Elliott, Karl Kroeber, Charles Moskos, Joe Parkhurst, Bob Rehder, Calvin Skaggs, Merrill Skaggs, and Ken and Carol Stocker. Special thanks are owed Myron Donald, Ed Nigh, and Ron Rodin for reading the whole manuscript and Ivan Dee for the faith he showed in the book from the time he first saw sample chapters of it and for his many improving editorial suggestions, both large and small.

I wish to thank too the Arizona Board of Regents and the Earhart Foundation (particularly its director Tony Sullivan) for a semester's sabbatical leave and a grant which together allowed me to concentrate on completing the work. I also appreciate the contributions of Rex Adams, Anita Almond, Peggy Flyntz, and José Noriega during the production of the book.

J. H. M.

Index

Agriculture, 26–27, 72, 118
Albany Plan, 168–169, 182–183
Albion's Seed: Four British Folkways in America (Fisher), 14
American culture: cooperation and, 30; economic rewards and, 16, 50–51, 53; freedom of movement and, 84–92; friendliness and, 210–212; frontier and, 20, 53–54, 93–107; geography and, 16–23, 25–26, 87–89; immigration and, 26–30, 33, 60–92; independence and, 10–13, 14; labor and, 54–55; land availability and, 53–55; mobility and, 16, 20–21, 149; origins of, 13–36; population and, 27–30, 55–56, 61–62; race and, 34, 62–63, 163, 207–211; regional culture, 14; religious freedom and, 16, 33, 140; settlers and, 22–23; slavery and, 34, 58–59, 106–107, 209; social mobility and, 69–71; technology from Europe and, 221; unilingualism and, 86; wilderness and, 16–21, 72–78, 100–101, 111–115; work and, 34, 37–59. *See also specific topics.*
American Dictionary of the English Language, 72, 81
American Philosophical Society, 103
American Statistical Association, 73

America's British Culture (Kirk), 14
Andrews, Charles M., 149
Appalachian Mountains, 20, 53, 90
Argentina, 31–32, 89–90
Aristocracy, 29, 148, 159–160, 213; in England, 69–71, 141, 178
Articles of Confederation and Perpetual Union, 168, 169
Associations, 103–105
Autobiography (Franklin), 57
Aztecs, 30

Basques, 159
Belief, 4–5, 220–226; as set, 5, 220. *See also specific types.*
Belief-behaviors: definition, 4; immigrants and, 60–61. *See also specific beliefs.*
Benét, Stephen Vincent, 78
Bolívar, Simon, 190
"Booming," definition of term, 100
Boston Tea Party, 185
Bowditch, Nathaniel, 102
Braddock, Edward, 171
Bradford, William, 45, 46
Brazil, 24; geography, 83, 114; independence, 188; military and, 188–189; population, 27; slavery in, 32, 34, 53, 83, 161, 170; sovereignty and, 170–171
British North America Act, 187
Bunyan, Paul, 73
Bush, George, 133

255

Canada, 25, 32–33; costs of government in French colony, 171; geography of, 26, 84, 114; immigration to, 26; independence, 187; military and, 174; mobility in, 84–85; population, 27, 85; sovereignty and, 170–171; "two nations," 162–163
Carter, Jimmy, 133
Celts, 159
Character and Opinion in the United States (Santayana), 68
Checks and balances, 215
Chibcha, 31
Clemens, Samuel L., 72
Colden, Cadwallader, 150
Colonies, American, 33, 37–59; costs of government in, 171–173; elections and, 175–176; legislative power and, 181; military and, 174, 175; military self-reliance, 34; population and, 27–30, 55–56, 61–62; religious freedom in, 202–203; "royal colonies, " 173; "virtual representation" and, 177–178; wealth and, 175, 179. *See also* American culture.
Colonization: comparisons of different countries, 24–28
"Common Sense" (Paine), 14
Compendious Dictionary of the English Language, 72
Constitution of the United States, 165–166, 169, 192–193; separation of church and state, 198–199, 201
Coolidge, Calvin, 145
Cooper, James Fenimore, 78
Cooper, William, 156–157
Cooperation, 30
"Counterculture," 223
Crévecoeur, Michel-Guillaume-Saint-Jean de: *Letters from an American Farmer*, 131
Cultural decline, 223–225
Culture: definition of, 3–9; generations and, 7. *See also*

American culture; Historical culture.
Cumberland Gap, 90

Declaration of Independence, 142–143, 169
Degler, Carl, 149
Delaware, 204
Douglas, William O., 146
Drug abuse, 223
Dulany, Daniel, 177–178
Dwight, Timothy, 80–81

Edison, Thomas, 102
Education: "multiculturalism," 224; public schools, 224; self, 102
Egypt, ancient, 6
Eisenhower, Dwight D., 132
Elizabeth II, 70
Emerson, Ralph Waldo, 71
Enculturation, 8. *See also* Culture.
England: aristocracy and, 69–71, 141, 178; birthright and, 178–180; church and state in, 198; colonial policies, 24–28, 166–190; elections and, 175–176; immigration policies and, 26–27; inheritance and, 151; lack of constitution, 192–193; sovereignty and, 166–168; "virtual representation," 177–178
Equal freedom, 222
Equality: of birthright, 141–146; European philosophers and, 145–146
Erie Canal, 88

Family values, 223
Faulkner, William, 125–126
Federalist, The, 219
Fisher, David Hackett, 14
Fitzgerald, Scott, 155
France, 24, 25, 32–33
Franklin, Benjamin, 49, 57, 99–100, 102, 103, 117, 119–120, 217–218; *Autobiography*, 123–124, 181–182; letter to a friend, 129–130; on

majority rule, 196; "On the Providence of God in the Government of the World," 125, 126
Frazier, Alice, 70
Frontier beliefs, 93–107; "getting ahead," 94–95, 100; mutual reliance and, 95–100, 103–105; self-reliance, 95, 102

Generations: change and, 7; "races" of Europe and, 208
Georgia, 59, 205
Giants in the Earth (Rölvaag), 75–77
Gran Colombia, 190
Great Awakening, 126–128
Greene, Jack P., 148
Greetings: mutual reliance and, 95; work and, 52

Harding, Warren G., 134
Harrison, Lawrence E.: *Who Prospers? How Cultural Values Shape Economic and Political Success*, 221
Harrison, William Henry, 145
Hawthorne, Nathaniel: *House of the Seven Gables*, 151–152
Headright system, 56
Hemingway, Ernest, 155
Henry, John, 73
Historical culture: beliefs and, 4–5; organic nature of, 8
Homestead Act, 53, 54
Human nature, beliefs on: goodness and, 212–213; power and, 213–219; race and, 207–211

"I Have a Dream" (King), 75
Immigrant beliefs, 60–92, 170; freedom of movement, 61, 71; improvement and, 61, 63–65, 71–73; opportunities and, 61, 69–71; past versus future, 73–75, 79; pre-emigration beliefs, 66–68; progress, 73–75; social mobility and, 69–71

Immigration: American culture and, 26–30, 33, 60–92; to Canada, 26; push and pull of, 66–67; religious and moral beliefs and, 115–117; self-selected, 27, 86, 130; to Spanish America, 26
Improvement: definitions of, 72. See *also* Immigrant beliefs.
Incas, 5, 30–31, 86
Indentured servitude, 56–58
Independence: for Brazil, 188–189; for Canada, 187–188; for Spanish America, 189–190

James, Henry, 212; "Daisy Miller," 213
Jamestown, 38–43
Japan, 5
Jefferson, Thomas, 123, 135; separation of church and state, 200
Jews, 205

Kennedy, John F., 144–145
King, Martin Luther, Jr., 75
"Kingdom of New Spain," 25, 31
"Kingdom of Peru," 26, 31
Kirk, Russell, 14
Krutch, Joseph Wood, 217

Labor, land and, 53–55
Land Ordinance of 1785, 53
Landes, David S.: *Wealth and Poverty of Nations*, 221
Language in America, 86, 208, 220
Lend-Lease program, 96
"Levellers," 13
Lewis and Clark expedition, 20
Lincoln, Abraham, 136–139, 170, 197
Locke, John, 145–146; "Fundamental Constitutions of Carolina," 145

Madison, James, 197, 215, 218–219
Magna Carta, 192
Majority rule, 194–198
Marshall, George C., 97
Marshall Plan, 96–98

Marxism, 215
Maryland, 173, 204
Massachusetts, 203, 206; immigration and, 46. *See also* Plymouth Plantation.
Mayas, 30
Mayflower Compact, 15
McKinley, William, 134
Melting pot, 66
Moral beliefs. *See* Religious and moral beliefs.
"Moral imagination," 4
Moral relativity, 207
Mormons, 205
Morrill Act, 54

National Road, 90
Native Americans, 21–22
New Amsterdam, 61–62
New England, 80. *See also* Plymouth Plantation.
New Hampshire, 204
New Jersey, 204
"New World," 21, 25
New York, 61–62, 80, 203
North America, geography of, 16–23, 25–26, 87–89
North Carolina, 38, 204

Oregon Trail, 90
Organizations, 103–105

Paine, Thomas, 14; "Common Sense," 61, 122
Palmer, R. R., 166
Pampas, 89–90
Paris Peace Conference, 74
Pedro I, Dom, 188
Pedro II, Dom, 188
Penn, William, 62
Pennsylvania, 62, 71, 173
Philanthropy, 99
Pilgrims, 43–47
Pinckney, Charles, 169
Pioneers, The (Cooper), 78
Plymouth Plantation, 43–47

Political beliefs, 165–205; least possible government, 191–192, 223–224; majority rule, 194–198; separation of church and state, 198–205; sovereignty, 166–190; taxation without representation, 11, 14, 172–173, 183–185; written constitution, 192–193
Portugal, 24, 161, 188
Practical improvement, 221–222
Private ownership: at Jamestown, 41–43; at Plymouth, 45–47

Quakers, 205
Quebec, 33

Race, 34, 62–63, 163, 207–211
Reform Bill of 1832, 176
Religious and moral beliefs, 108–147; belief in God, 108–111; chosen country, 132–140, 225; equality of birthright, 141–146; Great Awakening, 126–128; immigration and, 115–117; nature and, 111–120; polls about, 109–110; right and wrong, 120–131
Responsible individual, 222
Revolution: nature of, 6
Rockefeller, John D., 150–151
Roe v. Wade, 223
Rölvaag, Ole Edvart, 75–77, 82–83
Roman Catholics, 205
Roman Empire, 29
Roosevelt, Franklin D., 96, 100, 135, 136
Roper Center of Public Opinion Research, 224–225

Santayana, George, 68
Second Continental Congress, 187
Self-made men, 102
Separation of church and state, 198–205
Smith, John, 38–43, 194
Social beliefs, 148–164; class and, 153–157; property and, 150–153,

158; socialism and, 156–158; wealth and, 150–153
South Carolina, 38
Sovereignty: in America, 169–190; in England, 166–168; states and, 186; taxation without representation, 11, 14, 172–173, 183–185
Spain, 24, 25–26; conquests of, 30–31, 160–161; nobility and, 159
Spanish America: caudillos, 190; conquest of, 30–31, 160–161; geography of, 25–26, 114, 189–190; immigration to, 26; independence of, 189–190; military and, 31–32, 174, 189; mobility in, 85–86; sovereignty and, 170–171, 189
Stamp Act Congress, 185
State constitutions, 203–205
Stroessner, Alfredo, 190

Taxation without representation, 11, 14, 172–173, 183–185
Taylor, Ann, 158
Thomas, George, 96
Thoreau, Henry David, 121
Tocqueville, Alexis de, 101, 110; *Democracy in America*, 170
Truman, Harry S, 96
Twain, Mark, 72

United States: communication technology and, 91–92; geography of, 16–23, 25–26, 87–89; mass production in, 105; natural resources of, 118–120; railroads in, 91; rivers in, 87–88; seal of, 135; trails in, 90

Virginia, 38, 203. *See also* Jamestown.
Virginia's House of Burgesses, 172
"Virtual representation," 177–178
Volunteerism, 98–99, 101

Walden (Thoreau), 121
Warren, Earl, 146
Washington, George, 123, 134, 169, 187; Farewell Address, 226
Webster, Noah, 72, 81
"Welcome Wagon," 212
Whitman, Walt, 112, 163; "To Think of Time," 121
Wilderness, 16–21, 72, 74, 100–101; literature and, 75–78; religion and, 111–115
Wilderness Act (1964), 74
Wilderness Road, 90
Wilson, Woodrow, 74, 139
Winslow, Edward, 45
Work: greetings reflecting, 52; at Jamestown, 38–43; manual labor, 48–49, 51; material benefits of, 50–51, 53; at Plymouth, 45; primary beliefs and, 37–59; in Thirteen Colonies, 47–53
Work beliefs: benefit and, 50–51; at Jamestown, 38–43; at Plymouth, 43–47; as primary, 37, 48–49; wilderness and, 49–53
Wright, Orville, 102
Wright, Wilbur, 102

Yale University, 80–81
Yellowstone Park, 74

Zorach v. Clauson, 146

A NOTE ON THE AUTHOR

John Harmon McElroy has taught at eight universities in the United States, Colombia, Poland, and, as a Fulbright Professor of American Studies, in Brazil and Spain. His other works include an edition of Washington Irving's biography of Columbus, a study of the formation of American culture (*Finding Freedom*), and an edition of Walt Whitman's accounts of his experience in the Civil War (*The Sacrificial Years*). In the 1980s he was the founding president of Solidarity Tucson, a support group for the Polish workers' movement Solidarity. A professor emeritus of the University of Arizona, where he taught American literature for many years, he and his wife, Onyria Herrera McElroy, live in Tucson, Arizona.